ART & DESIGN

ACADEMY GROUP LTD
42 LEINSTER GARDENS, LONDON W2 3AN
TEL: 0171-402 2141 FAX: 0171-723 9540

EDITOR: Nicola Kearton
ASSISTANT EDITOR: Ramona Khambatta
EDITORIAL: Cristina Fontoura
ART EDITOR: Andrea Bettella
CHIEF DESIGNER: Mario Bettella
DESIGNER: Alistair Probert

SUBSCRIPTION OFFICES:
UK: VCH PUBLISHERS (UK) LTD
8 WELLINGTON COURT, WELLINGTON STREET
CAMBRIDGE CB1 1HZ
TEL: (01223) 321111 FAX: (01223) 313321

USA AND CANADA: VCH PUBLISHERS INC
303 NW 12TH AVENUE DEERFIELD BEACH,
FLORIDA 33442-1788 USA
TEL: (305) 428-5566 / (800) 367-8249
FAX: (305) 428-8201

ALL OTHER COUNTRIES:
VCH VERLAGSGESELLSCHAFT MBH
BOSCHSTRASSE 12, POSTFACH 101161
69451 WEINHEIM
FEDERAL REPUBLIC OF GERMANY
TEL: 06201 606 148 FAX: 06201 606 184

Subscription rates for 1995 (incl p&p): *Annual subscription price*: UK only £65.00, World DM 195 for regular subscribers. *Student rate*: UK only £50.00, World DM 156 incl postage and handling charges. *Individual issues*: £14.95/DM 39.50 (plus £2.30/DM 5 for p&p, per issue ordered).
For the USA and Canada: *Art & Design* is published six times per year (Jan/Feb; Mar/Apr; May/Jun; Jul/Aug; Sept/Oct; and Nov/Dec) by Academy Group Ltd, 42 Leinster Gardens, London W2 3AN, England and distributed by VCH Publishers, Inc., 303 N.W. 12th Avenue, Deerfield Beach, FL 33442-1788; Telefax (305) 428 8201; Telephone (305) 428-5566 or (800) 367 8249. Annual subscription price; US $135.00 including postage and handling charges; special student rates available at $105.00, single issue $26.95. Second-class postage paid at Deerfield Beach, Fl 33441. **POSTMASTER**: Send address changes to Art & Design, c/o VCH Publishers, Inc., 303 N.W. 12th Avenue, Deerfild Beach FL 33442-1788.
Printed in Italy. All prices are subject to change without notice. [ISSN: 0267-3991]
The full text of *Art & Design* is also available in the electronic versions of the Art Index.

CONTENTS

ART & DESIGN **MAGAZINE**

European Stamp Design: A Semiotic Approach to Designing Messages *by David Scott • Review of* Art & Design *recent and future issues*

ART & DESIGN **PROFILE** *No 45*

THE MULTIMEDIA TEXT
Guest-Edited by Nicholas Zurbrugg

Kathy ***Acker*** *After the End of the World • Warren* ***Burt*** *Compositional Linguistics • John* ***Cage*** *• Henri* ***Chopin*** *• Bob* ***Cobbing*** *• John* ***Conomos*** *The Movement of Shadows • Francesco* ***Conz*** *• Ian* ***Hamilton Finlay*** *• Ken* ***Friedman*** *Language and Culture in the Information Age • Gary* ***Genosko*** *In the Shadow of McLuhan • John* ***Giorno*** Eh Joe *• Jim* ***Krank*** *Punks One, Poets Nil • Stuart* ***Lynch*** *• Robert* ***Scanlan*** *Post-Modern Time and Place • Larry* ***Wendt*** *Narrative and the World Wide Web • Adam* ***Wolter***

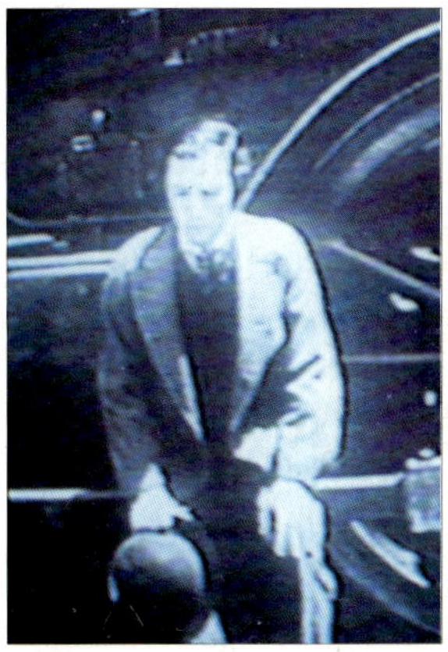

John Conomos, *Night Sky*, 1993, videotape (Buster Keaton)

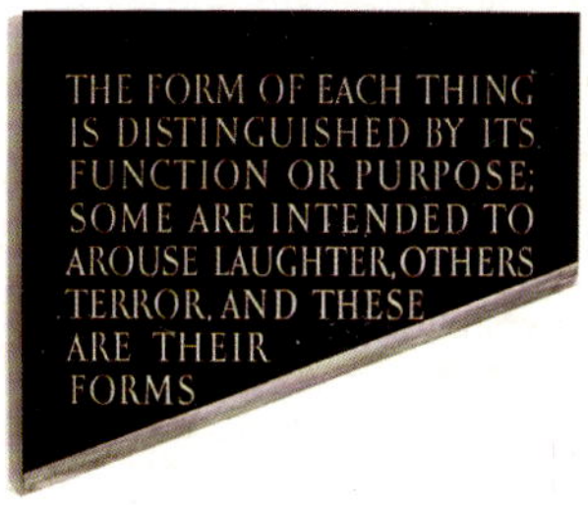

Ian Hamilton Finlay, *Four Guillotine Blades*, 1987 (Victoria Miro, London)

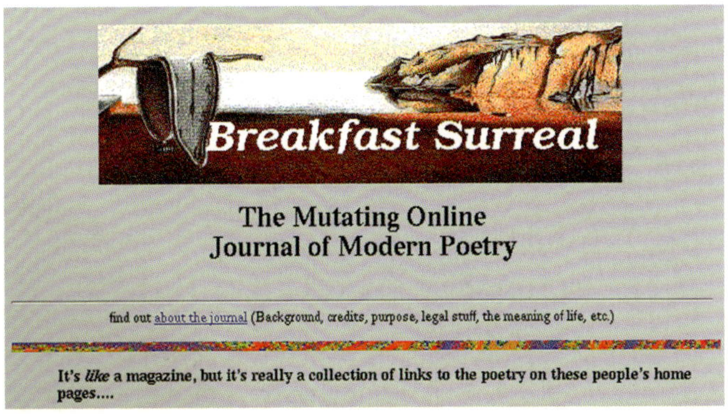

Larry Wendt, *URL: http://www.indirect.com/www/warren/surreal.html*

EUROPEAN STAMP DESIGN

A SEMIOTIC APPROACH TO DESIGNING MESSAGES

David Scott

Beautifully illustrated throughout, this unique book investigates the vital role postage stamps play in both shaping and reflecting national identity and the way they reflect the fundamental design developments within their period.

This is the first comprehensive study to use a semiotic approach to philatelic design, using the fundamental distinction between iconic, indexical and symbolic functions of signs to clarify the way stamp messages are structured and the ideological implications they carry. Focusing on the traditions of five different European countries – Britain, France, The Netherlands, Switzerland and Ireland – the book shows how national icons evolve, how commemorative issues reflect fundamental design as well as cultural concerns, and how many famous artists, such as MC Escher, Hans Erni and Edmund Dulac, have contributed to the development of stamp design. A whole chapter is devoted to an analysis of the exotic British and French colonial issues designed by Dulac and Michael and Sylvia Goaman.

David Scott is Professor of French, Trinity College, Dublin, Ireland. He is author of *Pictorialist Poetics* (1988) and *Paul Delvaux: Surrealizing the Nude* (1992). An editor of the journals *Word and Image* and *L'image*, he is a regular contributor to *French Cultural Studies* and *The Irish Arts Review*. He is currently curating an exhibition on European Stamp Design for the Design Museum, London to take place from October 1995 until January 1996.

144 pages, over 1300 illustrations, many in colour, publication date: September 1995, Academy Editions, ISBN: 1 85490 420 5, £24.95

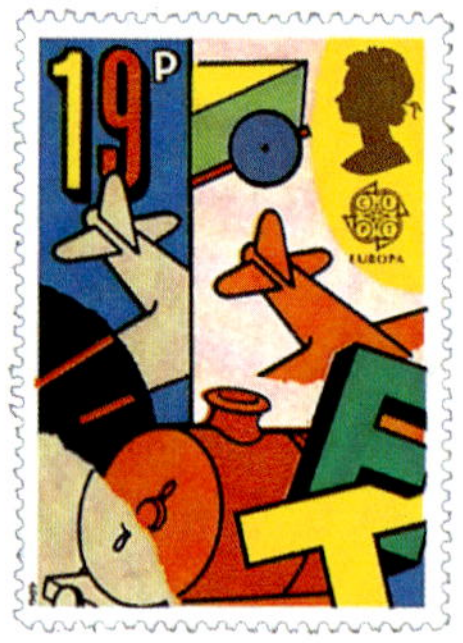

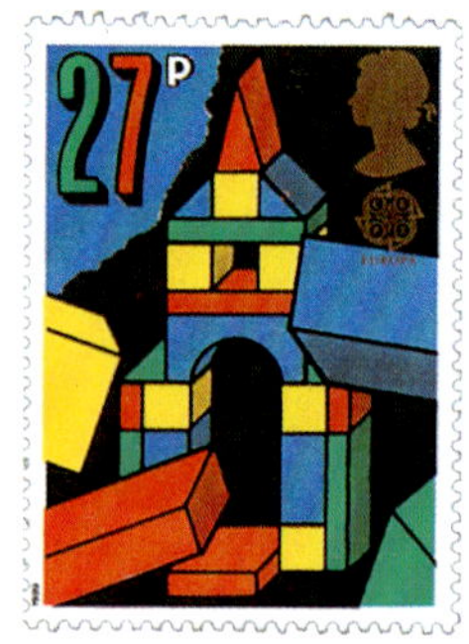

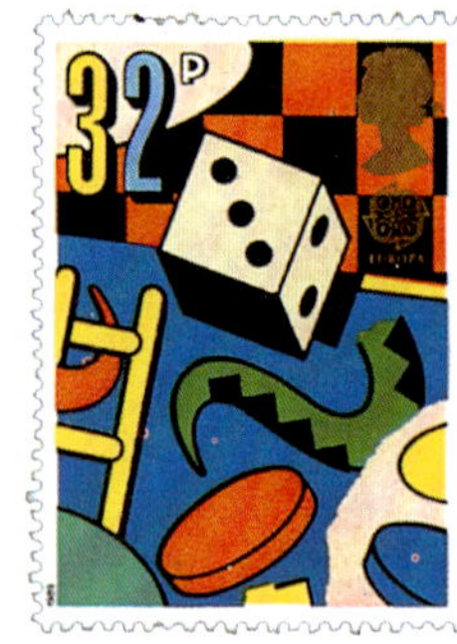

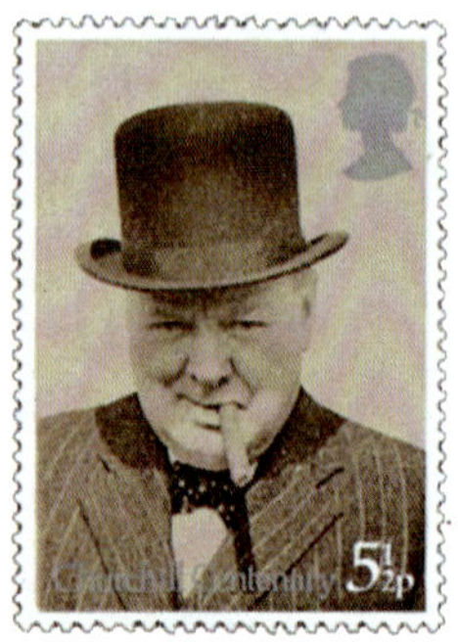
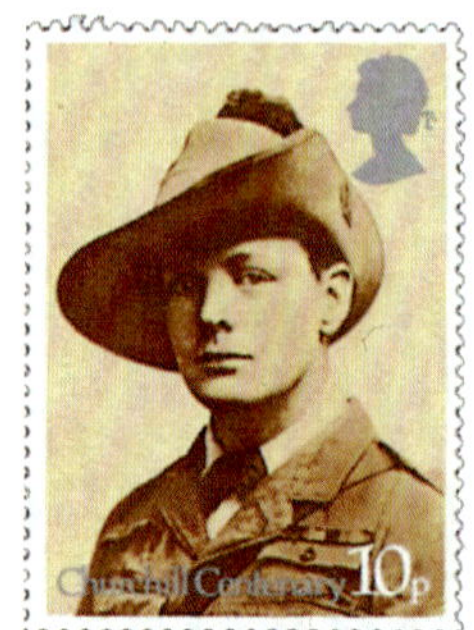
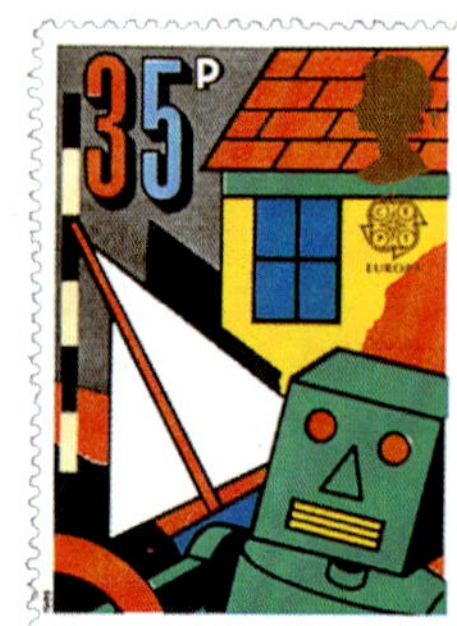

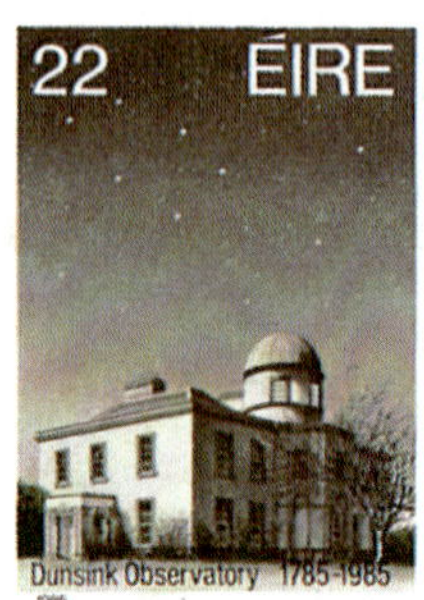

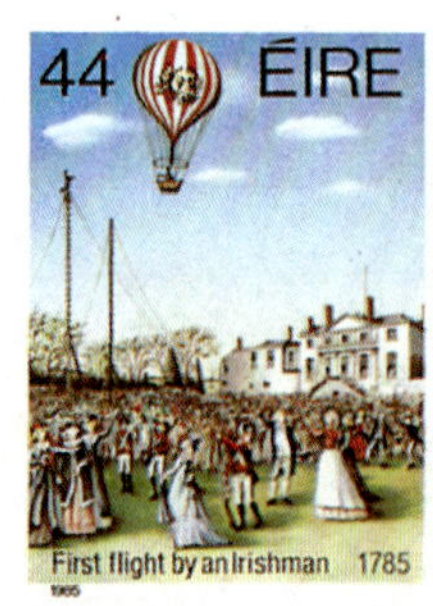

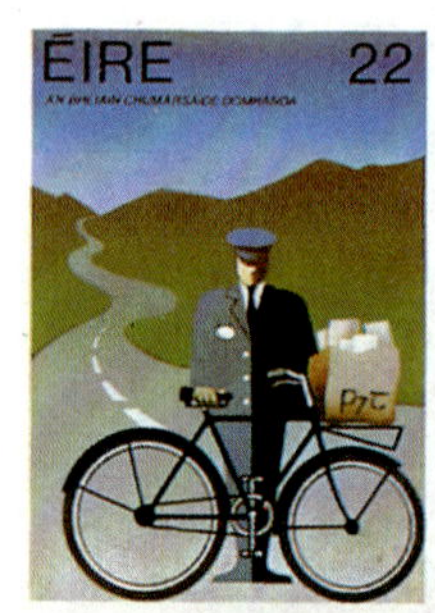

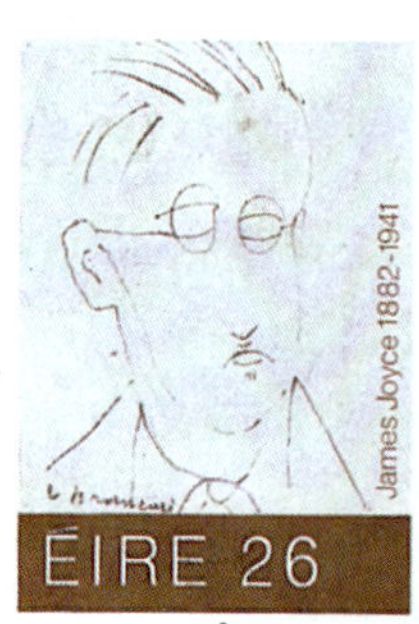

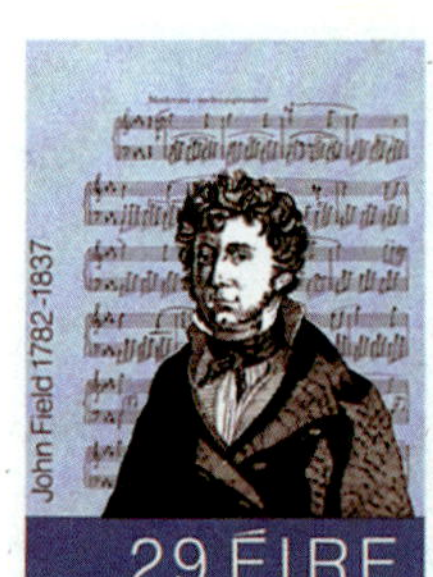

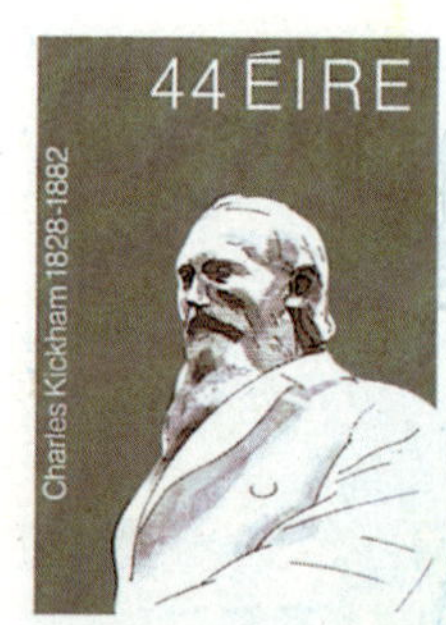

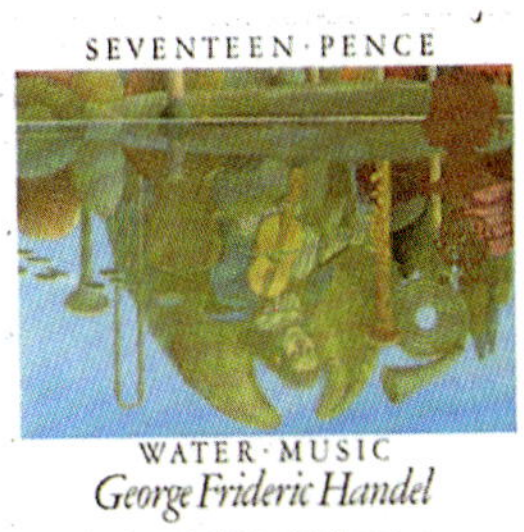
SEVENTEEN · PENCE
WATER · MUSIC
George Frideric Handel

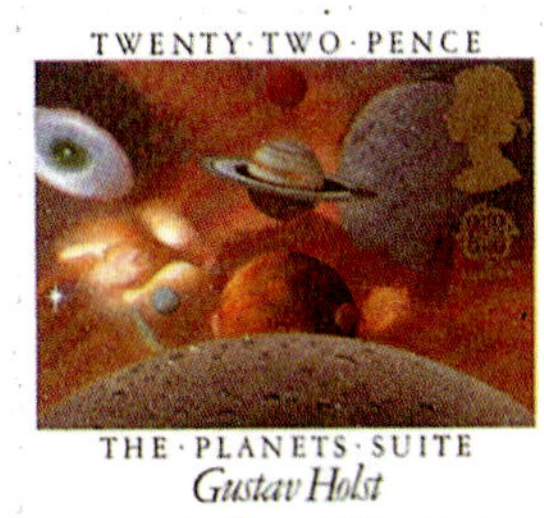
TWENTY · TWO · PENCE
THE · PLANETS · SUITE
Gustav Holst

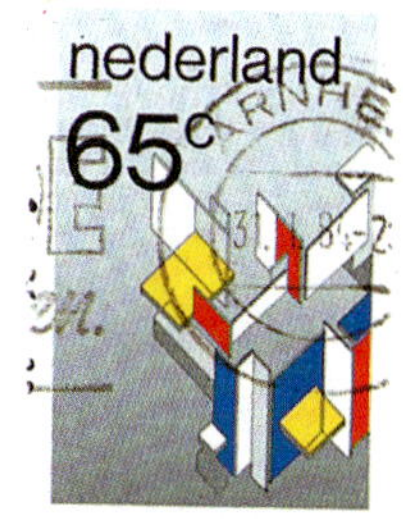
nederland
65c

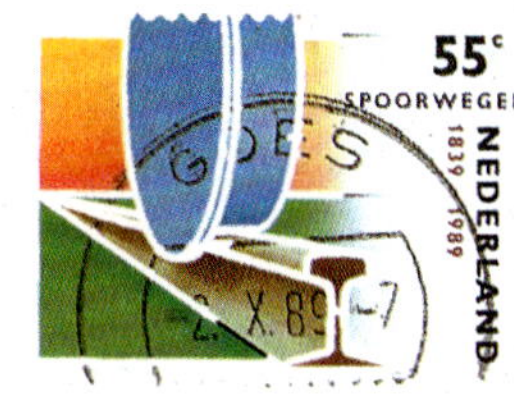
55c
SPOORWEGEN
1839 - 1989
NEDERLAND

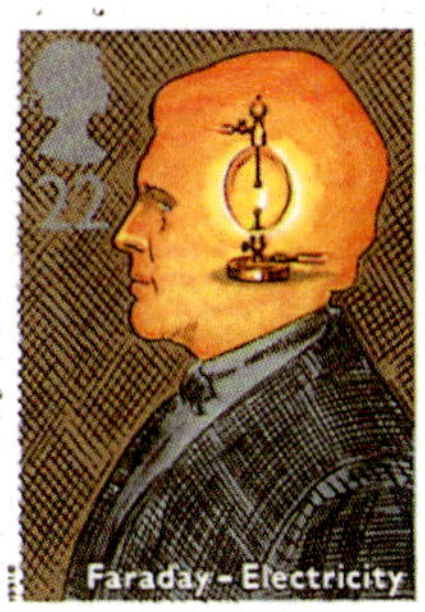
22
Faraday - Electricity

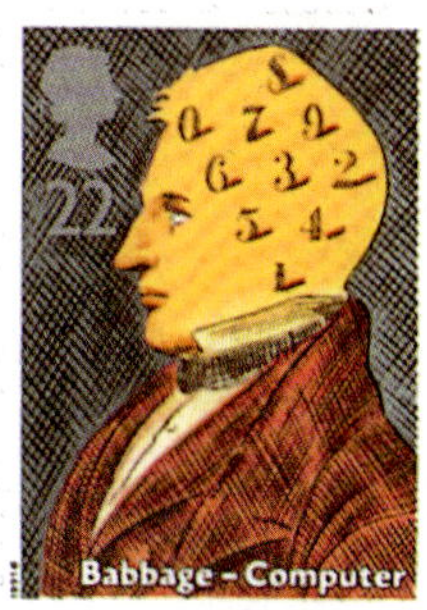
22
Babbage - Computer

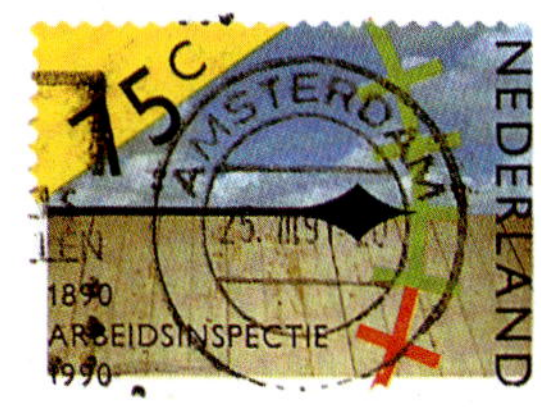
75c
NEDERLAND
1890
ARBEIDSINSPECTIE
1990

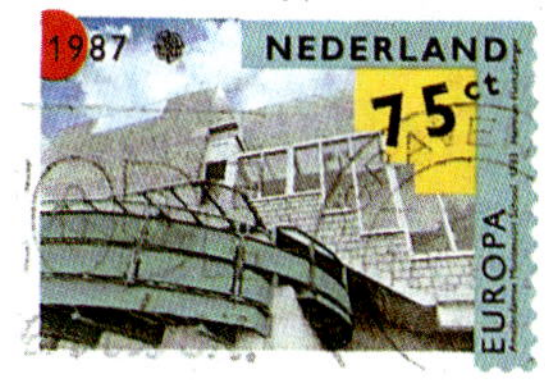
1987
NEDERLAND
75ct
EUROPA

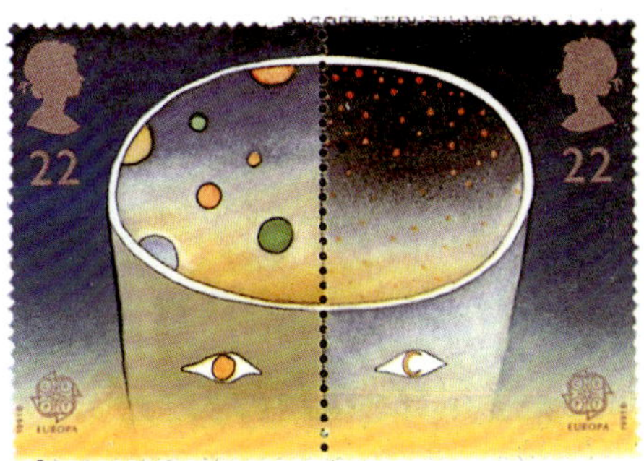
22
22
EUROPA
EUROPA

60ct
veilig verkeer
NEDERLAND

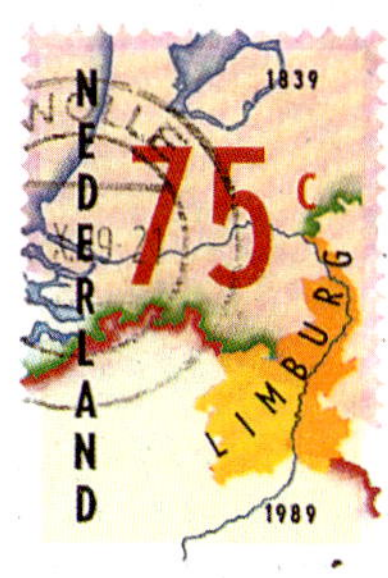
NEDERLAND
75c
1839
LIMBURG
1989

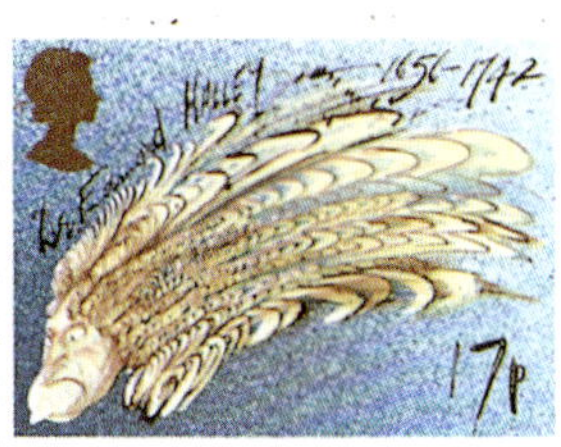
17p

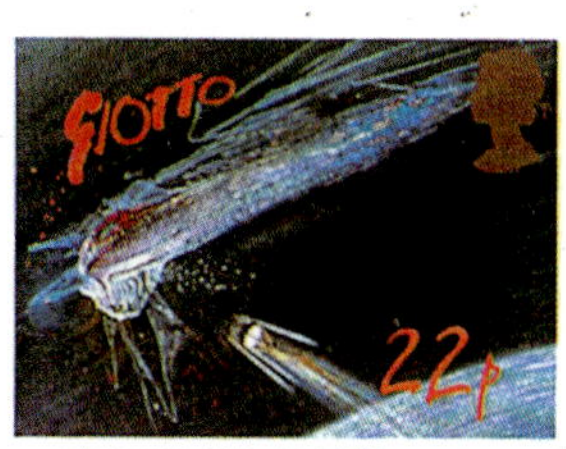
GIOTTO
22p

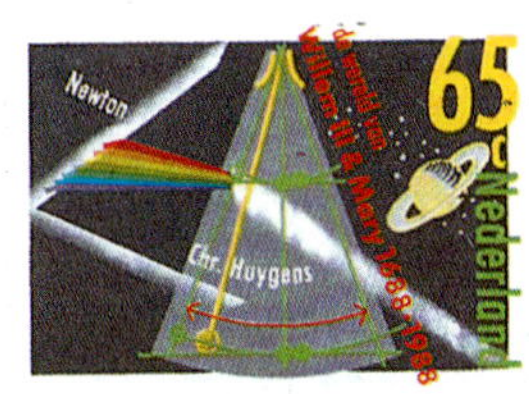
Newton
Chr. Huygens
65c
nederland

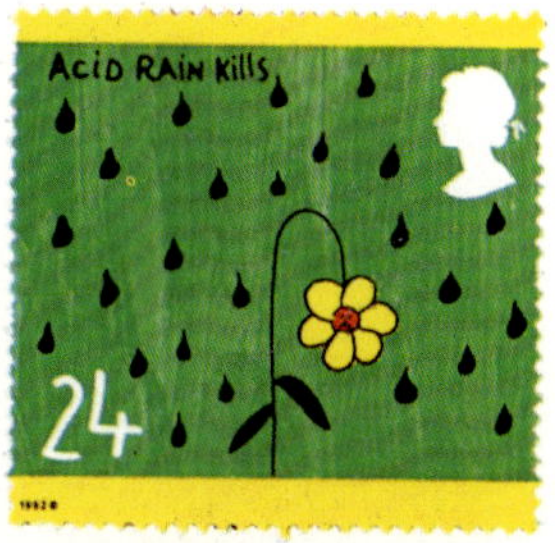
ACID RAIN Kills
24

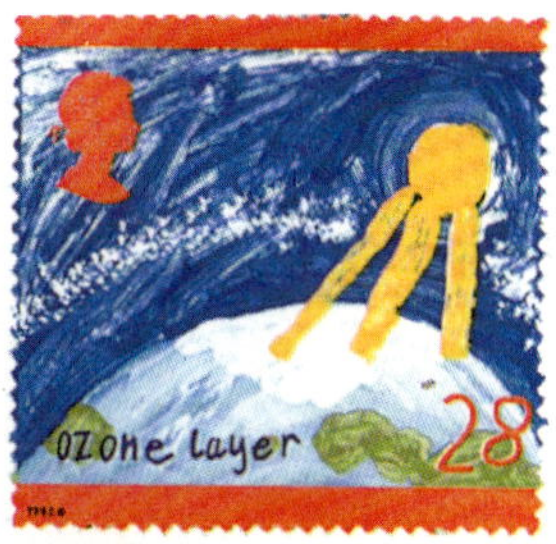
OZONE Layer
28

1994
PIET MONDRIAAN
NEDERLAND
70c

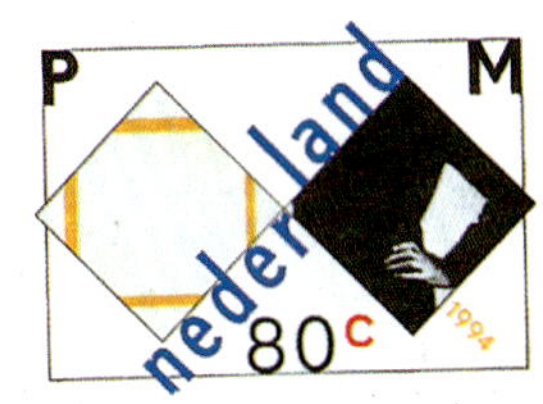
P
M
nederland
80c
1994

ART & DESIGN *recent issues*

PATRICK CAULFIELD

PAINTINGS 1963–1992

A & D Profile No 27

In the work shown at the 1992 retrospective exhibition 'Patrick Caulfield Painting 1963-1992' at London's Serpentine Gallery, Caulfield dignifies the ordinary, prosaic and unheroic side of urban life through his highly-stylised renditions of familiar pub, restaurant and domestic scenes. Normal banal views, or plain household objects are transformed into something magical by rich, lush colours and unexpected juxtapositions. The authoritative essay by Marco Livingstone and full colour reproductions of over 80 of his best known works, together with biographical details and a comprehensive bibliography make this volume an invaluable record of Caulfield's work.

PB 1 85490 180 X
Publication: 1992

FLUXUS

TODAY AND YESTERDAY

A & D Profile No 28

Guest-Edited by Johan Pijnappel

Fluxus, the first international, transmedia art movement this century is recalled in this special edition by a number of original members: Emmett Williams; John Cage; René Block; Jackson MacLow; Nam June Paik; Robert Filliou. Fluxus took the art world by storm in the early 60s and its spirit is still relevant in the 90s. Stemming mainly from Joseph Beuys and John Cage, the movement believed in the performing arts where inspiration could be drawn from the spiritual responses of the audience and where stimulation and change were the only constants. The text is comprised of articles, interviews and letters.

PB 1 85490 194 X
Publication: January 1993

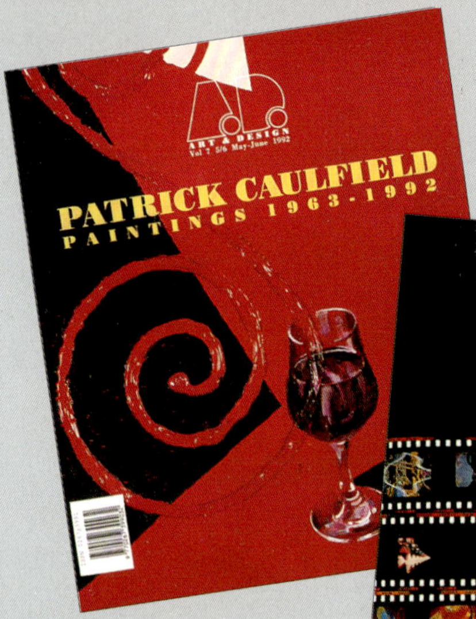

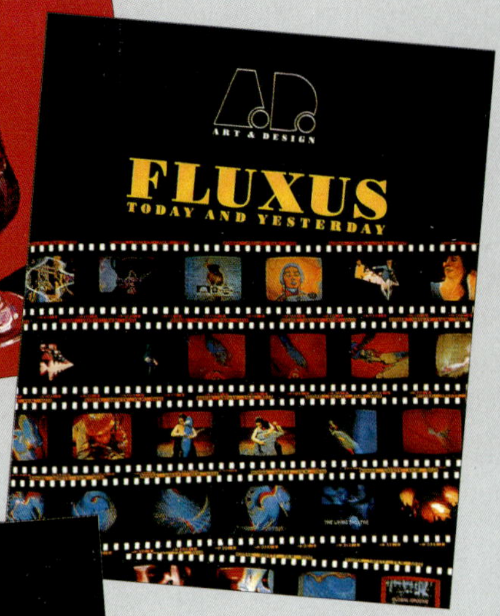

THE GREAT RUSSIAN UTOPIA

A & D Profile No 29

Guest-Edited by Victor Arwas

This profile gives a colourful overview of the work produced during one of the most artistically creative and prolific eras of the 20th century. Russian avant-garde art was an expression of a profound change in the sensibility of mankind – a search for a utopia. Victor Arwas, an expert on art and the decorative arts of the early part of this century, provides informative sections which cover: Avant-Garde Painting; Reliefs; Ceramics; Books; Graphics; Stage design; Collage; Photomontage; Photography. Work by Lissitzky, Rodchenko, Stepanova, Popova, Tatlin and Malevich, among others, is presented in full colour and biographies of over 30 artists are also featured.

PB 1 85490 182 6
Publication: March 1993

INSTALLATION ART

A & D Profile No 30

Guest-Edited By Andrew Benjamin

The term 'installation', defining site-specific sculpture, has in recent years established itself firmly as part of the vocabulary of contemporary visual arts. Central to most installation art is a notion of space as a visible material with properties such as wood or stone. Hitherto unpublished work is presented by Arakawa and Madeline Gins, with essays by Jean-François Lyotard, Thierry de Duve, the Museum of Installation, London, Corinne Diserens on Gordon Matta-Clarke. The issue also features work by James Turrell, Judith Barry, Richard Artschwager, Anya Gallaccio, Joseph Kosuth, Cady Noland, Andrew Sabin, Donald Judd, Wolfgang Laib.

PB 1 85490 213 X
Publication: May 1993

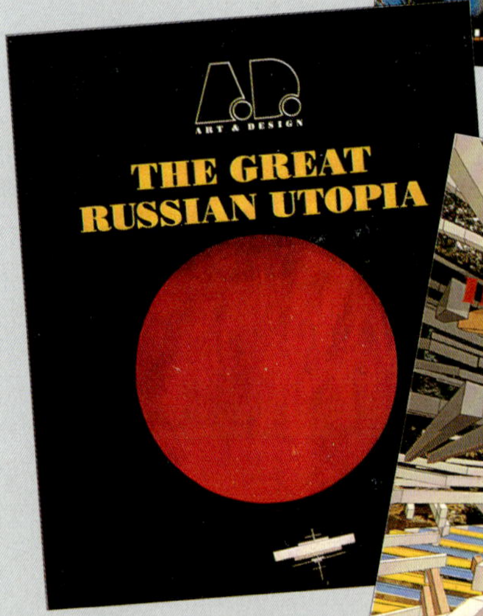

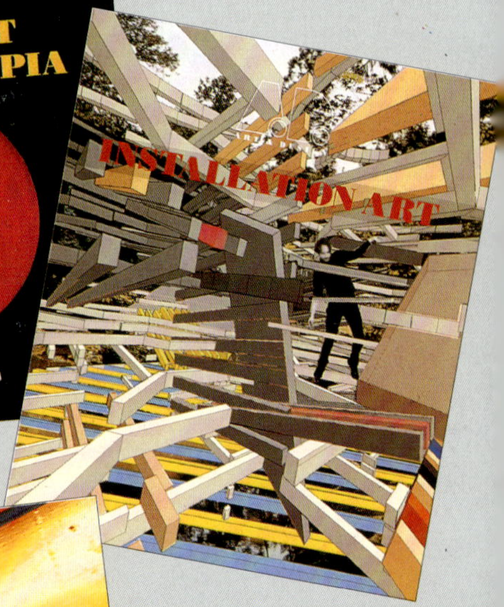

WORLD WIDE VIDEO

A & D Profile No 31

Guest-Edited by Johan Pijnappel

Video art represents the dematerialisation of art predicted by artists such as Marina Abramovic. This issue features work by Vito Acconci, Marina Abramovic, Bill Viola, Gary Hill, Francesc Torres, Keith Piper and the Ponton Euopean Media Art Lab. The experiments of Nam June Paik and Wolf Vostell in the 60s precipitated others such as artists like Nan Hoover, Bill Viola, Tony Oursler and General Idea who used video as a flexible and direct medium and were ignored for a long time. Towards the year 2000, the importance of dissolving traditional borders between art and society becomes clearer still.

PB 1 85490 214 8
Publication: July 1993

TIME & TIDE

THE TYNE INTERNATIONAL EXHIBITION OF CONTEMPORARY ART

A & D Profile No 32

A special issue produced with the 1993 Tyne International Exhibition of Contemporary Art in Newcastle, *Time and Tide* explores the nature of temporary installation and site works. The issue includes in-depth presentations of pieces by 15 internationally renowned artists including: Vito Acconci; Christine Borland; Gonzalo Diaz; Orshi Drozdik; Tony Fretton; Nan Goldin; Rodney Graham; Rémy Zaugg. With essays by Brian Hatton and Corinne Diserens, the issue contains a rich combination of specially designed artists' pages, writings and photographs of in situ work.

PB 1 85490 215 6
Publication: September 1993

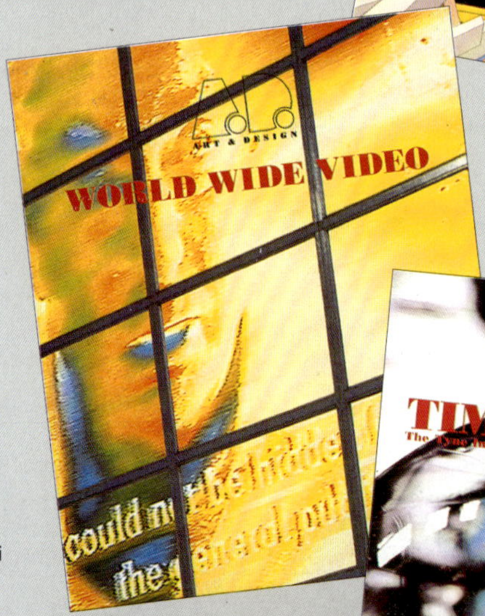

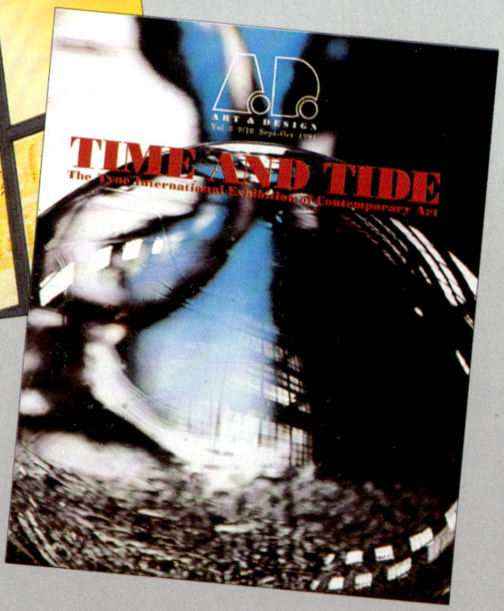

PARALLEL STRUCTURES

ART, DANCE AND MUSIC IN THE TWENTIETH CENTURY

A & D Profile No 33

Guest-Edited by Clare Farrow

From Matisse's Jazz compositions to Anish Kapoor's sculptural dance, this issue explores the relationship between art, dance and music and includes a variety of collaborations between choreographers, composers and artists from the early decades of the century right up to the present day. Articles range from a study of Parade and its debts to Futurist performance, jazz and the silent cinema, to the 'white' paintings of Robert Ryman; collaborative works by Merce Cunningham and John Cage and performances designed by artists such as Robert Rauschenberg and Jasper Johns.

PB 1 85490 216 4
Publication: November 1993

A REINHARDT, J KOSUTH, F GONZALEZ-TORRES

SYMPTOMS OF INTERFERENCE, CONDITIONS OF POSSIBILITY

A & D Profile No 34

Guest-Edited by Clare Farrow

This issue, based on the Camden Arts Centre exhibition in London, brings together the work of artists from three generations: Ad Reinhardt (1913-1967), Joseph Kosuth (b1945) and Felix Gonzalez-Torres (b1957), demonstrating how each artist has adopted a critical stance and sought to redefine artistic traditions. Kosuth's work can be seen as being a bridge between that of Reinhardt and Gonzalez-Torres, and this publication illustrates and reflects on the notion of passage from one generation to another.

PB 1 85490 217 2
Publication: January 1994

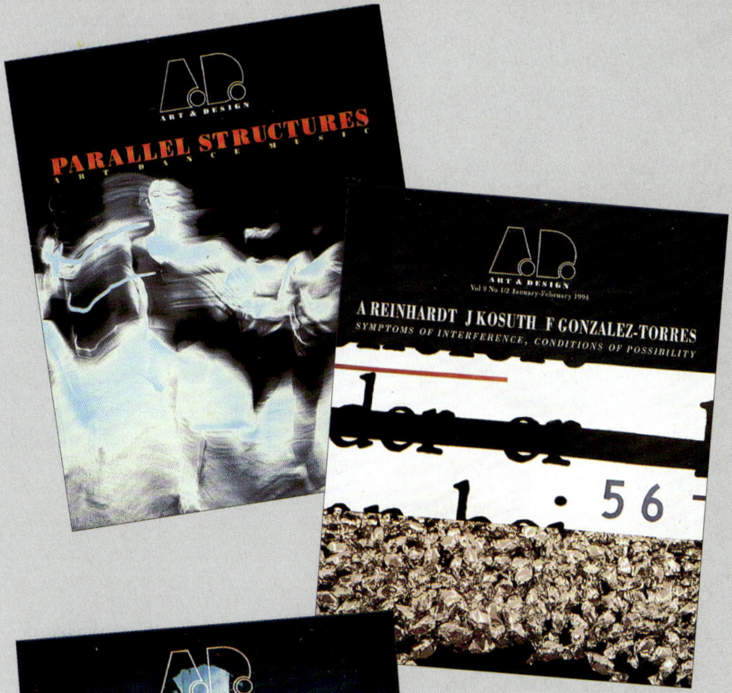

NEW ART FROM EASTERN EUROPE

IDENTITY AND CONFLICT

A & D Profile No 35

Guest-Edited by Paul Crowther

Exploring how political and social transformations in Eastern Europe have found effect in all areas of art practice since the end of the Cold War, this issue points to the interaction between Eastern European artists and their own traditions and the diversity of media and contemporary theory developed in the West. Material is drawn from several Eastern European countries including the Czech Republic and Slovakia, Slovenia, Croatia, Poland and Russia, with features on Neue Slowenische Kunst and Irwin, Ilya Kabakov, writings by Slavoj Zizek and an interview with Milan Knizak.

PB 1 85490 218 0
Publication: March 1994

ART AND THE NATURAL ENVIRONMENT

A & D Profile No 36

This issue explores how contemporary artists have attempted to recapture a closeness with nature. Tickon in Denmark, initiated by Alfio Bonanno as a 'total amalgam of art and nature', includes work by internationally renowned land artists such as Andy Goldsworthy, Chris Drury and Karen McCoy who have designed site specific work. Barbara Matilsky discusses the History of Environmental Art and features on David Nash, Wolfgang Laib, the Boyle Family and Mierle Laderman Ukeles demonstrate how environmental issues are highlighted by artistic interventions.

PB 1 85490 219 9
Publication: May 1994

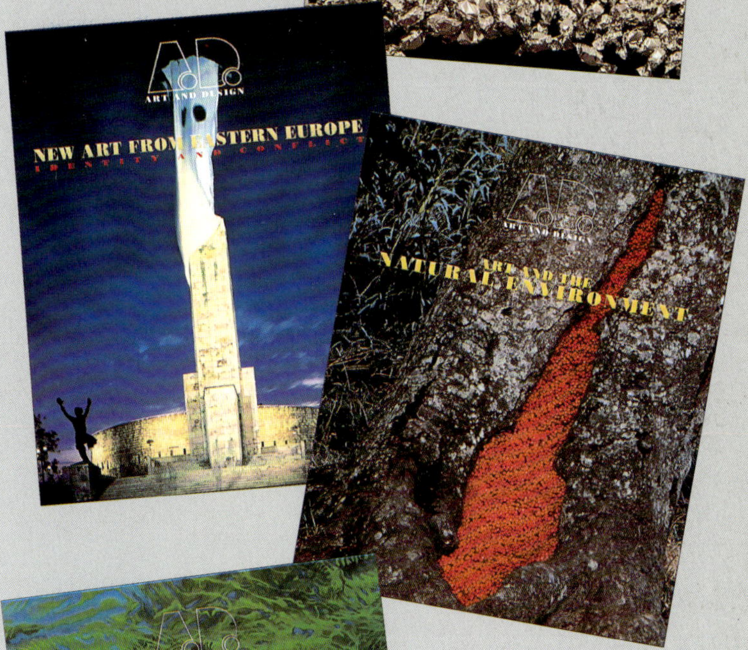

NEW ART FROM LATIN AMERICA

A & D Profile No 37

Guest-Edited by Oriana Baddeley

Recent exhibitions and publications have attempted to describe the cultural production of Latin America as a definable entity, existing outside national or international contexts. This issue examines the affect that accepted characteristics of 'Latin Americanness' have on the identity of artists practising today. Reflecting the diversity of cultural production and critical debate surrounding contemporary Latin American art, contributions include essays on Alfredo Jaar, Eugenio Dittborn with Edward Lucie-Smith on Ricardo Cinalli, Chloe Sayer on Mexican popular art, and David Elliot on young Argentinian artists.

PB 1 85490 220 2
Publication: July 1994

PERFORMANCE ART

INTO THE 90S

A & D Profile No 38

Performance has always been a way of bringing to life the formal and conceptual ideas on which art is based. This issue emphasises the role of performance as a weapon against the conventions of established art and explores its continuing potential with special features on the teaching of Marina Abramovic, Annie Sprinkle's 'Post-Porn Modernism', British performance art in the 90s, the Notting Hill Carnival; interviews with leading Los Angeles performer Rachael Rosenthal and Black-American dancer Billl T Jones and essays by Simon Herbert on a performer's history of performance art, William Furlong on sound in art and Rose Garrard on women's performance.

PB 1 85490 222 9
Publication: September 1994

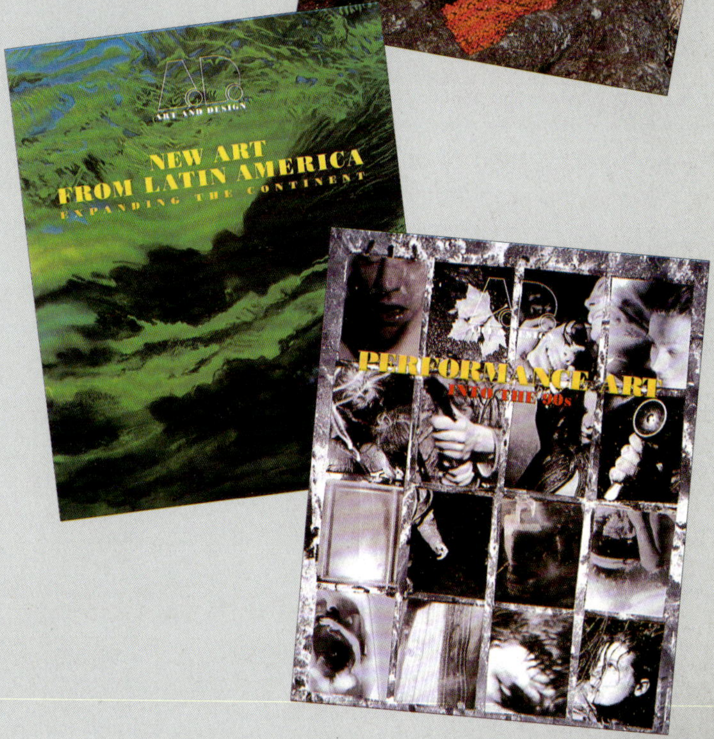

ART & TECHNOLOGY

A & D Profile No 39

Guest-Edited by Johan Pijnappel

Expanding upon the long standing relationship between man and machine, this issue explores the interaction between art and modern technologies demonstrating how artists have reacted to the newest developments. Projects from the 1960s to the present day give an overview of the different technological components that make up the art of our age. With contributions from some of the most important figures and institutions involved in the revolution in technological art, including Art Lab Tokyo and ZKM Karlsruhe, this issue shows that the 1990s is an era when science, engineering and art have come closer together than at any time since Leonardo da Vinci.

PB 1 85490 221 0
Publication: October 1994

BRITISH ART

DEFINING THE 90s

A & D No Profile 41

Contemporary British art has been reaching wider audiences in recent years at home and abroad. This issue highlights the various aspects of particular interest and activity which make the British art scene distinctive and exciting. Contributors include: Andrew Wilson on new painting; Tim Etchells on aspects of British Live Art; Oriana Baddeley interviewing John Keane, the Gulf War artist; Petrine Archer-Straw interviewing Eddie Chambers on Black art in Britain; Jeffrey Kastner on Matts Gallery and the phenomenon of artist-run spaces; Liam Gillick on the internationalisation of recent British art and Andrew Renton on Antony Gormley's Angel.

Paperback 1 85490 229 6
Publication: March 1995

ART & CULTURAL DIFFERENCE

HYBRIDS AND CLUSTERS

A & D Profile No 43

Guest-Edited by Nikos Papastergiadis

In the post-colonial era, the boundaries of art which traditionally supported the white western male have been slowly eroded, allowing a wider range of voices to be heard. But how deep has such a change gone and is a genuine multicultural approach possible within the terms of the institution of art? This issue discusses local and global notions of art in an era of nationalism, mass migration and socio-economic globalisation. With an evocative selection of writing by artists, poets and critics including John Berger, Irit Rogoff, Nestor Garcia-Canclini, Jimmie Durham and Juan Davila, this issue offers a broadly illustrated account of this area of crucial concern.

PB 1 85490 226 1
Publication: July 1995

THE CONTEMPORARY SUBLIME

SENSIBILITIES OF TRANSCENDENCE AND SHOCK

A & D Profile No 40

Guest-Edited by Paul Crowther

The sublime has long been familiar as an aesthetic of nature and landscape and it now figures as a major element in many aspects of post-modern sensibility. This issue addresses key aspects of the current debate in relation to contemporary art. It offers general theoretical articles addressing the links between art and the sublime made by Lyotard and by feminist thinkers. It also considers the relevance of the sublime to artists such as Malevich and Rothko along with contemporary work by Damien Hirst, Cornelia Parker and Philip Taaffe, thus raising questions involving contemporary attitudes to such topics as nature, violence and sexuality.

Paperback 1 85490 223 7
Publication: January 1995

THE IDEAL PLACE

A & D Profile No 42

Guest-Edited by Philip Peters

Published in collaboration with Philip Peters of the HCAK Institute in The Netherlands, this issue analyses the concept of place in art today through the work of 24 artists including Art & Language, Ricardo Brey, Renée Green, Matt Mullican, Stephen Willats, Robin Winters, Lawrence Weiner and Remy Zaugg. 'Place' and 'Placement' have played an important part in the practice of a great many artists, of differing characters and generations, as exemplified by Duchamp and Carl André. Including specially commissioned texts by Henk Oosterling, David Elliott and Andrew Wilson, this issue explores the utopian question, 'is there an ideal place, and could or should a place exist?

PB 1 85490 225 3
Publication: May 1995

PHOTOGRAPHY IN THE VISUAL ARTS

A & D Profile No 44

Guest-Edited by John Stathatos

This issue is devoted to a survey of photography and the photographic image in the contemporary visual arts. In the last decade, photography has emerged as one of the most innovative visual media; whether representing opportunistic infiltration by photography, or conversely, its co-option by the wider visual arts, the results have proved both vigorous and exciting. Including work by Jeff Wall, Peeter Linnap, Catherine Yass and Susan Trangmar, this issue concentrates on the areas of photography currently of greatest interest to practitioners in the visual arts, and challenges the boundaries of the socially and artistically acceptable through the use of photographic imagery.

PB 1 85490 224 5
Publication: September 1995

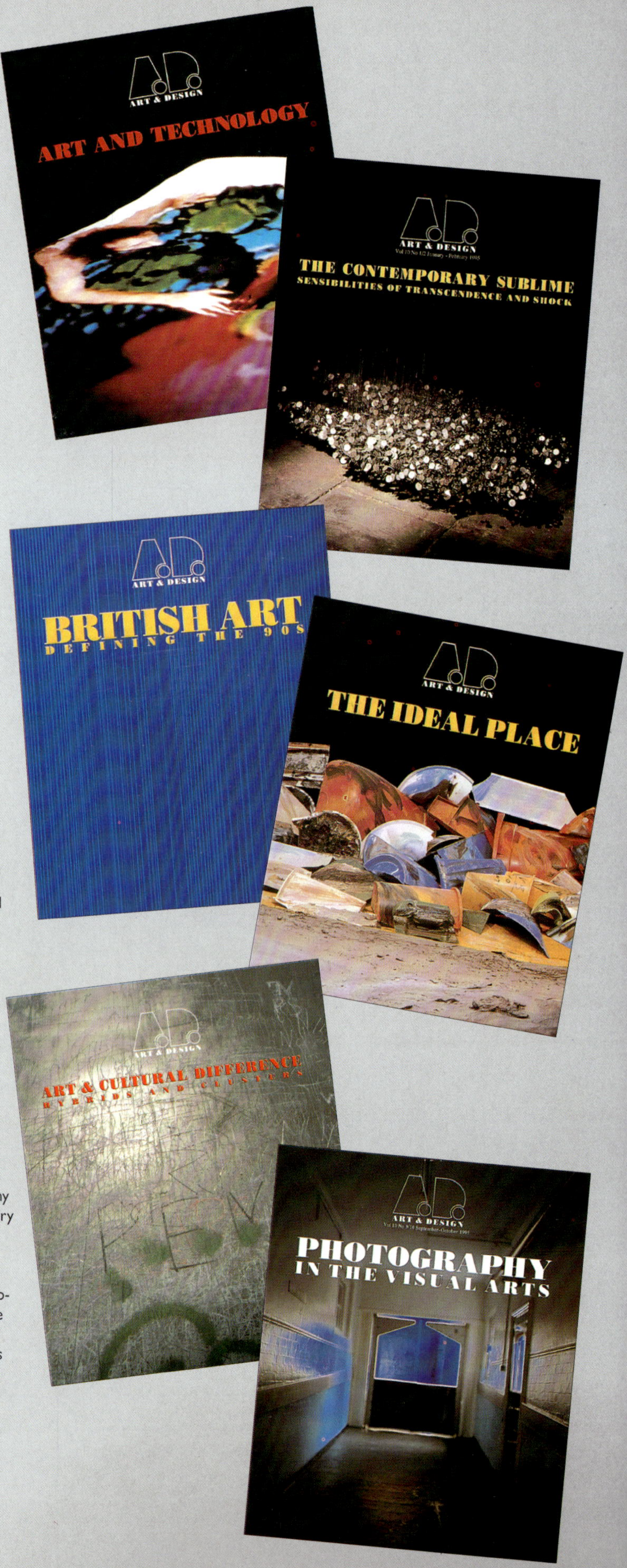

PUBLIC ART

A & D Profile No 46

Guest-Edited by Amanda Crabtree

Public Art has moved on from the common perception of sculpture in parks and plazas to become one of the most hotly debated areas of development in contemporary art at the present time. This issue looks at how artists react to the idea of monumental art today, accentuating the relationship between art, politics and social activism; Miriam Rosen investigates the potential of recent developments in communication such as Cyberspace, Superhighways and The Internet; Jeff Kastner in an interview with Mary Jane Jacob examines recent community-based projects in the United States and in particular at what has been termed 'new genre' public art; Valérie Mavidorakis considers the history of public commissions from Rodin to Serra and from Baquie to Rachael Whiteread and the infamous house.

PB 1 85490 230 X
Publication: January 1996

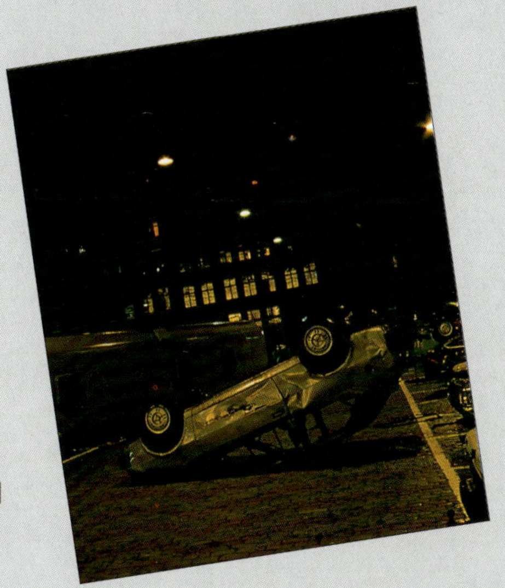

ABSTRACT EROTICISM

A & D Profile No 47

Guest-Edited by Michael Petry

The domain of Eros touches the lives of all; gender, sexuality and corporeality cannot fend off the erotic impulse, the object of desire is unique to each subject, yet Eros worms its way into every molecule. Depictions of Eros in the technological age have moved beyond the barrier of pornography with its insistent use of the figure to a more abstract treatment. This issue of *Art & Design*, aims to explore a visual language that evokes this abstract concept yet remains erotic. With invited 'love letters' from many famous writers including Kathy Acker, Peter Ackroyd, Fiona Pitt-Kelcey and Susan Sontag, work by artists including Janie Antoine, Matthew Barney, Louise Bourgeois, Helen Chadwick, Gary Hill and Rebecca Horn and writings by Thomas McEvilley among others, this issue is a celebration of Eros triumphant

PB 1 85490 231 8
Publication: March 1996

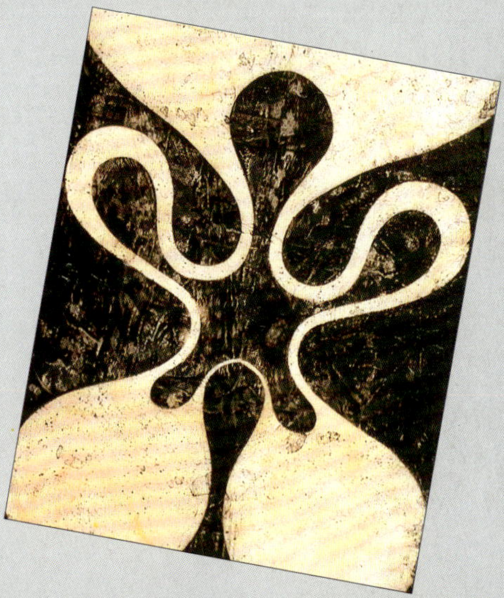

For further information please contact Academy Group Ltd, 42 Leinster Gardens, London W2 3AN Tel: (0171) 402 2141 Fax: (0171) 723 9540
VCH, 8 Wellington Court, Wellington Street, Cambridge CB1 1HZ, United Kingdom. Tel: (01223) 321111 Fax: (01223) 313321
USA and Canada: VCH Publishers Inc, 303 NW 12th Avenue, Deerfield Beach, FL 33442-1788, USA. Tel: (305) 428 5566/(800) 367 8249 Fax: (305) 428 8201/(800)367 8247
All other countries: VCH, PO Box 10 11 61, 69451 Weinheim, Federal Republic of Germany. Tel: (06201) 606 446/447 Fax: (06201) 606 184.

PAINTING IN THE AGE OF ARTIFICIAL INTELLIGENCE

A & D Profile No 48

Guest-Edited by David Moos

Gathering together a formidable collection of writings by both artists and writers, this issue explores the position of painting today. Painting has had to reaffirm itself in an age where different media and approaches proliferate, where the possibilities of communication in the fields of artificial intelligence are infinite. Specific painters have been chosen whose work will endure or continue to prove vital for the immediate future of painting and its development as a medium, both materially and conceptually. Including features on more historical figures such Willem de Kooning, Philip Guston and Joan Mitchell, established contemporary painters such as Chuck Close, Sigmar Poke and Robert Ryman as well as younger contemporary artists such Helmut Dorner, Peter Halley, Imi Knoebel, Juan Uslé and Jonathan Lasker, the issue provides a perceptive framework to some of the best work being carried out today.

PB 1 85490 232 6
Publication: May 1996

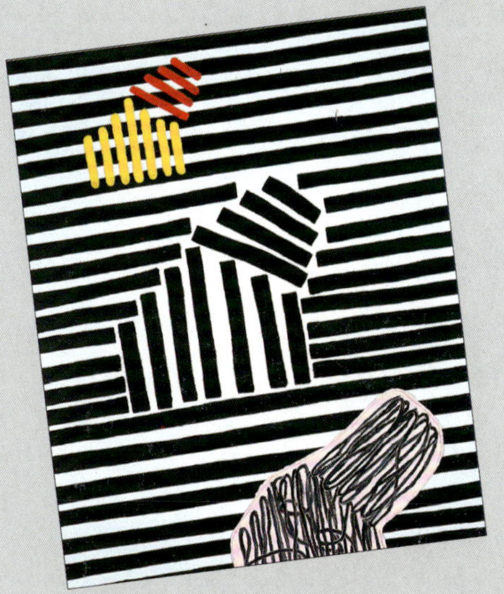

THE MULTIMEDIA TEXT

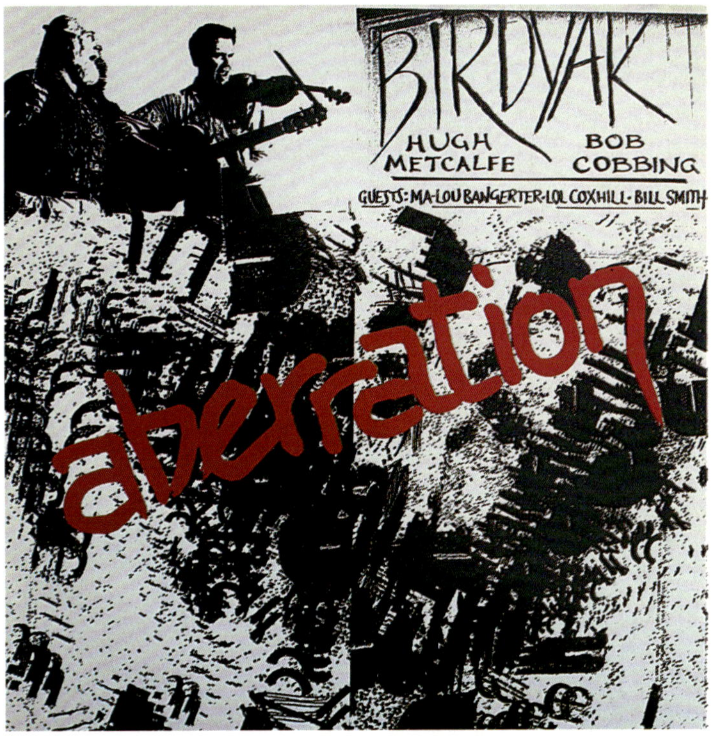

Hugh Metcalfe and Bob Cobbing, Birdyak, *1988*

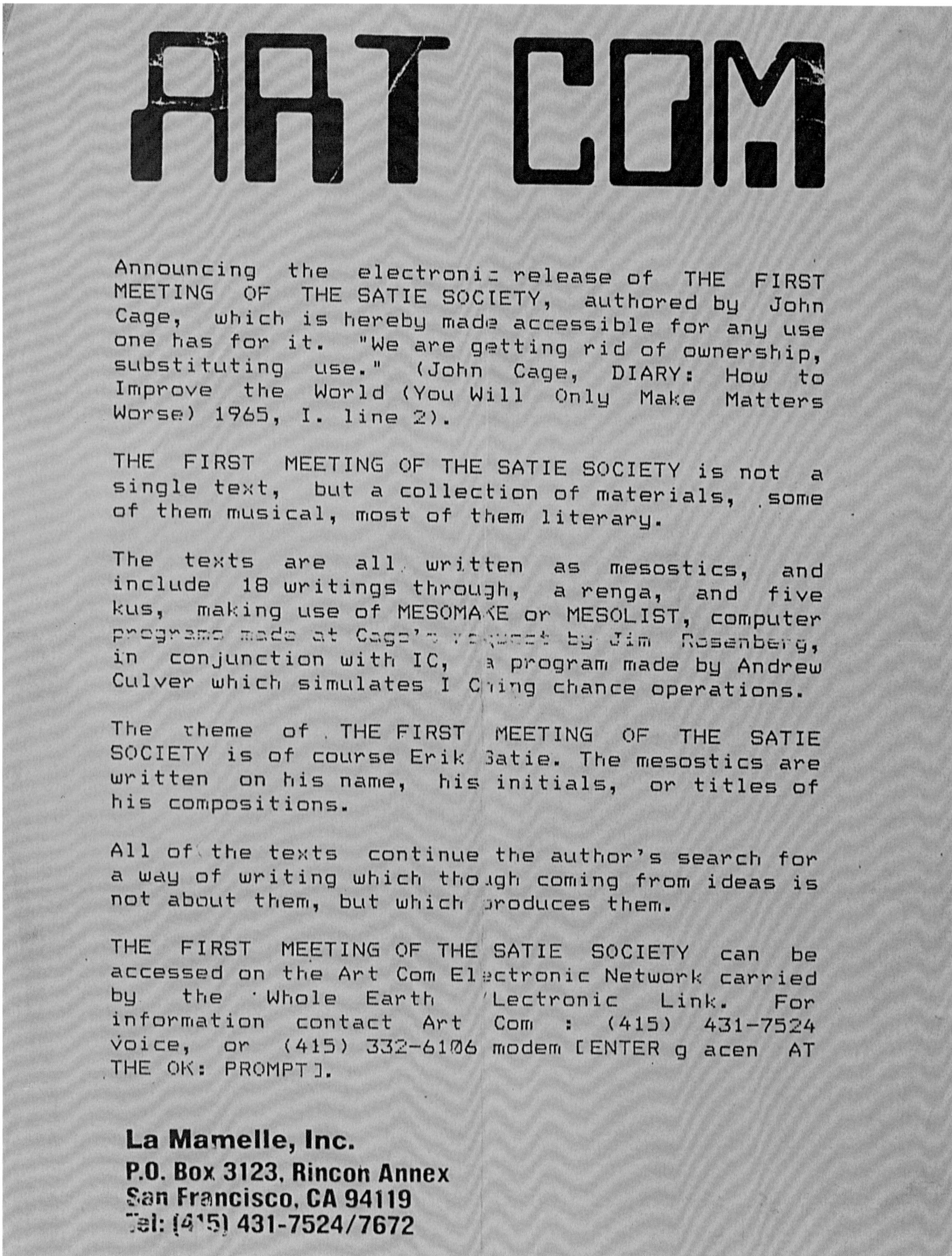

ART COM

Announcing the electronic release of THE FIRST MEETING OF THE SATIE SOCIETY, authored by John Cage, which is hereby made accessible for any use one has for it. "We are getting rid of ownership, substituting use." (John Cage, DIARY: How to Improve the World (You Will Only Make Matters Worse) 1965, I. line 2).

THE FIRST MEETING OF THE SATIE SOCIETY is not a single text, but a collection of materials, some of them musical, most of them literary.

The texts are all written as mesostics, and include 18 writings through, a renga, and five kus, making use of MESOMAKE or MESOLIST, computer programs made at Cage's request by Jim Rosenberg, in conjunction with IC, a program made by Andrew Culver which simulates I Ching chance operations.

The theme of THE FIRST MEETING OF THE SATIE SOCIETY is of course Erik Satie. The mesostics are written on his name, his initials, or titles of his compositions.

All of the texts continue the author's search for a way of writing which though coming from ideas is not about them, but which produces them.

THE FIRST MEETING OF THE SATIE SOCIETY can be accessed on the Art Com Electronic Network carried by the Whole Earth 'Lectronic Link. For information contact Art Com : (415) 431-7524 voice, or (415) 332-6106 modem [ENTER g acen AT THE OK: PROMPT].

La Mamelle, Inc.
P.O. Box 3123, Rincon Annex
San Francisco, CA 94119
Tel: (415) 431-7524/7672

John Cage, Flyer for The First Meeting of the Satie Society

Art & Design

THE MULTIMEDIA TEXT

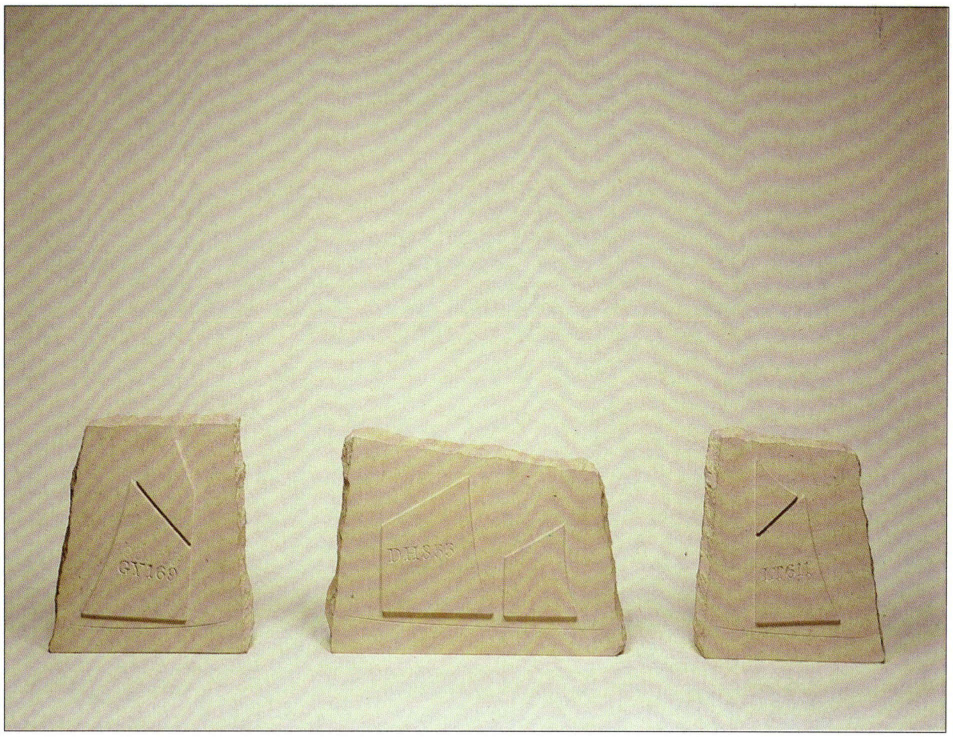

Ian Hamilton Finlay, Three Sails, *stone – left: 32.5x28.5x7cm, middle: 30.5x42.5x7cm, right: 30.5x26.5x7cm (Victoria Miro Gallery, London)*

ACADEMY EDITIONS • LONDON

Acknowledgements

We would like to thank Nicholas Zurbrugg for putting together this fascinating issue of Art & Design. **Nicholas Zurbrugg** is Professor of English and Cultural Studies at The School of Arts and Humanities, De Montfort University, Leicester, and is author of *The Parameters of Postmodernism* (Routledge). **Kathy Acker** is a San Francisco-based novelist. Her works include *Don Quixote, Blood and Guts in High School, Great Expectations, Empire of the Senseless, In Memorium to Identity* and *Pussy, King of the Pirates* (forthcoming Grove, 1995). **Warren Burt** is a Melbourne-based American composer, writer and artist. *Writings from a Scarlet Aardvark*, his collected essays, is published by Frog Peak Music, New Hampshire. **John Cage** is recognised as America's most significant avant-garde composer, performer and theoretician. **Henri Chopin** is one of the pioneers of sound poetry and concrete poetry. The editor and publisher of the reviews *Cinquième Saison* and *OU*, he is also the author of this movement's first substantial history, *Poésie Sonore Internationale* (Jean-Michel Place). **Bob Cobbing** is one of the foremost sound poets and avant-garde publishers in England. His Writer's Forum editions have published work by many experimental writers. **John Conomos** is a Sydney-based video artist and theorist. He lectures in Film Theory and Video at the College of Fine Arts, The University of New South Wales, Sydney. Editor of *Scan* + he is writing a history of Australian video. **Francesco Conz** is the publisher of large-scale fabric multiples by multimedia artists. **Ian Hamilton Finlay** is one of Europe's foremost concrete and visual poets, and language artists. His Wild Hawthorn Press has published the magazine *Poor Old Tired Horse* and a succession of poem-cards, poem-prints and bound and folding poem-booklets. His recent work encompasses urban and garden installations. **Ken Friedman** is Associate Professor of Leadership and Strategic Design at the Norwegian School of Management NMH. He is also director of the Nordic Centre for Innovation, a joint research centre of the Norwegian School of Management NMH, University of Lund and University of Art and Design Helsinki. **Gary Genosko** is an independent Canadian researcher. He is the author of *Baudrillard and Signs* (1994) and the editor of *The Guattari Reader* (1995). **John Giorno** is a New York-based sound poet and language artist. Giorno Poetry Systems have published a series of LP and video anthologies of work by the New York avant-garde, and Giorno is also the author of poem-prints published by Editions Francesco Conz (Verona) and by George Moulder Fine Arts (New York). **Jim Krank** is a Brisbane writer, working on a screen adaptation of Antonin Artaud's later years, *Sanatorium Under the Sign of the Swastika*. **Stuart Lynch**, a former member of the Butoh dancer Min Tanaka's Mai-Juku Performance Company, is an international dance performer presently based in both Denmark and Australia, where he works in collaboration with dancer/choreographer Tess De Quincey. **Robert Scanlan** is Literary Director of the American Repertory Theatre in Cambridge, Massachusetts and also heads the Dramaturgy Program at the Institute for Advanced Theatre Training at Harvard University. He has collaborated with Philip Glass on the world premier of the opera *Orphée* and was dramaturg for Robert Wilson's staging of Ibsen's *When We Dead Awaken*. **Larry Wendt** is a San José-based sound poet and text-sound composer who has performed throughout Europe, America and Australia. He edited the international CD anthology *Vocal Neighbourhoods* for *Leonardo Music Journal* (Vol 3, 1993). **Adam Wolter** is a Brisbane-based computer artist. He exhibits at the Peter Bellas Gallery, Brisbane, and at the Irene Sutton Gallery, Melbourne.

Documentary photography: Graham Coulter-Smith. Unless otherwise stated, all images are courtesy of the artists: p40 Courtesy of BFI Stills, Posters and Designs; pp46-55 courtesy Victoria Miro Gallery, London.

Front Cover: Collage of images from within The Multimedia Text *by various artists;*
Inside Covers: Henri Chopin, L'Esprit des Lois*, Poésies, 1989, detail*

EDITOR: Nicola Kearton ASSISTANT EDITOR: Ramona Khambatta EDITORIAL: Cristina Fontoura
ART EDITOR: Andrea Bettella CHIEF DESIGNER: Mario Bettella DESIGNER: Alistair Probert

First published in Great Britain in 1995 by *Art & Design* an imprint of
ACADEMY GROUP LTD, 42 LEINSTER GARDENS, LONDON W2 3AN
Member of the VCH Publishing Group
ISBN: 1 85490 227 X (UK)

Art & Design Profile 45 is published as part of *Art & Design* Vol 10 11/12 1995
Art & Design Magazine is published six times a year and is available by subscription

Distributed to the trade in the United States of America by
NATIONAL BOOK NETWORK, INC, 4720 BOSTON WAY, LANHAM, MARYLAND 20706

Printed and bound in Italy

Contents

ART & DESIGN PROFILE No 45

THE MULTIMEDIA TEXT

Guest-Edited by Nicholas Zurbrugg

Nicholas Zurbrugg Introduction 6

Kathy Acker After the End of the Art World 7

Warren Burt Compositional Linguistics: 20th-Century American Composers and the Text 10

John Cage *interviewed by Nicholas Zurbrugg* 16

Henri Chopin *interviewed by Nicholas Zurbrugg* 20

Bob Cobbing *interviewed by Nicholas Zurbrugg* 32

John Conomos The Movement of Shadows: Video as Electronic Writing 38

Francesco Conz: Multiplying the Text *interviewed by Nicholas Zurbrugg* 42

Ian Hamilton Finlay *interviewed by Nicholas Zurbrugg* 46

Ken Friedman Language and Culture in the Information Age 56

Gary Genosko In the Shadow of McLuhan 60

John Giorno On Playing Samuel Beckett's *Eh Joe* 64

Jim Krank Punks One, Poets Nil: Steven Jesse Bernstein, Lydia Lunch and Henry Rollins 68

Stuart Lynch *interviewed by Nicholas Zurbrugg* 72

Robert Scanlan Post-Modern Time and Place: Wilson/Müller Intersections 76

Larry Wendt Narrative and the World Wide Web 82

Adam Wolter: 'Fairly Strictly a Computer Artist' *interviewed by Nicholas Zurbrugg* 92

INTRODUCTION

Nicholas Zurbrugg

Remarking how most people are completely unaware of 'the real quality of 20th-century creativity' and of the ways in which this century's most visionary artists have consistently undermined and intertwined disciplinary 'categories', the French sound poet Henri Chopin emphasises how Luigi Russolo was 'a painter, a composer and an investor', Pierre Albert-Birot was a 'typographer, a sculptor, a poet and a dramatist', and Arp was 'the same – several disciplines'.

Considered conservatively, Russolo, Albert-Birot, Arp and Chopin himself are all 'undisciplined' artists, in the sense that their art seems too big for its disciplinary boots – a cuckoo, as it were, straddling several incompatible nests. Considered more positively, the art of such multidisciplinary creators is supremely significant as work annunciating, inaugurating and consolidating some of 20th-century culture's most essential, creative and conceptual transitions. At the inner margins of the new, and at the outer margins of the old, their work typifies the most significant live-ends of the supposedly dead-end 'Post-Modern condition'.

Ironically, as Ian Hamilton Finlay observes, mainstream criticism repeatedly neglects or rejects any 'range of interests' that challenges its prejudices, preconceptions and taboos. Yet for Finlay, elementary awareness of the 'western tradition' of ornamental gardens suggests that there is nothing surprising about the gesture of integrating art, text and gardens. Only the 'rigid separation' of such materials seems shocking. Likewise for Chopin, familiarity with Russian or Oriental song suggests that there is no 'frontier between poetry and music', just as pre-typographic books suggest the inseparability of word and graphic design. In this respect, there is nothing 'avant-garde' about the multimedia sensibility insofar as it confirms our culture's oldest traditions. On the other hand, the technological innovations of the early, mid and late 20th century have witnessed profoundly new aesthetic possibilities. If as Brion Gysin remarked, writing has long seemed 'fifty years behind painting', it has perhaps begun to close this gap in the age of what he called 'machine poetry'.

The most positive impulses in Post-Modern creativity offer three successive responses to the modernist multimedia and multi-textual avant-garde. As Jasia Reichardt's ground breaking exhibition 'Between Poetry and Painting' (1965) demonstrated, the textual experiments of the Dadaist and Futurist poets and painters led directly to the more self-consciously constructivist aesthetic of the Lettrist, concrete and visual poets of the 60s – the poets published by Ian Hamilton Finlay's magazine *Poor Old Tired Horse*, by Bob Cobbing's *Writer's Forum* editions, and by Henri Chopin's *Revue-Disque OU*.

Exploring the impact of the poem on and off the page, within what Cobbing calls 'a more total approach', as record or as three-dimensional object, as 'real time' or 'reel time' performance or collaborative event, and as sonic or iconic environment, the early work of Finlay, Cobbing and Chopin typifies the initial, heroic phase of the Post-Modern multimedia intertext. As Melbourne-based American composer Warren Burt suggests, the experiments of Harry Partch, John Cage, Jackson MacLow, Kenneth Gaburo and Robert Ashley typify the comparable multimedia textual aesthetic informing American composition, 'blurring the boundaries between . . . music and language'.

The second wave of Post-Modern multimedia art consists of those projects expanding 'first wave' innovation by taking the text off the page into other domains; in the case of Finlay into 'proposals for buildings', in the case of Cage into work for the 'Whole Earth 'Lectronic Link', in the case of Chopin into collaborations with younger computer-poets and computer-composers such as Larry Wendt and Marc Battier.

As American Repertory Theatre Literary Director Robert Scanlan indicates, this second wave of multimedia creativity concurrently precipitated new forms of multimedia theatre, such as Heiner Müller's and Robert Wilson's extraordinary collaborative variations upon works by Shakespeare and Laclos. Subsequent new directions in radical verbal/visual theatre include New York sound poet John Giorno's offstage/on-stage video performance of Beckett's *Eh Joe*, and Copenhagen and Sydney-based Butoh dancer Stuart Lynch's *Paradance Fable*; a performative response to an essay from Baudrillard's *The Ecstasy of Communication*.

Extending the scale and substance of the multiple print with his innovative fabric editions, Verona publishers and photographer Francesco Conz's collaborative orchestrations of past and present verbal/visual work by European and American Fluxus, visual poetry, sound poetry and new music pioneers similarly encourage 'multimedia artists . . . real children of their epoch' to take their work into various kinds of 'new direction'.

Far from witnessing the decline of multimedia intertextual creativity, the 70s and 80s clearly signal the widespread consolidation of the early Post-Modern avant-garde's energies and experiments. As Sydney video artist John Conomos observes, new technologies have in turn allowed artists such as Jean-Luc Godard and Chris Marker – as well as artists of Conomos' generation – to explore 'electronic writing'; re-translating historical and autobiographical themes in a domain between 'literature, the visual arts and the new electronic media'.

More recently, young 'third wave' high-tech practitioners such as Brisbane computer-artist Adam Wolter have once again reassessed and realigned past and present iconography and thematics, juxtaposing linear and numerical variants of classical iconography within electronic installations such as Wolter's *Mesh*.

While Canadian theorist Gary Genosko, San José high-tech performance poet Larry Wendt and Oslo-based Fluxus veteran Ken Friedman discuss the uncertain potential of 'third wave' computer and net culture, San Francisco novelist Kathy Acker considers the more subversive and abrasive aspirations of the Australian feminist high-tech collective, VNS Matrix, and the hyper-bacchanalian San Francisco punk rock band, Tribe 8. Acker cites both groups as 'signs of birth'; 'Funky feminism' reaching beyond the 'straight white male' clichés of 'old punk'.

Addressing other aspects of what one might call third wave punk culture, Brisbane writer Jim Krank argues that whereas the 'old punk' lyrics of Henry Rollins and Lydia Lunch stagnate in self-conscious 'macho bullstuff', the neglected poetry and rock collaborations of the late Steven Jesse Bernstein offer one of the most forceful recorded 'spoken word' performances of the last two decades.

Encompassing visual text and sound text, visual and sound installation, theatrical, musical, cinematic, video and computer performance, and the extremes of high tech net-text and low tech punk text, the potential of multimedia intertextual composition has never been more challenging or more diverse. Among such practices, perhaps, one encounters some of the more rewarding manifestations of late Post-Modern creativity.

AFTER THE END OF THE ART WORLD

Kathy Acker

> 'What about you?' he asks. 'What do you teach?'
> 'History', Max Thor says. 'History of the future.'
> Silence. Bernard Alione gazes at Max Thor, motionless.
> His voice is unrecognisable now.
> 'Is it very different?' he asks.
> 'There's nothing left', Max Thor says.
> *'So I don't say anything. The students go to sleep.'*[1]

The Leila Wallace-Reader's Digest Foundation, a funding organisation in the United States, supports poetry centres directly and indirectly by underwriting writers', especially poets', tours. It is one of the largest organisations of its kind. For a tour, the organisation pairs a national and a local writer, then sends the two to local centres throughout the United States.

This year I was asked to be one of the national writers. I was sent to read and to give workshops in Buffalo (New York), Milwaukee, the eastern part of North Carolina, New York City and San Francisco.

I have privately named my tour *The Tour of Death*. Two of the five centres I visited – the North Carolina Network and San Francisco's Intersection – closed after the local writer, Bob Gluck, and I read there. The venue in Milwaukee is surviving due only to its excellent bookstore; only the New York centre, St Marks-in-the-Bowery, an historical monument, is relatively economically healthy. When I say *Tour of Death*, I am not speaking only about the economics of art in the United States, I use the word *death* for other reasons. Though all the poetry centres purported to be community centres, almost all were run by upper-middle class Caucasian women. Moreover, this same social group made up almost 80 per cent of our audiences throughout the tour. To say the least, this is not the composition of my usual audience.

Given the present political and economic configuration of the United States, it is no wonder that the business of poetry, of all literary writing and of art is in trouble. Government funding of the arts is almost over; people, not only artists, are frightened of poverty. To those who are deeply scared, even including artists and art funders, art increasingly seems of minimal importance. Art is being marginalised to the point of extinction: I did not need *The Tour of Death* to show me this; to show me how thoroughly economics and politics determines culture.

What the Leila Wallace-Reader's Digest tour did show me was the extent to which the artists themselves are responsible for the marginalisation and perhaps extinction of what is known in the United States as *the art world*. Perhaps the political shift from the centre to the extreme right which we have been – and are experiencing – in this country has been interiorised by artists and other art-workers. Certainly, as the political spectrum has shifted, so not only the poets, not only the literary industry, not only the artists and art-dealers, but the whole network named *high culture*, in its desperate attempt to defend art to government officials and to an indifferent populace, has moved closer to conservatism. Any 'experimentalism' is out; art that does well economically is in. As I have said, fear rules. And we who work to actualise the imagination are scared to death to admit what we know every day of our lives: that our work is no longer necessary to our society as our society is now defining itself.

This is what I mean, finally, by *The Tour of Death*. We will not admit that what was once known as the art world, insofar as it had a community and therefore a cultural existence – in that it was not just a playground of the rich for the rich – is over. The middle class who served the backbone of the art world is becoming conscious of its own demise; people are realising that they can no longer afford the mortgages on the homes they bought during times of former affluence, nor can they afford to send their children to college; decent medical care is a luxury; homelessness the spectre in front of their eyes. The once staunch middle-classes do not have the leisure to attend poetry readings.

It is all over.

You have asked me to write about 'new developments in literature and art', especially performance art, and I can begin by writing only one thing: art, except as a playground for the rich, is dead.

Duras: 'There's nothing left . . . So I don't say anything'.

Let us look elsewhere.

I am not talking about the death of the art world. Of high art. That has already been announced in several places and, prior to its announcements, has taken place. I am presenting signs of birth.

What I knew, when I grew up both as a child and as a young writer in New York City, was a white male-dominated art world. Since it's mythic hero was the American cowboy, it was a community which denied all possibilities of community. In the United States, we are still living under the banner of the cowboy: that myth has led us to supra-individualism, nationalism and group paranoia.

Just as nothing comes out of nothing, so that which is cannot die. It changes form. Then it is not true that there is no longer any art. Rather, the old formations known as art or the art world have passed away. And those who were not heard or who were barely heard in those old glorious cowboy days are now being heard more and more. Listen.

> I think that we always wanted to get our work, our projects, out of the closeted, mundane, safe, boring, irrelevant art world and out into the streets, gutters, schools . . . [by means of] . . . underground press, pirate radio, raves . . . All this has happened.

Francesca da Rimini, AKA gashgirl, is speaking. Her cohorts, Josephine Starrs, Julianne Pierce and Virginia Barratt, form the Australian-based computer artists VNS Matrix.

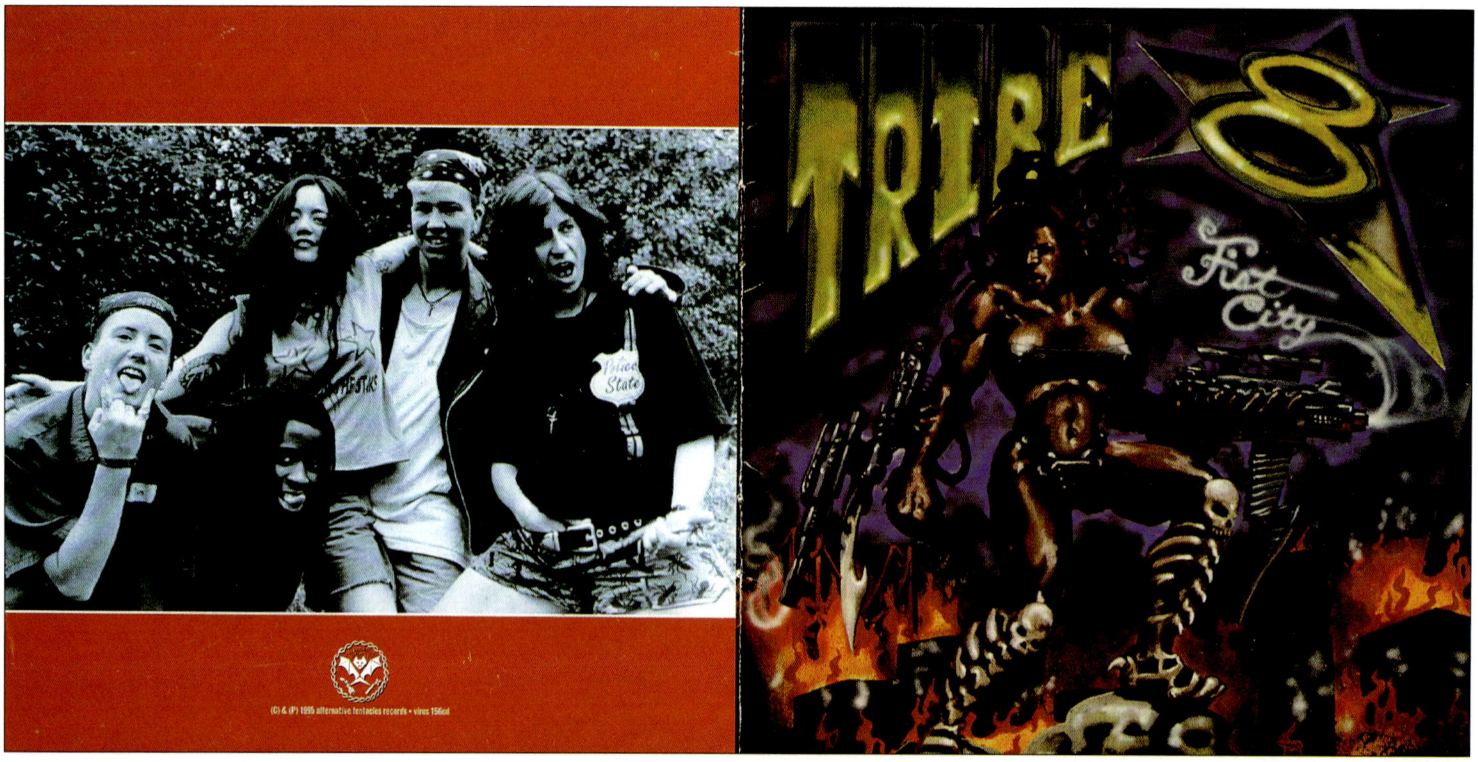

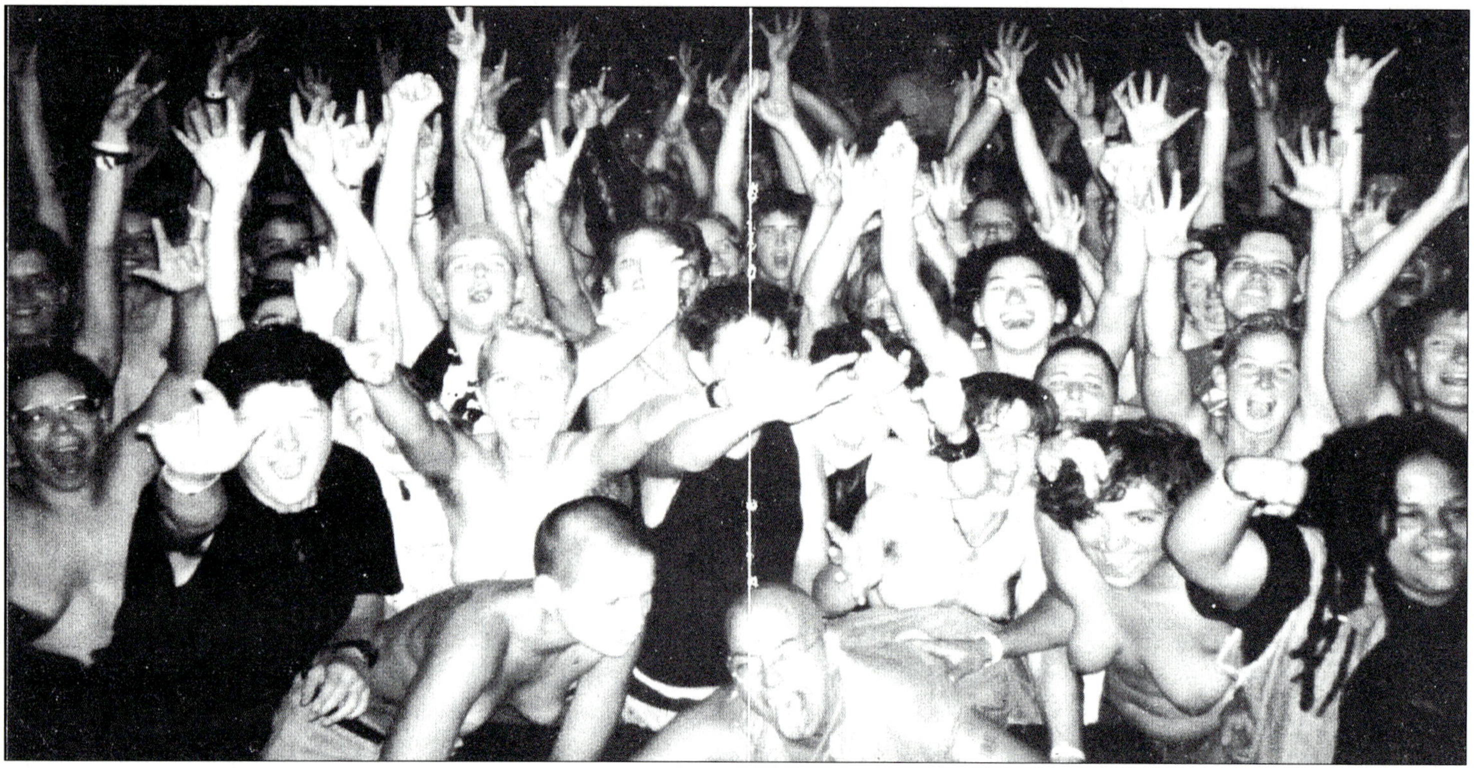

FROM ABOVE: Tribe 8, Fist City *CD (Alternative Tentacles Records, San Francisco), front and back cover; Fans at a Tribe 8 concert*

> We are sick of how women continue to be invisible in popular culture. We are sick of boyzland. Whether or not culture is boyzland, that's how the media portrays it. We want to undo the male hold on technology, the gendering of technology as male, and at the same time, we want to be among those who are giving young women a model of feminism they can relate to. Funky feminism.

VNS Matrix commenced their technology plot by writing a manifesto which they plastered on the streets of Adelaide and Sydney. It was also sent via fax and e-mail to all sorts of women, including me. I will never forget returning home, one day last year, to page after page of the *Cyberfeminist Manifesto for the twenty-first Century* which begins, 'We are the modern cunt positive anti-reason unbounded unleashed unforgiving . . . '

I spent a year trying to trace these strange women; finally, through a mutual friend, RosieX who produces the magazine *Geek girl*, they contacted me.

I am gossiping; I am also pointing to change. Cowboys and financiers run the old art world and that world gave birth, as its artists, to cowboys and financiers. Now that world is over, the women who are making culture are working within and by means of networks of friendship. Moreover, their work is producing friendship. For instance, the *Cyberfeminist Manifesto for the twenty-first Century* caused a friendship to spring up between VNS Matrix and myself.

At the moment, VNS is creating an actual computer game, *All New Gen*. Its mission, according to its makers, is to 'sow the seeds of new world disorder'.[2]

Almost halfway across the physical world but next door in the virtual, Lynn Breedlove, Lynn Flipper, Lynn Slade, Leslie Mah and Lynn Payne of Tribe 8, the hottest band in San Francisco, are transforming their audiences into packs of maddened Bacchantes. The first time I saw Breedlove on stage, a few years ago, I thought I was seeing one of the dreams I had had when a girl. The venue was *Slim's*, one of the best in San Francisco; there was an A&R convention in town. Breedlove appeared wearing neo-New Romantic garb: a white pirate shirt and tight black leather pants. She was a boy version of Patti Smith. Off came the shirt. On one of her breasts, the word *anarchist*. On the other, *fag*. As in the first story of the Old Testament, words made reality: Tribe 8, playing something like music but more raucous, more discordant, proceeded to flash knives, display handcuffs, all the stage gear of the bad boys who were no more, while the audience in rapture (except for some A&R men quivering in the corner) threw off their shirts. Meanwhile, Breedlove had her hand down her leathers. These pants burst open; out jumped a huge dark grey strap-on. A girl leaped on the stage and started to suck . . .

Is it art? Now listen to Lynn:'I was raised on white man's art. I'm redefining what art is to me. Tribe 8 is part of a whole movement . . . '

Me: 'What movement?'

Breedlove: 'A grass roots punk movement. Not like the old punk that was straight white male centred'.

Me: 'How would you define this new punk?'

Breedlove: 'It consists of spoken word, literature especially 'zines, music. The main thing is that we're doing it for ourselves, creating culture our ways. There's no one way anymore. Whereas the media is creating a homogenous culture'.

When I asked thee Holy Queen of the Net, ex-fem of the magazine *Mondo 2000*, St Jude, who lives only in the country of the virtual, what happened to the old art world, she replied,

'The artists killed it off. They defined themselves too narrowly. That culture of which art was a part failed me. It gave me nothing. I have had to do it on my own.'

Breedlove said the same thing: now all of us are making our culture for ourselves in the face of the monolithic media. Many of us are working by means of, and for, friendship. As is the case with this article.

Notes

1 Marguerite Duras, *Destroy, She Said*, Grove, New York, 1986, p76.

2 'VNS Matrix', *Geekgirl*, No 001 (1995), ed RosieX, King's Cross, Sydney, Australia.

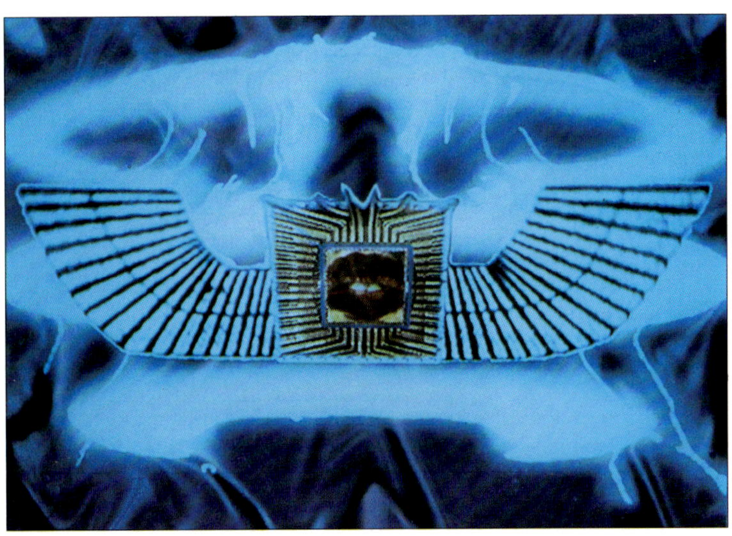

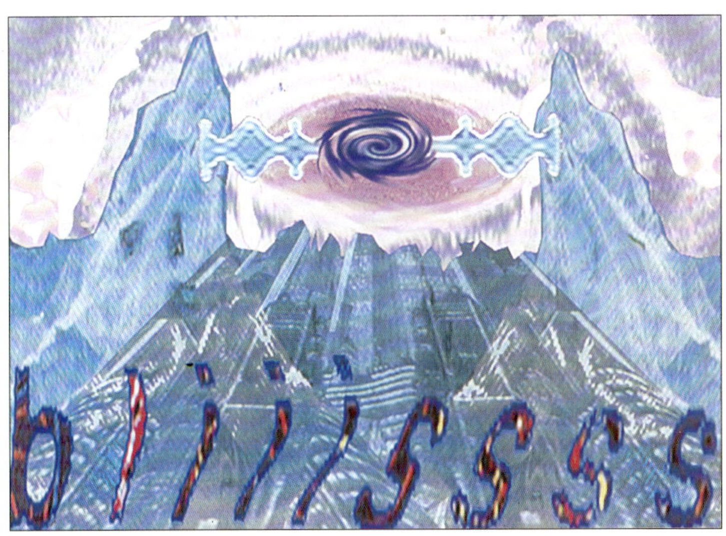

VNS Matrix, L to R: 'Silicon Angels', lightbox image from All New Gen *installation; 'Fractal Mountains of Bliss' from* All New Gen, *interactive artwork*

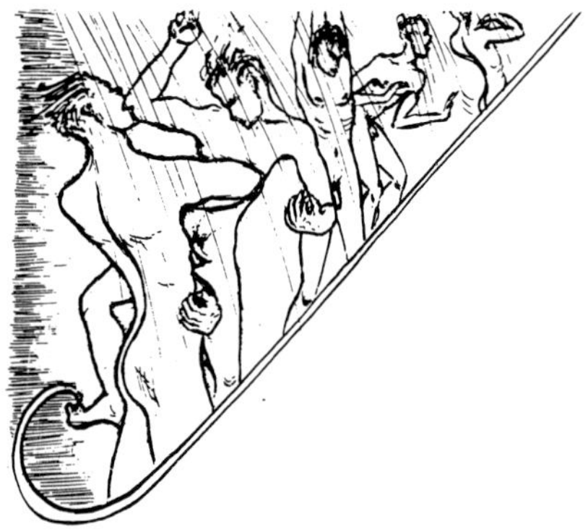

JULY 16--

(Sketch of shower takers-- p. 12) There is a strange alliteration in the three principal desires of bums. Food and flops are the two most important, but they get the least attention in conversations.

"They go to bed at night talking about it and they get up in the morning talking about it."

Right you are, my lad.

One well-made chap, with a pair of statuesque "shoulders," "featherless," as the 'bos say, gets endless ribbing. It is especially brazen in the shower room.

"Don't you worry, honey, I'll fix you up tonight!"
----------------(music, p. 12)-------------------

He accompanies the words with a well-directed pat.

Horseplay and wild repartee follow. They are a safety valve.

Another subject, which runs a close second in popularity, concerns the gifts and instincts of various farm animals.

Tonight I say, I believe without any tinge of morality: "An eighteen-year-old boy in colonial Massachusetts was hung for that."

"Well, boys, they can't hang you for the old stand-by,"
--------------------(music, p. 12)--------------------
is the reply.

Another big paleoka cups his hand out in front of him:

"Yeh--Meet the wife!" he grins.
----(music, p. 12)--

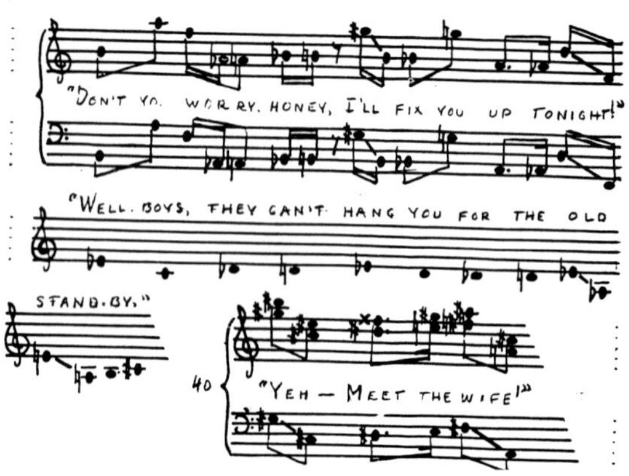

Text and drawings from Harry Partch's Bitter Music. *Reproduced with permission of Danlee Mitchell, The Harry Partch Foundation*

it is unorthodox shows a most unfortunate lack. . . . "

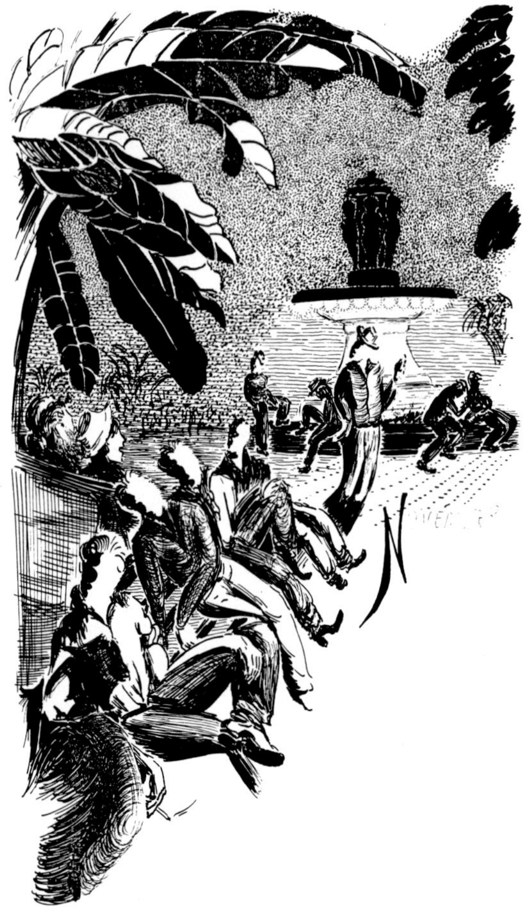

NOVEMBER 29--BANANA CENTER, CENTRAL PARK, EL-LAY--

(Sketch of Banana Center-- p. 62) This became Pershing Square in the war-mad days, but it is still Central Park to me and still "Cannibal Island" to the skidway.

"May I speak to you?"

"Surely."

"Have you been saved?"

"I'm sorry, but your subject doesn't interest me."

The young man bows and walks away, and I mentally collapse from astonishment. Such passivity before pagan resistance is unlike evangelical votaries.

Endless, endless movement. Loitering figures--lingering, lurking.

Some have been heard to say that no respectable person would allow himself to be seen in the park after dark. Huh! I walk about under the thousand shadows of the bamboo and banana trees with utter unconcern.

Here, Saint Francises tempt birds by day.

Here, Saint Pauls tempt God by night.

COMPOSITIONAL LINGUISTICS

20TH-CENTURY AMERICAN COMPOSERS AND THE TEXT

Warren Burt

One of the distinguishing features of 20th-century art has been the blurring of boundaries between formerly separate artistic disciplines. This has been especially so with the distinction between music and language. From the experiments of early 20th century avant-gardists such as Christopher Brennan (Australia), FT Marinetti (Italy) and Kurt Schwitters (Germany), up to the present work of such contemporary performance poets as Chris Mann and Amanda Stewart (Australia), Larry Wendt (USA) or Henri Chopin (France), the musical use of language has had a rich and distinguished history. Some of the most extreme and interesting work in this field has been undertaken by a group of mid-century American composers. More than many others, their work involved (and for some of them, continues to involve) a rigorous need to combine 20th-century music-compositional techniques with linguistic materials, creating a body of work characterised by its uniqueness and complexity.

This article will look briefly at the work of a half dozen mid-century American composers – Harry Partch, Kenneth Gaburo, John Cage, Jackson MacLow, Robert Ashley and Benjamin Boretz – each of whom approached the intersection of language and music in a different manner, and all of whom additionally produced visual art works as accompaniments to their sound and text works.

Harry Partch (1901-74) is best known for his amazing collection of handmade instruments, tuned to a harmonic system of his own devising, and used in his dozen or so full length music-theatre works. Less known is that Partch started out by searching for a way to embody the music he heard in the inflections of everyday American speech. This work eventually led him to reject the Western 12-tone equal tempered tuning system as it was inadequate to express the nuances of speech. He had already decided this as early as 1928. In 1935, however, forced into a homeless existence due to extreme poverty, Partch produced a musical journal, *Bitter Music*, a work which for the last time used the piano and its scale.

Bitter Music is a work that combines narrative, music and drawing to tell the tale of one person's homelessness during the deepest days of the Great Depression. Most of the text is straightforward prose but occasionally, when the inflection of the speech is particularly unique, a musical line is added. This music is usually only a series of pitches meant to be played on a piano in order to give the speaker the pitches of the inflections of the words in question. In later parts of the work, the piano part becomes more elaborate, beginning a dialogue with the speaker but never losing its role as a guide to speech inflections.

Bitter Music was never published in Partch's lifetime. A contract for its publication was cancelled due to paper shortages during World War II; a pity as it was a seminal work in many ways. In its combining of words, music and drawing, it was a very modest yet powerful *gesamtkunstwerk*; in its narrating of a spiritually-infused poverty-inspired wandering, it anticipated Kerouac and the beats by two decades; it had as strong a pro-gay rights stance as any book published at the time, and it combined all these into an extremely powerful and moving intimate theatre. Partch called *Bitter Music* a 'literary experiment'. He wanted a single performer to play the piano in an intimate setting, reading the words and playing the music. A words and music only (without the drawings) version of *Bitter Music* is currently available from the University of Illinois Press. In 1991, the author, in collaboration with pianist Sheila Learmonth, performed 85 minutes of extracts from *Bitter Music* and later recorded them for the Australian Broadcasting Corporation.

One of the most radical approaches to the language/music issue was taken by the multidisciplinary Kenneth Gaburo (1926-93), a composer, writer, director, performer, graphic artist and publisher. Gaburo was associated with Partch at various stages in their careers, and in 1980 directed the first ur-text version of Partch's 1954 music theatre piece *The Bewitched*. Inspired by studies in linguistics and cognitive psychology, by the late 50s Gaburo had coined the term 'compositional linguistics' to describe work which treated language as music and music as language. Early works of this sort, such as *Antiphony IV* (1967), a chamber piece for tape (of vocal and electronic sounds) and acoustic instruments, broke texts up into their constituent phonemes, and subjected these to the same rigorous serialisation techniques that composers were using for pitch and other musical parameters at the time.

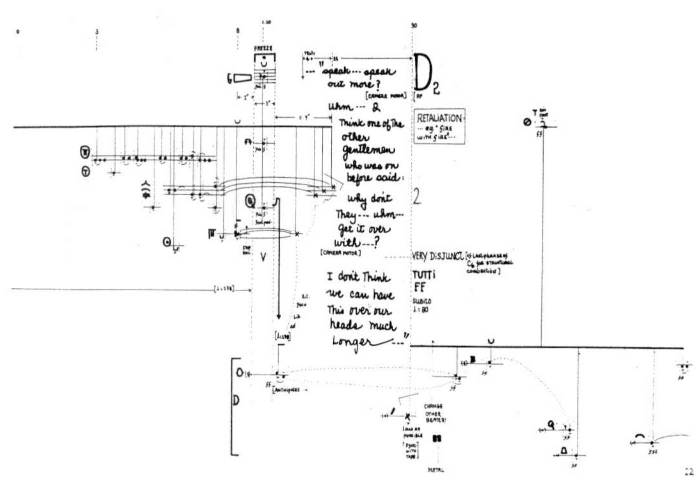

Kenneth Gaburo, Antiphony IV*, 1967*

Later works, such as *Maledetto* (1967-69), a theatrical masterpiece for seven speaking voices, combine narrative, phonemic break-up, strict and aleatoric uses of musical forms such as canons and hocketing, singing and much dramatic interplay with double, triple and quadruple entendres, to create a swirling texture of language

wroth with twone nathandJoe
A
Malt
jhEm
Shen

pftJschute
sOlid man
that the humptYhillhead of humself
is at the knoCk out
in thE park

Jiccup
the fAther
Most
hEaven
Skysign

Judges
Or
deuteronomY
watsCh
futurE

pentschanJeuchy
chAp
Mighty
cEment
and edificeS

the Jebel and the
crOpherb
flYday
and she allCasually
ansars hElpers

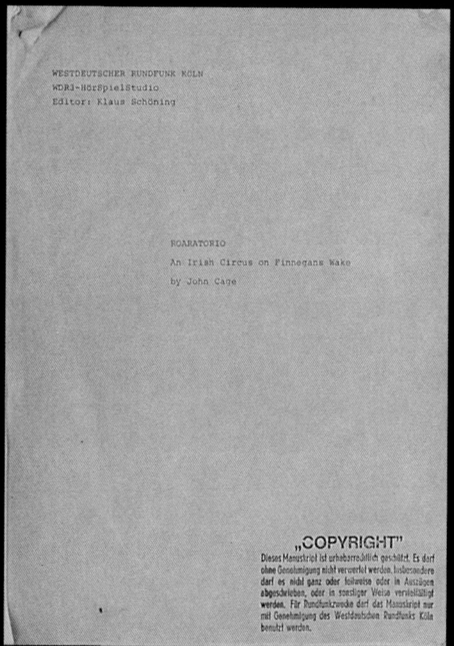
WESTDEUTSCHER RUNDFUNK KÖLN
WDR3-HörSpielStudio
Editor: Klaus Schöning

ROARATORIO
An Irish Circus on Finnegans Wake
by John Cage

„COPYRIGHT"
Dieses Manuskript ist urheberrechtlich geschützt. Es darf ohne Genehmigung nicht verwertet werden. Insbesondere darf es nicht ganz oder teilweise oder in Auszügen abgeschrieben, oder in sonstiger Weise vervielfältigt werden. Für Rundfunkzwecke darf das Manuskript nur mit Genehmigung des Westdeutschen Rundfunks Köln benutzt werden.

LEFT: Extract from Roaratorio *by John Cage, 1979; ABOVE: Cover of Roaratorio*

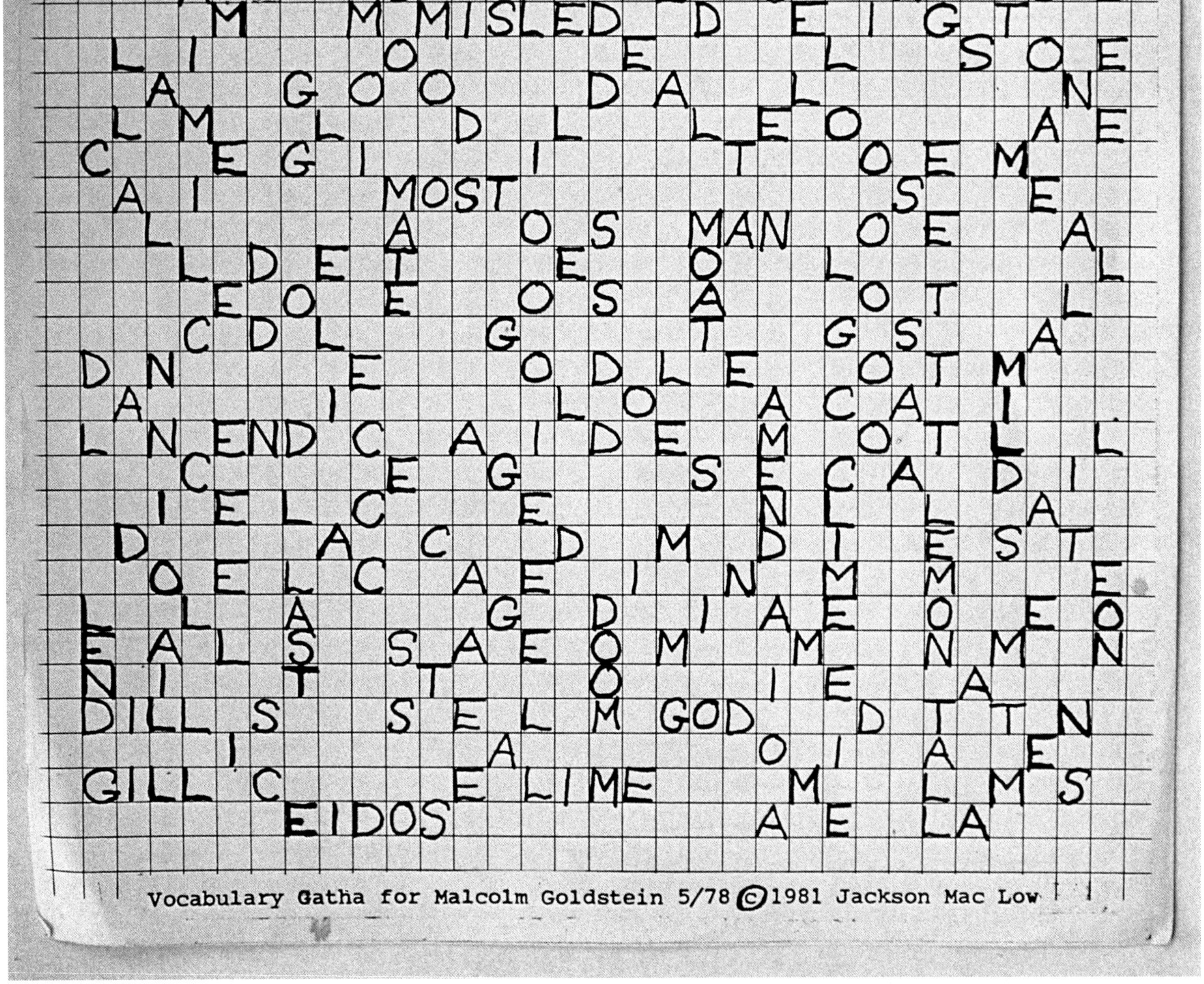
Vocabulary Gatha for Malcolm Goldstein 5/78 ©1981 Jackson Mac Low

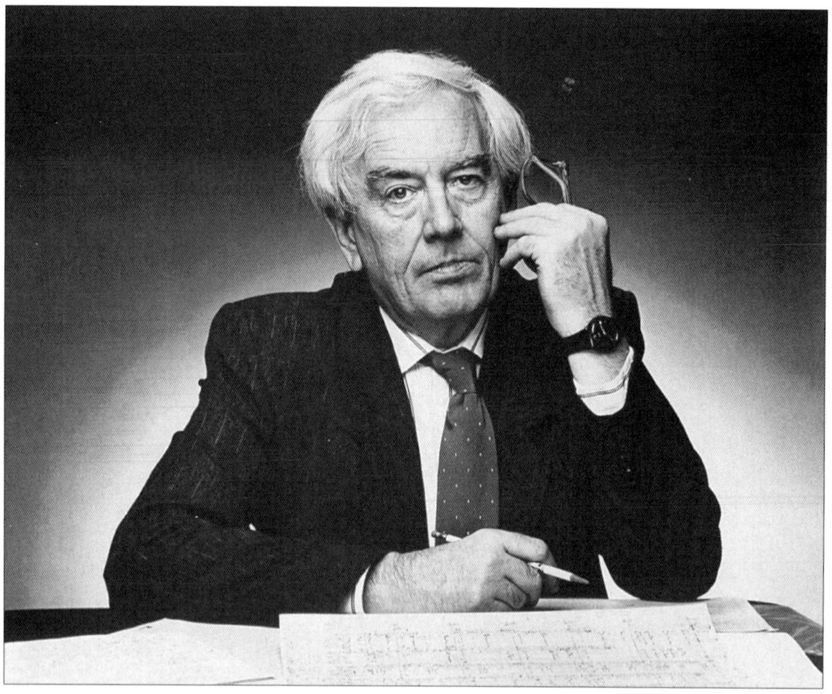

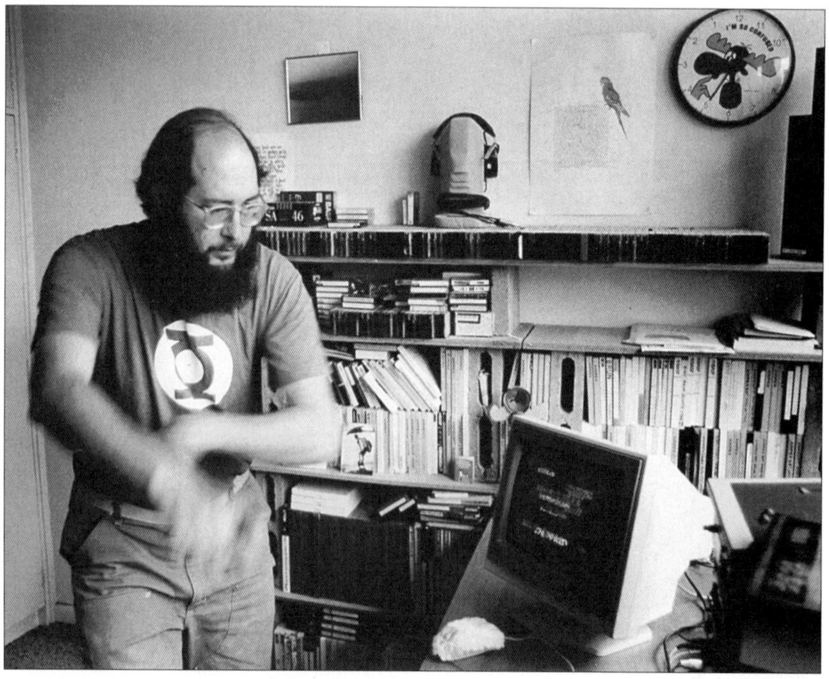

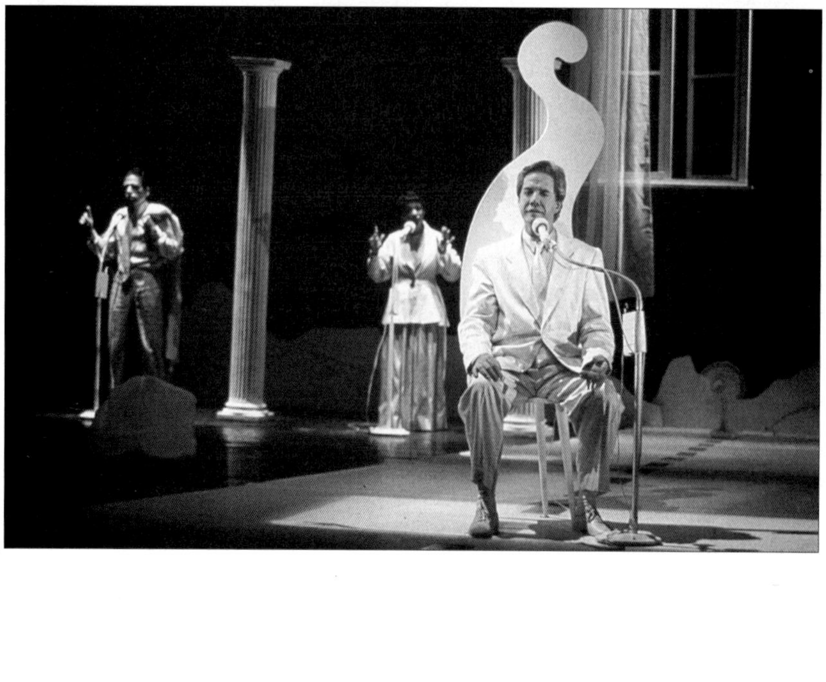

FROM ABOVE: Robert Ashley, photo Jack Mitchell, 1989; Warren Burt rehearses Continuously Retitled, *1992, photo Lyn Pool; John Cage,* eL/AFICIONADO, *photo Dan Rest, 1994*

around the humblest of subjects, the lowly machine screw.

By the time of Gaburo's last works, such as 'Ago', from *Pent/Agony* (1982) for solo reader, and *Mouthpiece II* (1992) for voice and concrete sounds on tape, his use of musically-structured language had combined with his intense concern with sexual politics to produce highly controversial works which are searing in their intensity. Delivered in a tense voice straining with emotion, Gaburo's 1987 Melbourne performance of 'Ago' (which was recorded by the Australian Broadcasting Corporation) was a powerful performance, the mention of which still provokes heated reactions. No less controversial and radical in his approach to language was John Cage. In *Empty Words* (1974) Cage followed Norman O Brown's idea that grammar and syntax represented the military organisation of language, and proceeded to systematically deconstruct Henry David Thoreau's 'Journal' into randomly ordered phrases, words, syllables and finally individual letters. A complete performance of 'Empty Words' would take about 11 hours, and was at one point performed as an all-night reading for an audience that could listen or sleep as they wished.

Perhaps Cage's most complex language/music composition was *Roaratorio, an Irish Circus on Finnegans Wake*, (1979), a piece for radio which used the text of Joyce's classic, *Finnegans Wake*, as both material and structure. From the text Cage extracted a number of 'mesostics', a poetic form he invented, which can use a number of chance techniques in its construction. He then learned to read these fragmentations in a unique manner. Accompaniment sounds were provided by the *Wake* itself. Cage compiled a listing of all the sounds mentioned in the *Wake*, indexing them by where they occurred in the text. As many of these as possible were recorded. Since Cage's mesostics had worked through the original Joyce text in linear order, it was then possible to determine where in the final mix a sound mentioned in the *Wake* would appear, by determining where in Cage's reading of his mesostics that page would appear. The resulting ultra-dense 64-track mix was then combined with live performances by Irish folk musicians to create a work which is dazzling in its intensity and never less than fascinating and beautiful.

Jackson MacLow (b 1922), composer and poet, studied with Cage in the early 1950s, first coming to prominence as the poet who most systematically applied Cage's chance techniques to language. MacLow's text works, such as *The Pronouns* (1964), are works of fairly abstract process-derived poetry which can be used to create full scale theatrical works. In *The Pronouns*, dancers use the text as an 'image-bank' to create a series of theatrical and choreographic gestures, which may or may not make sound, which are then performed both with and without the readings of the texts, to make a richly referential multidisciplinary performance. In other MacLow's works, such as his *Iran-Contra Hearings* (1988), simpler processes, such as letters-to-pitches translation schemes, are used to produce works for musical instruments. Another technique is revealed in *The 8-Voice Stereo Canon Realisation of The Black Tarantula Crossword Gathas* (1973). Here, MacLow used a vocabulary from another writer (Kathy Acker) to produce a text in the form of a crossword, which was then used as a score for a dense, but extremely non-dramatic reading on eight simultaneous tape tracks. The number and kinds of structures MacLow has invented for processing language and generating texts is staggering. Indeed, few composers have produced anywhere close to the variety of structures MacLow has made and used during his career.

Pre-eminent among contemporary American opera composers is Robert Ashley (b 1930), whose engagement with text extends to his student days at the University of Michigan, where he studied linguistics as well as music. Ashley's work combines deceptively straight narrative with music that often refers to pop archetypes. On closer examination of the texts, however, a very strict rhythmic organisation emerges. This rhythm is then used to structure all aspects of the piece, many of which have improvisatory components.

Ashley's most recent production, *Now Eleanor's Idea*, a series of four 90-minute operas produced in November 1994 at the Brooklyn Academy of Music, departed from the driving half-spoken/half-sung solo narrative Ashley had used in his earlier *Perfect Lives*, and used instead a kind of vibrateless chanting on a very limited range of pitches, but sung by professional singers. This kind of singing/chanting allowed the rhythmic aspects of the writing to have prominence. Also, through the use of electronics, the electronic-music accompaniment tracks of the piece could follow the rhythms of the voice, so that much of the piece would be informed by characteristics of the text. *Now Eleanor's Idea* also references a number of late-20th century literary genres, such as personal ads, spy novels, the 'low-rider' automobile culture of southwestern Hispanic-Americans and soap operas, concluding with a transcendental Buddhistic vision of the structure of the universe, ecstatically sung/chanted (in the Brooklyn performance) by the amazing Joan LaBarbara.

Less well known than his colleague's work, but no less profound, is the small but carefully considered linguistic output of composer, theorist and improviser Benjamin Boretz (b 1934). Primarily known for his earlier, highly structured serial instrumental and computer music, or for his more recent challenging free improvisational work, Boretz's *Language, as a Music* (1978), and *If I Am A Musical Thinker* (1981), are well wrought formulations of musical-linguistic aesthetic positions. *If I Am A Musical Thinker* is a small manifesto in defence of musical intellectualism. Like works by Partch and Gaburo, it combines words and drawings by someone primarily regarded as a composer. *In Language, as a Music*, various discourses from philosophical academies to 1940s Brooklyn street jive (a clear predecessor to rap), from a Borgesian fairy tale to a sparse set of invocations each beginning with an urgent 'listen!' are used to question the whereabouts of the boundary between language and music. One of the movements is an unaltered excerpt from Boretz's piano composition *My Chart Shines High Where the Blue Milks Upset* (1977). Placed in context of the word play of other sections, the prose-like nature of Boretz's piano writing become apparent.

This concern for embodying a musicality of prose, or of speech, is a characteristic shared by Boretz with all the other composers mentioned here, as well as with others such as Dane Rudhyar (1899-1987), who early in the century called for a music not based on dance forms, but on the rhythms and inflections of both the everyday and ecstatically heightened speech. What composers have brought to the interface of language and music has been a kind of cross-disciplinary structural rigour and complexity that has often not been the case with similar works made by colleagues from the literary or visual arts. This rigour, in the end, may be their unique contribution.

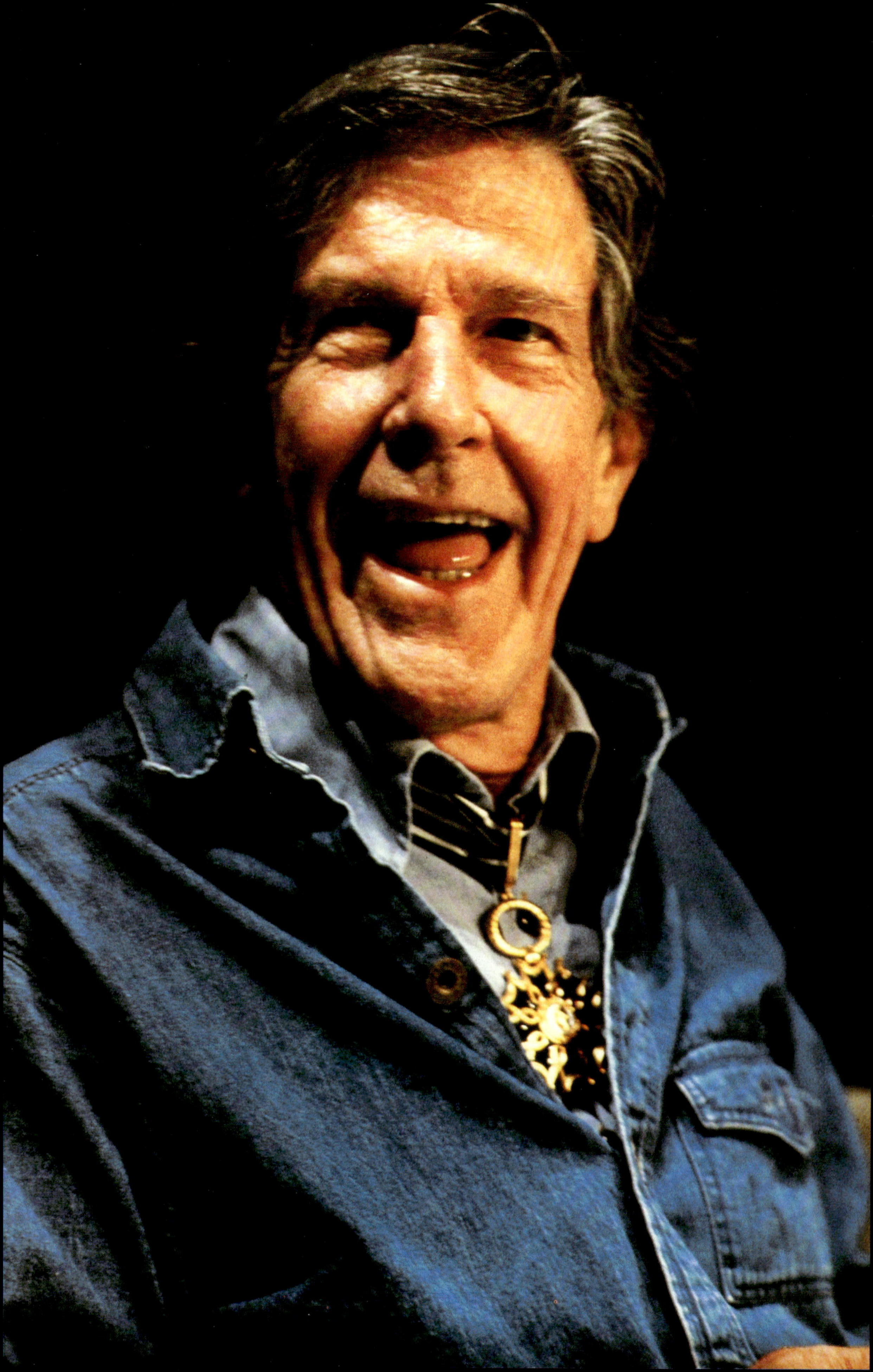

JOHN CAGE

Interviewed by Nicholas Zurbrugg

Nicholas Zurbrugg – *Perhaps I could begin by asking you what projects you are presently working upon?*

John Cage – One of my most recent projects is called *The First Meeting of the Satie Society*. It consists of a plurality of texts which are conceived of as presents for Erik Satie. For instance, I made 18 writings through *Essay on Civil Disobedience* by Henry David Thoreau. All these texts are in the form of mesostics, but the string words for the mesostics are titles of compositions by Erik Satie. Thoreau's present is written on the title *Messe des pauvres*, since Satie was known as 'Monsieur le Pauvre', and Thoreau said that the best thing a man can do for his culture when he is rich is to carry out the projects he had when he was poor. So I thought of poverty as a bond between Thoreau and Satie and so on with the others. I also used a text by Chris Mann to write mesostics. I think of Mann's work as fresh and a new direction in poetry. And Satie said 'Show me something new, I'll begin all over again!' I have managed to make all of this material – which is over 200 pages – accessible electronically through an organisation in San Francisco called 'The Well', which means 'Whole Earth 'Lectronic Link'. I believe that the people who started 'Well' started the Whole Earth Catalogue earlier in the century. So now, no matter where one is, one can contact this work.

I am also working on *Europera*, an opera without a libretto. There is no plot. It is a collage of all the theatrical elements, and nothing is related intentionally to anything else. The lighting does not light the activities, but is independent of them. The singers will be singing arias of their choice. The instruments will be playing bits and pieces of actual, say, flute and oboe parts from the literature. Hence, the instrumental music will be played at the same time as the arias, but will not accompany them. It comes from submitting an unabridged dictionary to chance operations, like I could read a page of the dictionary until one of the words on the page suggest some kind of action. Just yesterday we were able to get through all the actions of the ten singers in *Europera One*, which is an hour-and-a-half long. I think what happens both in succession and simultaneously can be

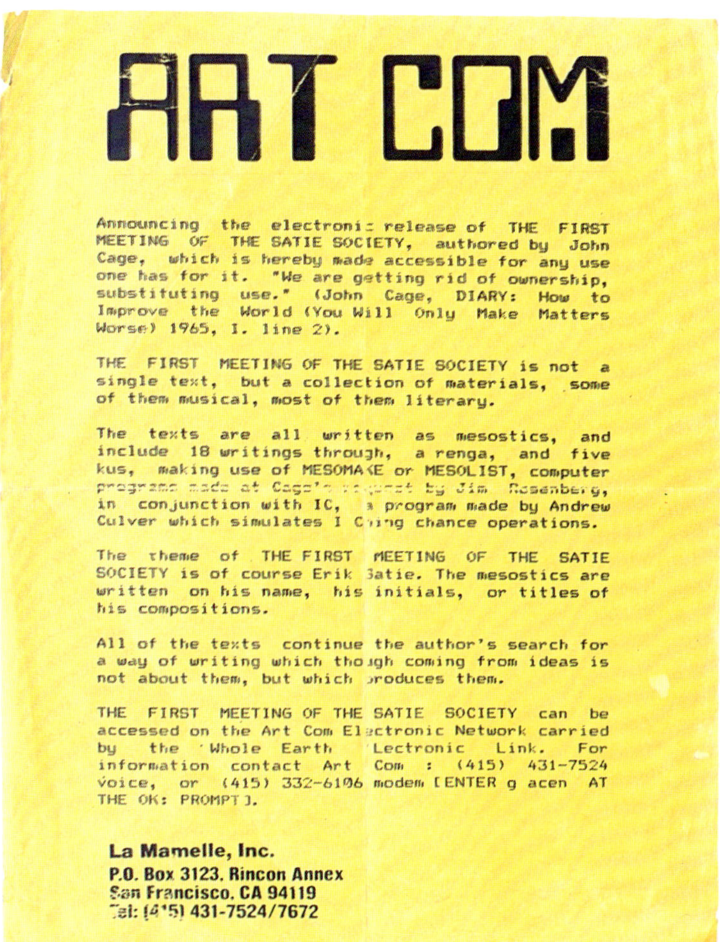

ART COM

Announcing the electronic release of THE FIRST MEETING OF THE SATIE SOCIETY, authored by John Cage, which is hereby made accessible for any use one has for it. "We are getting rid of ownership, substituting use." (John Cage, DIARY: How to Improve the World (You Will Only Make Matters Worse) 1965, I. line 2).

THE FIRST MEETING OF THE SATIE SOCIETY is not a single text, but a collection of materials, some of them musical, most of them literary.

The texts are all written as mesostics, and include 18 writings through, a renga, and five kus, making use of MESOMAKE or MESOLIST, computer programs made at Cage's request by Jim Rosenberg, in conjunction with IC, a program made by Andrew Culver which simulates I Ching chance operations.

The theme of THE FIRST MEETING OF THE SATIE SOCIETY is of course Erik Satie. The mesostics are written on his name, his initials, or titles of his compositions.

All of the texts continue the author's search for a way of writing which though coming from ideas is not about them, but which produces them.

THE FIRST MEETING OF THE SATIE SOCIETY can be accessed on the Art Com Electronic Network carried by the 'Whole Earth 'Lectronic Link. For information contact Art Com : (415) 431-7524 voice, or (415) 332-6106 modem [ENTER g acen AT THE OK: PROMPT].

La Mamelle, Inc.
P.O. Box 3123, Rincon Annex
San Francisco, CA 94119
Tel: (415) 431-7524/7672

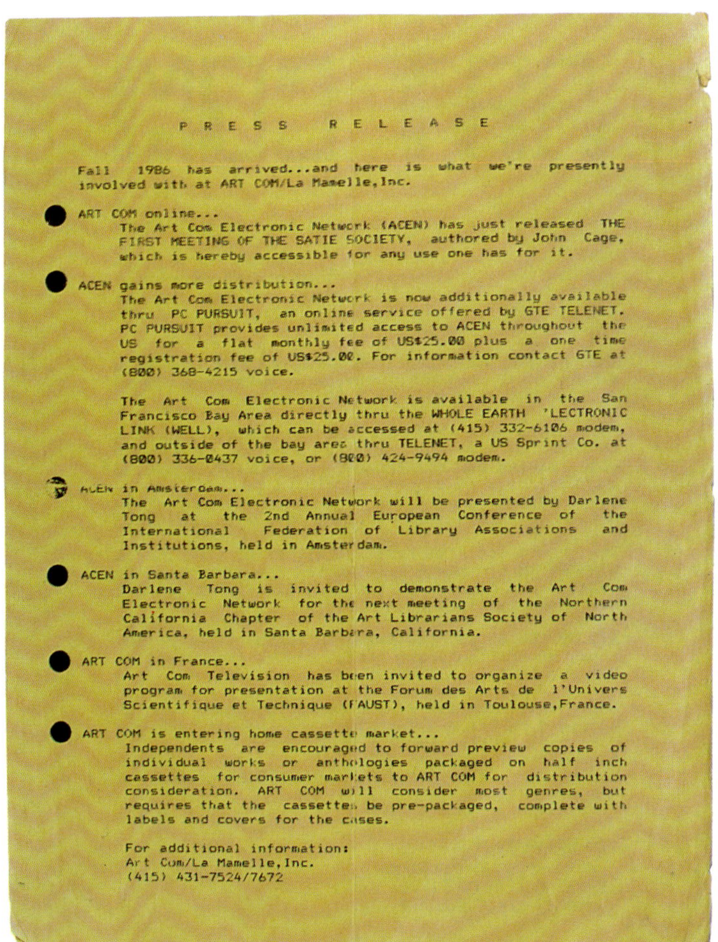

P R E S S R E L E A S E

Fall 1986 has arrived...and here is what we're presently involved with at ART COM/La Mamelle, Inc.

- ART COM online...
  The Art Com Electronic Network (ACEN) has just released THE FIRST MEETING OF THE SATIE SOCIETY, authored by John Cage, which is hereby accessible for any use one has for it.
- ACEN gains more distribution...
  The Art Com Electronic Network is now additionally available thru PC PURSUIT, an online service offered by GTE TELENET. PC PURSUIT provides unlimited access to ACEN throughout the US for a flat monthly fee of US$25.00 plus a one time registration fee of US$25.00. For information contact GTE at (800) 368-4215 voice.

  The Art Com Electronic Network is available in the San Francisco Bay Area directly thru the WHOLE EARTH 'LECTRONIC LINK (WELL), which can be accessed at (415) 332-6106 modem, and outside of the bay area thru TELENET, a US Sprint Co. at (800) 336-0437 voice, or (800) 424-9494 modem.
- ACEN in Amsterdam...
  The Art Com Electronic Network will be presented by Darlene Tong at the 2nd Annual European Conference of the International Federation of Library Associations and Institutions, held in Amsterdam.
- ACEN in Santa Barbara...
  Darlene Tong is invited to demonstrate the Art Com Electronic Network for the next meeting of the Northern California Chapter of the Art Librarians Society of North America, held in Santa Barbara, California.
- ART COM in France...
  Art Com Television has been invited to organize a video program for presentation at the Forum des Arts de l'Univers Scientifique et Technique (FAUST), held in Toulouse, France.
- ART COM is entering home cassette market...
  Independents are encouraged to forward preview copies of individual works or anthologies packaged on half inch cassettes for consumer markets to ART COM for distribution consideration. ART COM will consider most genres, but requires that the cassettes be pre-packaged, complete with labels and covers for the cases.

  For additional information:
  Art Com/La Mamelle, Inc.
  (415) 431-7524/7672

OPPOSITE: John Cage, photo courtesy Francesco Conz; ABOVE: Flyer for The First Meeting of the Satie Society

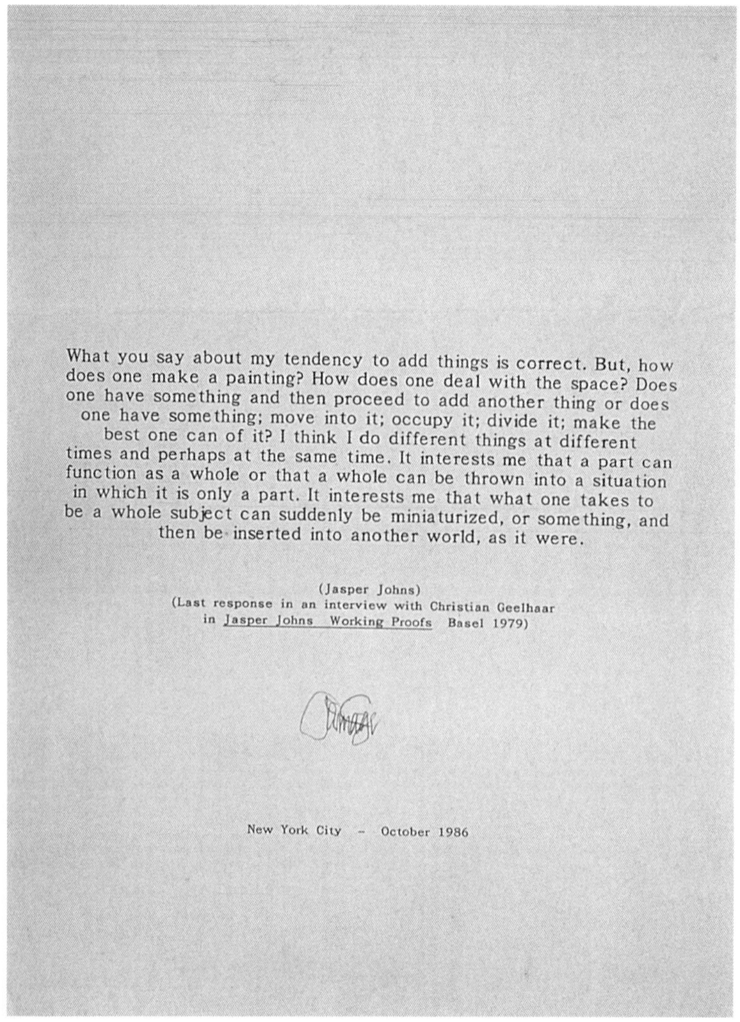

What you say about my tendency to add things is correct. But, how does one make a painting? How does one deal with the space? Does one have something and then proceed to add another thing or does one have something; move into it; occupy it; divide it; make the best one can of it? I think I do different things at different times and perhaps at the same time. It interests me that a part can function as a whole or that a whole can be thrown into a situation in which it is only a part. It interests me that what one takes to be a whole subject can suddenly be miniaturized, or something, and then be inserted into another world, as it were.

(Jasper Johns)
(Last response in an interview with Christian Geelhaar in Jasper Johns Working Proofs Basel 1979)

New York City - October 1986

Jasper Johns's last response in an interview with Christian Geelhaar in Jasper Johns's Working Proofs *(Basel 1979). Source text for* Mesostic *illustrated p19.*

said to be surprising and unexpected. It is actually in a form of theatre with which I am unfamiliar. I look forward to experiencing it.

Are any other people working with similar forms of theatre? Would this relate to things that Robert Wilson has done?
– Well, Robert Wilson's work takes a long time and very little happens. It is also an interesting form of theatre. But it is almost at the other extreme of what I am doing, because here, every four minutes a wealth of material is changing. It is very complex.

So would it be fair to say that you are interested in the connections that arise between the complex materials in these works?
– Well, the connections are multiple. And since there is no intention, the multiplicity of possible interpenetrations is very great. It is like the puns in *Finnegans Wake* – things go in almost any direction.

A lot of critics have recently argued that the present 'Post-Modern' age is rather gloomy and an age in which there are not any more connections and meanings or whatever. But it seems to me that what you are describing is very affirmative.
– I hope so. I had a really alarming experience, I think it was last week. I am a member of the American Academy Institute of Arts and Letters, and was asked to be on a committee giving awards to composers. There were seven of us, and I had to listen in one day – even disliking as I do recordings – to 60 pieces of music. All of it – not all of it literally, but most of it – was what is now called neo-Romantic material. It was as though we were living in the 19th century! It was unbelievable. Many people seem to have learned nothing from the 20th-century experience. Maybe it is peculiar to music? I am afraid it may exist in poetry too. What do you think?

I am not quite sure about poetry. I think in art there is a return to this neo-Expressionism, and in theoretical works people say there is no advance possible, and that all one can do is synthesise the past in a fairly unadventurous manner.
– Well, I am in disagreement.

This is a vast question, but is it possible to say what the most important lessons of the 20th century experience might be?
– I think that a great deal of our experience comes from the large use of glass in architecture, thus our experience is one of reflection and collage and transparency. And I think those elements are very important and very different from a life which has less glass in it!

One problem that arises here, is that some theorists say that everything has become very flat and suggest that we are living in a culture of surfaces, without depth and without significance.
– No, we see several things at once!

as it Were

anotHer world

A whole or
The best one can of it

suddenlY
sOmething

move
miniatUrized

or
Something
A whole or that
You
Add things is correct

that a whole can Be
hOw does one
occUpy
a siTuation in which it is
soMething and then
mY
funcTion as
anothEr
whole caN
aDd
onE
iNto it

a whole Can be
onlY a part

aT the same time

Or does one
function As
another worlD

Do
Time
and tHen proceed to
dIvide it

oNe
a paintinG

Mesostic *from Jasper Johns's text, illustrated p18*

So it is a rich simultaneity?
– It is very rich. Instead of seeing one thing, it is as though we lived constantly in Rome where you see many centuries interpenetrating.
Well, I think you wrote many years ago that our souls have become 'electronic', able to assimilate many experiences. Just to go back to technology, do you see that as being of equal importance to, say, the experience of glass?
– Well, it is like transparency. I remember once when I was giving a performance with David Tudor of what we called 'live' electronic music. There was one machine under my control which was not plugged in. But it worked anyway!

How did it work?
– It worked as though it were plugged in. And I said to David, 'Isn't that strange? and he said, 'No. It's because it's so close to the others that are plugged in'. It was vibrating sympathetically! That is amazing! But that is like transparency and reflection. I do not think we know all the words yet which describe the effect on the other senses. I mean to say, we could accept the word 'collage' in music. 'Transparency' becomes a little more difficult, and 'reflection'. 'Collage', I think, is of the essence of work in the arts in the 20th century. And for someone who is a neo-Romantic, collage is impossible. They simply do not accept it. They think you should carry one thing through to the end – like a stone wall!

I sometimes think even that is an illusion, because even if you are reading a so-called 'linear novel', it is quite possible to jump about, and, as it were, knock the text out of line.
– Yes. With my mesostics I am able to put a source text in the computer, and then, following the rule of the mesostics – which is to not commence the second letter of a string until the second line, and so on, or not to permit either letter between two letters of a string – I am able to analyse such a text with the computer, so that I have a list of all the words throughout the source that satisfy the mesostic rules, and then, through the use of chance operations, to write a text which comes first from here and then from there. I find it fascinating. I did it recently for a longish text from an interview with Jasper Johns about ways of making a painting. It goes on and on, and it interested me because though it comes from ideas, it produces other ideas. There comes a kind of fertilisation of ideas.

Do you ever find the idea of working with a computer at all contradictory? The idea of 'mechanised chance' seems a little paradoxical, does it not?
– No, I like it very much!

New York, 27 January 1987

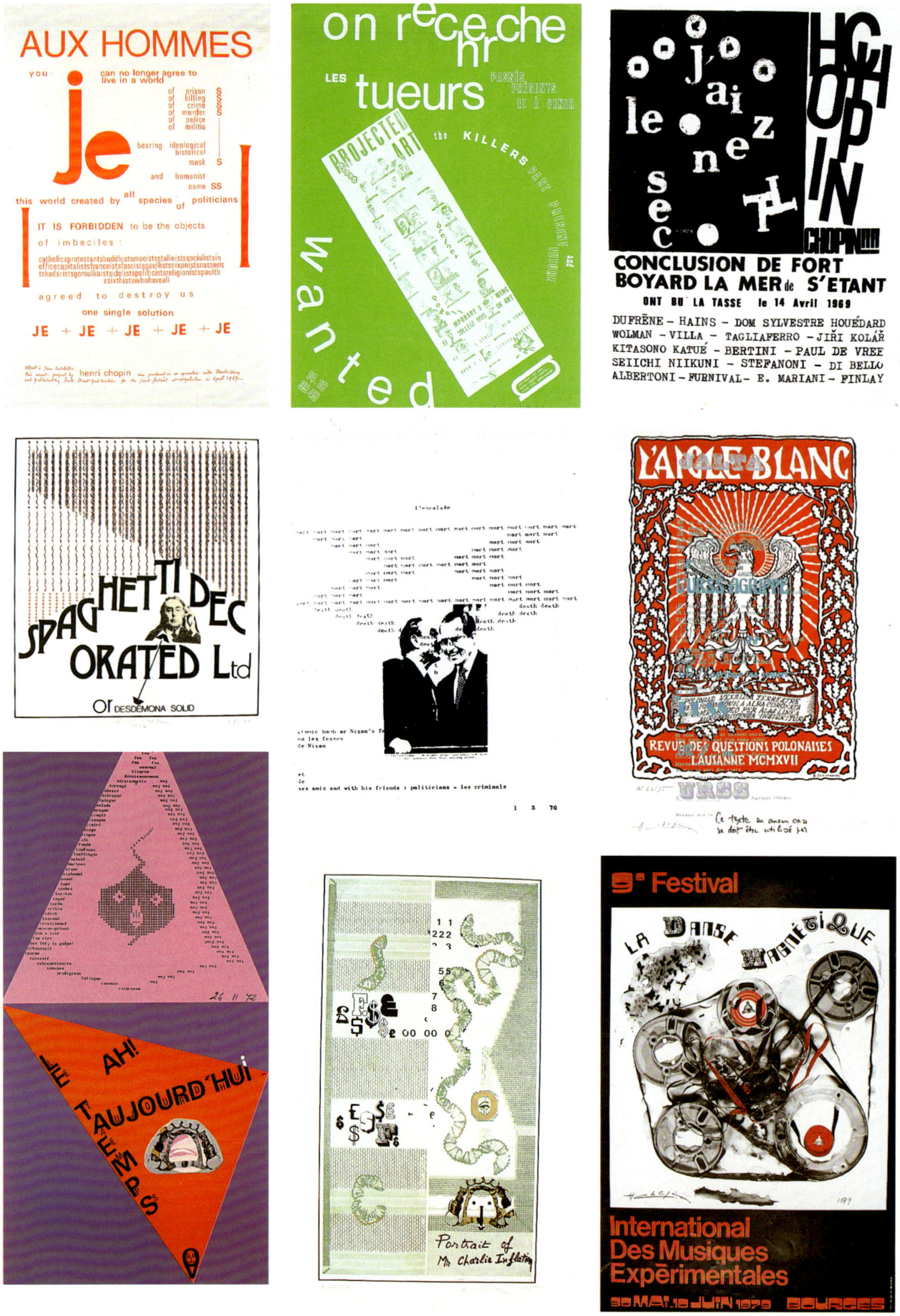

Henri Chopin, Screen Prints 1967-92

HENRI CHOPIN

Interviewed by Nicholas Zurbrugg

Nicholas Zurbrugg – *Henri, you have worked for many years as one of the pioneers of sound poetry. How exactly would you define its characteristics?*

Henri Chopin – The main characteristic of sound poetry is its use of electronic tape recording technology – media which did not exist commercially before 1950. In a sense it has a very long history because it represents the rediscovery of the vast oral, rhetorical traditions – of everything typical of poetic activity before the invention of printing. Sound poetry is in turn created with a machine – tape recorders – machines which reveal the particular qualities of the voice and our capacity to project poetry towards the listener, beyond the book. That is its general quality. We subsequently discovered the way in which the tape recorder's microphone could become a means of multiplying the voice, just as the microscope multiplies our medical awareness of blood. Once there was just blood – now we are aware of thousands of blood cells. Likewise, as our recordings and our vocal modifications have revealed, there are thousands of variations in the voice.

How did you first start working with recorded sound?

– In the beginning, in France, I wanted to be a singer, and I was one for a while. Then I worked in the theatre. In other words I was interested in the voice. Then in the years between 1944 and 45, I was directly influenced by the songs of the Soviet army. When I was in the USSR in 1945 I was greatly impressed by the men and women I heard singing in Russian or singing improvised songs. Later in 1948 and 49 when I was in Vietnam, I was also greatly impressed by Oriental chanting and recital. All of these ancient vocal traditions fascinated me long before the availability of the tape recorder. When I discovered the tape recorder in the early 50s, it was quite a shock! At the time, poetry was a written form, and once I began recording my poetry, I found writing very inadequate. I wanted to modify the values of the word in order to enter the domain of the recording.

At that point, in 1956, I was in contact with Maurice Lemaître, the Lettriste, and was corresponding with André Breton. Neither one nor the other – the Lettriste or the Surrealist – offered me very interesting solutions. They seemed to have very traditional responses to the possibilities of orality and vocal projection. The more I studied vocalic values from 1955-57, the more I gradually abandoned the written word in order to explore vocal values in their own right – either in semantic or non-semantic materials.

In one of your early poems, Présence, *in the review* Poésie Nouvelle *of 1957, there is a long section with the words* 'marchons marchons marchons' *– 'on and on and on'. Does this exemplify this sort of partially semantic, partially abstract composition?*

– Yes. I can remember exactly when it was written. It was in 1949 near the Boulevard Exelmans in Paris, when there was still a little train that ran overhead going *brm brm brm brm brm* all the time – and at the same time I wrote '*marchons marchons marchons marchons marchons*', following the rhythm of the train. It was a kind of pre-minimal music which also reflected my research on the repetitive songs of the Middle Ages – although my expertise and documentation were very limited at that time.

That is a little surprising perhaps. I would have thought you might have been influenced by the publications of the Dada movement.

– No, I knew nothing about Dada. In 1949, Dada was completely unknown and completely eclipsed by Surrealism. The little we knew of Dada was via Aragon, Breton and Paul Eluard, who had all been Dadaists before they became Surrealists. It was all very vague – nobody knew what Dada was, and nobody knew very much about Italian Futurism or Russian Futurism. It was only in the 50s that I learned about the Dada period from Michel Seuphor. Then in the 60s I learned more from Pierre Albert-Birot and Marcelle Cahn, the painter. But the general public was very poorly informed, and still is, moreover. But today there are books. Then there was nothing – just the triumph of Surrealism.

Eugene Jolas's review Transition *had published quite a lot of Dadaist, Surrealist and Futurist texts in Paris in the late 30s and early 40s.*

– It was completely forgotten. When Surrealism appeared, artists like Pierre Albert-Birot and Raoul Hausmann were completely forgotten and neglected. There were very few publications by them or about them. Moreover, when I began working with tape, I was living at the Ile de Ré, near La Rochelle – that is to say, I was completely isolated. Thanks to my wife, Jean, I knew of English writers like Eliot and Joyce, whose work was only published in French translation in isolated fragments. I found these editions second-hand rather than in major book shops. I remember finding a limited edition translation of Egan Pound's *Cantos*. At the same time there was the Surrealist regime, led by Breton, which hid everything – the research of *Der Stürm* in Germany, Pierre Albert-Birot's review *Sic*, the review *Ma* in Hungary, the review *Zenith* in Yugoslavia, the Flemish reviews *Het Overzicht* and *Ca Ira!* – all of which was absolutely unknown. I had to visit the artists themselves before I finally learned that their world was much more creative than Surrealism, and discovered the true art of the 20th century. As for the Italian Futurists, the fact that Marinetti was a great friend of Mussolini led him to be dismissed in turn – nobody knew anything about him. Nor indeed did anyone know about the Belgian poet who invented 'les informations' – radio news – Paul Vermée, who was married to Céline Arnault, who published *Ca Ira!* in Antwerp. All these things were completely

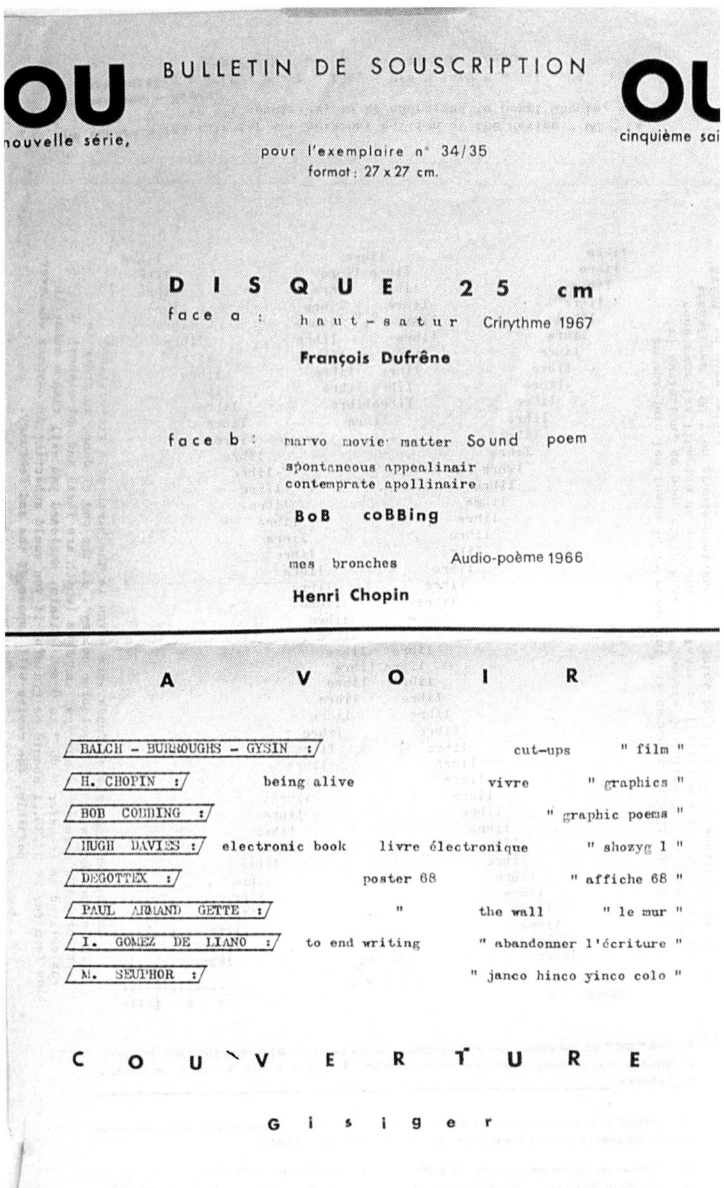

OU BULLETIN DE SOUSCRIPTION OU

nouvelle série, cinquième sai

pour l'exemplaire n° 34/35
format : 27 x 27 cm.

D I S Q U E 2 5 cm

face a : h a u t - s a t u r Crirythme 1967

François Dufrêne

face b : marvo movie matter Sound poem
spontaneous appealinair
contemprate apollinaire

BoB coBBing

mes bronches Audio-poème 1966

Henri Chopin

A V O I R

BALCH - BURROUGHS - GYSIN :		cut-ups	" film "
H. CHOPIN :	being alive	vivre	" graphics "
BOB COBBING :			" graphic poems "
HUGH DAVIES :	electronic book	livre électronique	" shozyg 1 "
DEGOTTEX :		poster 68	" affiche 68 "
PAUL ARMAND GETTE :		" the wall	" le mur "
I. GOMEZ DE LIANO :	to end writing		" abandonner l'écriture "
M. SEUPHOR :			" janco hinco yinco colo "

C O U ` V E R T U R E

G i s i g e r

Subscription form for Revue-Disque OU *34-35*

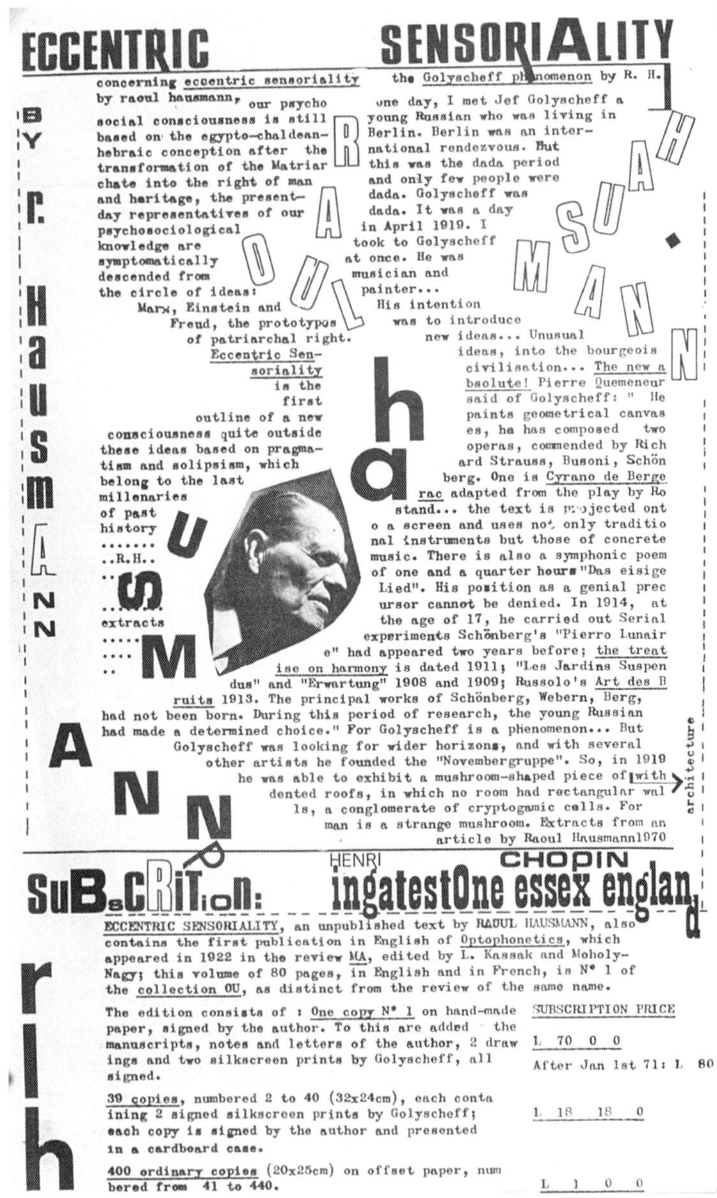

ECCENTRIC SENSORIALITY

BY r. Hausmann

concerning eccentric sensoriality by raoul hausmann, our psycho social consciousness is still based on the egypto-chaldean-hebraic conception after the transformation of the Matriarchate into the right of man and heritage, the present-day representatives of our psychosociological knowledge are symptomatically descended from the circle of ideas: Marx, Einstein and Freud, the prototypos of patriarchal right. Eccentric Sensoriality is the first outline of a new consciousness quite outside these ideas based on pragmatism and solipsism, which belong to the last millenaries of past history ....R.H.. .. .. extracts ....

the Golyscheff phenomenon by R. H.

one day, I met Jef Golyscheff a young Russian who was living in Berlin. Berlin was an international rendezvous. But this was the dada period and only few people were dada. Golyscheff was dada. It was a day in April 1919. I took to Golyscheff at once. He was musician and painter... His intention was to introduce new ideas... Unusual ideas, into the bourgeois civilisation... The new absolute! Pierre Quemeneur said of Golyscheff: " He paints geometrical canvases, he has composed two operas, commended by Richard Strauss, Busoni, Schönberg. One is Cyrano de Bergerac adapted from the play by Rostand... the text is projected onto a screen and uses not only traditional instruments but those of concrete music. There is also a symphonic poem of one and a quarter hours "Das eisige Lied". His position as a genial precursor cannot be denied. In 1914, at the age of 17, he carried out Serial experiments Schönberg's "Pierro Lunaire" had appeared two years before; the treatise on harmony is dated 1911; "Les Jardins Suspendus" and "Erwartung" 1908 and 1909; Russolo's Art des Bruits 1913. The principal works of Schönberg, Webern, Berg, had not been born. During this period of research, the young Russian had made a determined choice." For Golyscheff is a phenomenon... But Golyscheff was looking for wider horizons, and with several other artists he founded the "Novembergruppe". So, in 1919 he was able to exhibit a mushroom-shaped piece of architecture with dented roofs, in which no room had rectangular walls, a conglomerate of cryptogamic cells. For man is a strange mushroom. Extracts from an article by Raoul Hausmann1970

SuBsCRiTion: HENRI CHOPIN ingatestOne essex england

ECCENTRIC SENSORIALITY, an unpublished text by RAOUL HAUSMANN, also contains the first publication in English of Optophonetics, which appeared in 1922 in the review MA, edited by L. Kassak and Moholy-Nagy; this volume of 80 pages, in English and in French, is N° 1 of the collection OU, as distinct from the review of the same name.

	SUBSCRIPTION PRICE
The edition consists of : One copy N° 1 on hand-made paper, signed by the author. To this are added the manuscripts, notes and letters of the author, 2 drawings and two silkscreen prints by Golyscheff, all signed.	L 70 0 0 After Jan 1st 71: L 80
39 copies, numbered 2 to 40 (32x24cm), each containing 2 signed silkscreen prints by Golyscheff; each copy is signed by the author and presented in a cardboard case.	L 18 18 0
400 ordinary copies (20x25cm) on offset paper, numbered from 41 to 440.	L 1 0 0

Subscription form for Raoul Hausmann, Eccentric Sensoriality *(Collection* OU *1970)*

obscured by Surrealism, as was *Cercle et Carré* – the little magazine published by Seuphor in an edition of 300 or 400 copies. Nobody knew that Seuphor had published a poem to be thrown from aeroplanes! The press only discussed Surrealism. Thanks to Seuphor I discovered what had happened in the first half of the century's art. And thanks to Arthur Pétronio, I found out about the musical experiments preceding sound poetry. Pétronio's father was a great friend of Marinetti and Russolo and had created a kind of animated theatre – plays with 40-60 different roles, using mirror transformations – in the years before 1914! Pétronio himself was a friend of Kandinsky and of René Ghil – the poet who anticipated new phonetic machines in 1923. Pétronio was similarly neglected by the realists. I published a number of his texts in the review *Cinquième Saison*.

When did you meet the other sound poets that you subsequently published in Cinquième Saison *and* OU*?*
– It was only in 1960, when I returned to Paris, that I met Bernard Heidsieck, François Dufrêne – and one year later, Brion Gysin – who were all also researching oral poetry. Gysin was working with semantic permutations, Heidsieck's *Poèmes-partitions* were still semantic and Dufrêne's *crirythmes* – doubtless inspired by Artaud – explored the pure cry, without any semantic content.

Did you meet other Lettriste poets as well as Dufrêne?
– Yes, I met Maurice Lemaître, who had published two of my early books with Editions Caractères. But he only wanted to talk about Isidore Isou, and about himself. I had also come across Isidore Isou's *Introduction à une nouvelle poésie* of 1947, but I did not really find it satisfactory. In 1953 I met Altagor, the father of *méta-poésie* – a fascinating person who at the time was married to Maguy Lovalo – the daughter or granddaughter of Lucien Lovalo who created the role of Wozzeck in Berg's opera in 1925. I learned a great deal from her. We made a radio programme together in 1959, and in this way I discovered a great many things. All this offered alternatives to Surrealism, because, naturally, Surrealism only taught Surrealism, and for me that was without interest.

In 1960, a Polish painter introduced me to François Dufrêne. Our first meeting was extremely awkward, because he considered himself to be God's gift to orality. Only later did I discover Dufrêne's very real friendship. He was very young and very aggressive at that time. In 1961, thanks to Seuphor, I presented the first recordings of my work in public at the Galerie Mesure in Saint-Germain-des-Près – a gallery directed by Seuphor's son, Régis Seuphor – which exhibited work by artists such as Marcelle Cahn and Luc Piere. It was in this gallery, due to Seuphor, that I first heard Kurt Schwitters' *Ursonate* on a 78rpm record belonging to the Dutch painter César Domela, a friend of Van Doesburg and Mondrian. Domela lent me this record, and I played it in the gallery along with a recording of one of my first *audio-poèmes* – *Espace et Gestes*. In my introduction I said, 'Here's the past, Schwitters, which is purely phonetic, and here's the present, electronic poetry, by Chopin'.

This was simply a public presentation in the gallery – it was not broadcast by radio?
– No, public radio obviously took no notice of this, it was in the gallery. But the gallery's audience included Jacques Costine, who had founded the review *Contimporanul* in Romania in 1920 with Marcel Janco and Tristan Tzara. Those present included the Dadaist Marcel Janco; Madame Buffet-Picabia, Picabia's widow; Claire Goll, the widow of Ivan Goll; and Robert Altmann, the collector. There were only 50 people, but 50 very interesting people!

Was this your first recorded work?
– No, it was my third. I recorded *Pêche de Nuit* in 1957, at the Ile de Ré, and then *Vibrespace* followed by *Espace et Gestes* and *La Peur*.

Was your audience's response generally positive?
– Extremely positive! There was tremendous support from the older generation of artists. For example, some time later, I played *Pêche de Nuit* in the studio of the painter Suzanne Rodillon – I was there with Dufrêne on that occasion. An artist who had been listening to the tape gave me his address and said, 'Come to my studio and I'll give you a painting, because you've achieved with sound something which we could never have done'. So I went to visit him. It was Marcel Duchamp! I was so much in awe of him that I did not remind him he had promised me a painting! So yes – people were very curious to find out more about the new techniques that I was using.

There was also another artist at the Galerie Mesure who I have forgotten to mention, Jefrim Golyscheff, whom I only really got to know much later in Berlin, one of the fathers of serial music. In all the German and Austrian musical dictionaries he is hailed as the precursor of serial music by Busoni, Schoenberg and Richard Strauss, whereas he is unrecognised in France. He abandoned art in 1925 and worked as a physicist in France, the United States and Brazil, and then began to paint in 1964, and died, I think, in 1970. I could not initially understand why he encouraged and helped my research so much, and only later learned of his reputation as a composer – he was hiding his past. It is very curious, the first half of the 20th-century seemed to manifest a kind of artistic desire which only becames fulfilled in the second half of the century. Artists like Costine, Golyscheff and so on were interested in every aspect of 20th century creativity – and in a sense, my early work with sound poetry brought all of these aspirations together.

A little later, in 1962, in Antwerp, I met Paul Neuhuys, an extremely thin little man who made de luxe cigars for people like Churchill and the English and Dutch courts, while also editing the review *Ca Ira!* – a francophile alternative to the Flemish reviews in Antwerp – in which he had written one of the first substantial surveys of Dada in 1921. He was a great supporter of my work and did everything he could to make the future of sound poetry more accessible to a wider public. When I first met Paul Neuhuys, at an event that Paul de Vree and I had organised, this tiny man was informing an audience of 200-300 enormous Belgians: 'You don't understand anything at all!' It was a wonderful spectacle!

When did you meet Paul de Vree?
– I met him through the painter Luc Piere, in 1959, and published French translations of his articles on the avant-garde in *Cinquième Saison*. These were overviews of the international avant-garde, but focused particularly upon Belgium where there were two tendencies – the francophone Surrealists such as Magritte, Neuhuys and later, Mariën, and the Flemish Constructivists. It was very curious, a bit

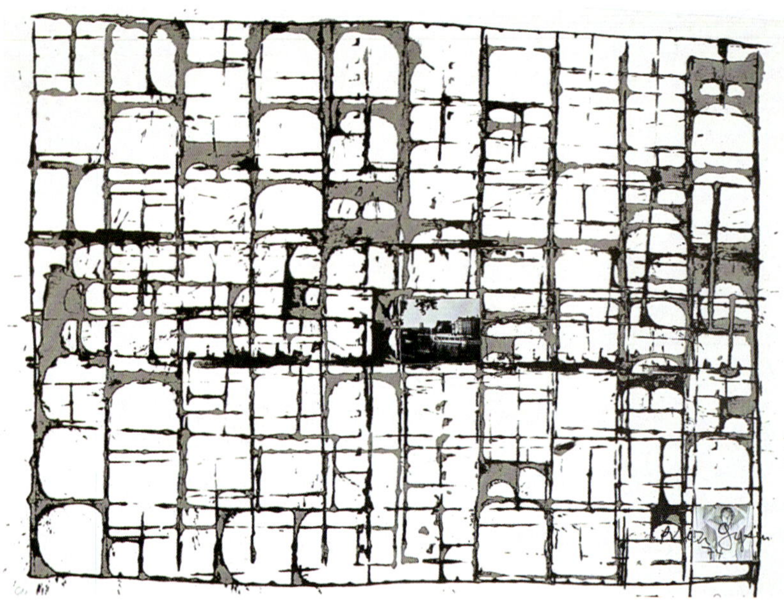

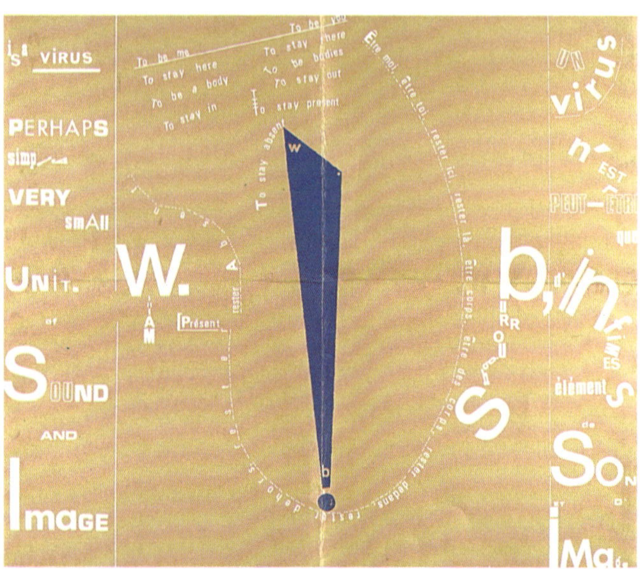

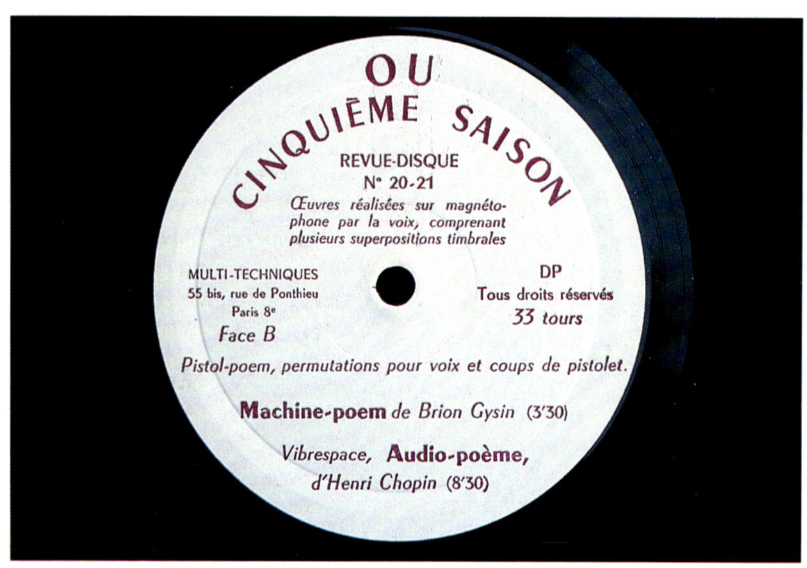

FROM ABOVE, L to R: William S Burroughs, Un Poème moderne, *Ruby Editions Portfolio 1, edited by Henri Chopin; Brion Gysin,* Untitled, *Ruby Editions Portfolio 4; Henri Chopin, Poster for William Burroughs 1971;* Revue-Disque OU *20-21, 1964*

like the present American situation, where New York is very literary and California is very oral. In 1962 Paul de Vree played me his audiovisual poems. I thought they were breathtaking and published them in my review *OU*. But they were particularly breathtaking when recorded by the actor Julien Schoenaerts who had – and has – one of the most remarkable voices I have heard. One can understand de Vree's problem though, in the sense that he, who would have been almost 80 now, was born too late to explore electronics.

When did you first begin to present direct performances as opposed to public presentations of prerecorded material?
Well, in 1960 I was invited by Jacques Poliéri, who worked in the theatre, to an avant-garde festival in Paris, where I presented a direct reading. There were only 30 people, but among them was a little old lady with a bag in her hand, like a housewife out shopping, who came up to me and kissed me. It was Marcelle Cahn, a fabulous painter, who had been part of the Cercle et Carré group in the 1930s. She had been very close to Mondrian and Léger, and introduced me to a whole world of pre-war avant-garde art. As a German Jew, she had remained in hiding in Paris throughout the Occupation, and thanks to the Galerie Mesure, had begun painting again in the 60s. According to her, the work I was publishing at that time corresponded directly to the spirit of her generation in the 40s.

That sense of continuity seems extremely important, particularly when certain critics like to claim that the Second World War totally annihilated all traces of the 20th-century avant-garde.
– Not at all, it was asleep. It was put to sleep on the one hand by Surrealism and on the other hand by the Communist party. Indeed, Aragon and Eluard were both Communists. Then the Surrealists fled to America, and when Surrealism finally began to run to a standstill in the 50s, the whole stifled avant-garde began to surface again.

In this respect Isou merits respect for launching the Lettriste movement in the late 40s.
– Unquestionably, but he came from central Europe and was much more informed than we were. He had a sort of genius for discovering independent spirits in Romania, Hungary and Yugoslavia. He knew a great deal, whereas we were absolutely unaware of all that. In this respect Lettrisme detonated a new awareness, alerting the world to something important. Finally, despite its great intentions, I think Lettrisme became an arrière-garde movement. Isou was completely indifferent to technological creativity, whereas the next generation, Spacagna, Sabatier and Altmann, were fascinated by these things.

Isou experimented with films, however, did he not? And did he not make a kind of early television art by placing paper cutouts on a television screen? Surely from time to time he experimented with technology?
– From time to time he was a precursor, certainly, there is no doubt about that! But he worked primarily for the page, rather than working with the microphone like Dufrêne. As for Lemaître, the last time I saw him in performance in Liège, in Belgium, he was with a choral ensemble. For poets like Heidsieck and myself there are no longer any need for such ensembles – tape recorders are our ensembles! Machines can record all vocal possibilities, and in this sense we no longer need traditional theatre. For example, even when singers have poor voices, technology can give them astonishing voices. On the one hand, technology offers the artificiality of mediocrity; on the other hand, it offers the possibility of valid research.

What were your general impressions of François Dufrêne?
– Dufrêne was already famous in Paris at 16 – he was a kind of Arthur Rimbaud, an extremely fascinating person. He began as a kind of genius, and towards the last four or five years of his life he began for the first time to research his precursors, particularly the rhetoricians – research which inspired his *Cantate des mots camés*. For me it was the reverse. I began by studying the past in order to move towards the present. When I first encountered Dufrêne nothing had any importance for him except Lettrisme. He left Isou in 1953 when Isou invited Maurice Lemaître to join his movement, whereas the lieutenant of Lettrisme was initially Dufrêne. In 1958 he began the Ultra-Lettriste group in collaboration with Robert Estivals's review *Grâmmes*. In the same year the first Lettriste record was published – *Maurice Lemaître présente le Lettrisme*. I was the only critic to support it, in *La Revue Lettriste* and in *Poésie Nouvelle*. In 1958 I also met the Brazilian poet Haraldo de Campos in Paris and learned about the development of concrete poetry in Brazil and Switzerland. But it was not until 1963, when Pierre Garnier published his review *Les Lettres* that the general public learned about concrete poetry.

In other words this epoch was doubly important, as the beginning of both sound poetry and of visual poetry as international movements?
– Yes, it was extremely international. Between the years 1959 and 1963 I was also a radio producer in Paris with Maguy Lovano for Paris-Inter. I also produced broadcasts in Belgium for French and Flemish radio, and in 1964 I produced broadcasts in Switzerland in Lausanne. In 1965 there was a very important exhibition, accompanied by radio, at Lund, near Malmö, in Sweden. In the same years I produced broadcasts in Czechoslovakia, at Brno. You can see how international these developments were!

Was Paris equally animated?
– Yes, there were a lot of events: the Festival organised by Poliési in 1960; my presentation of Schwitters's *Ursonate* and my *Espace et Gestes* in 1961 at the Galerie Mesure; in 1962 the sonorisation of the exhibition *L'Oeil de boeuf*, where I first met Bernard Heidsieck; in 1963 the sonorisation of the studio of Suzanne Rodillon; in 1964, 65, 66 and 67 the night-time sonorisation of Galerie Riquelme in the rue de l'Echaudé, where I exhibited the books of Pierre Albert-Birot, and organised the first Paris exhibition of Jiri Kolar, John Furnival and Melo e Castro. Then in 1967, Dufrêne, Wollman and I sonorised the kinetic art exhibition *Lumière et Mouvement* at the Musée d'Art Moderne, in which Julien Blaine and Jean-François Bory also exhibited poem-objects.

Did you have much contact with the Fluxus artists?
– I have always had very good relations with them, but I only published Alice Hutchins and Ben Vautier in *OU*.

How did you meet Brion Gysin?
– Bernard Heidsieck introduced us in 1963. He became a great

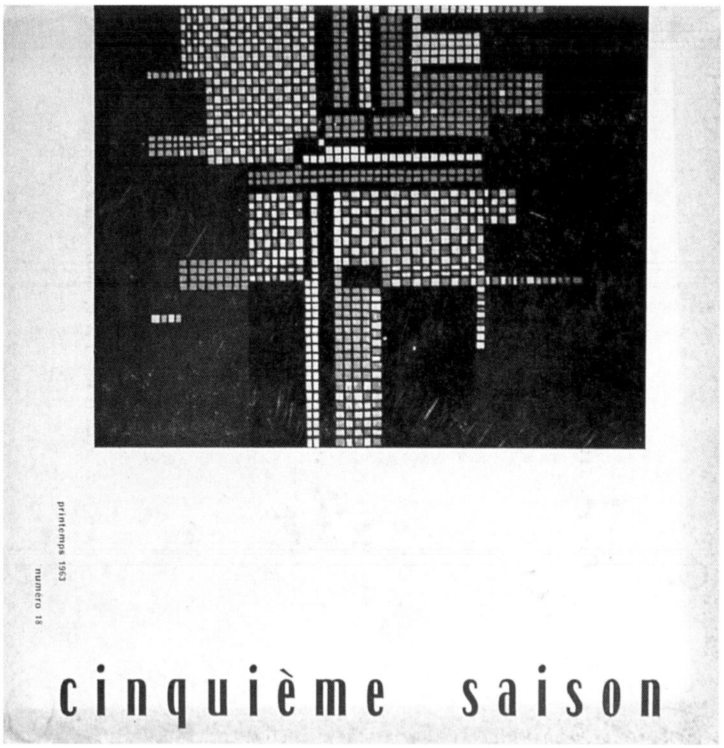

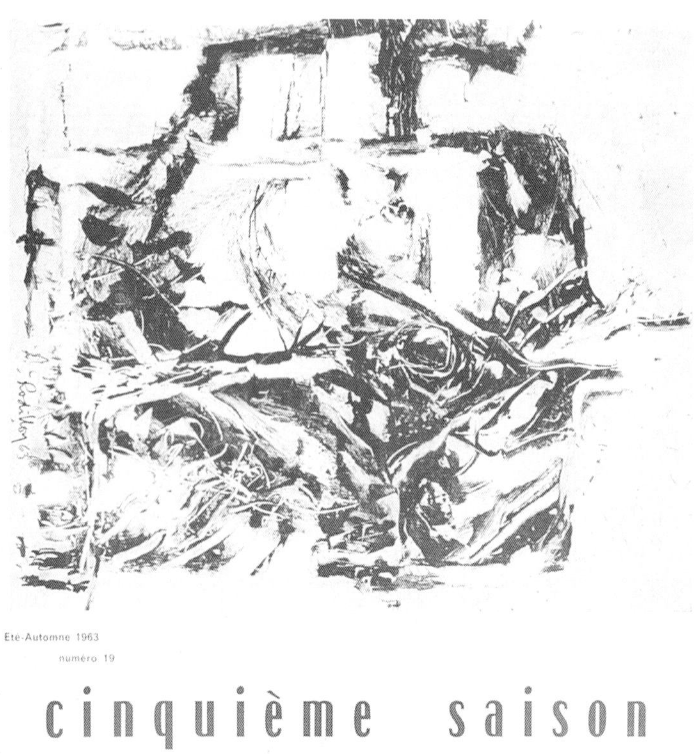

family friend and used to come about twice a month for lunch at Sceaux and then take the children for a walk! Through Brion I met Ian Sommerville, Antony Balch, Burroughs of course, and all of Burroughs's London circle. Brion was an enormously clever artist conceptually – he invented the permutations and the cut ups, after all. But it was Burroughs who developed the cut ups. He was a hard worker – Gysin less so, though he had fabulous ideas, such as the 'Dream Machine'. At the end of his life, when he was very, very ill, Brion showed me his drawings – drawings of very rare quality, and as powerful as those of Durer. But he only drew four of them. Brion, for me, was a master who never really worked.

How did you first contact the English concrete poets such as Dom Sylvester Houédard and John Furnival?
– In 1963 Dom Sylvester Houédard invited me to Prinknash Abbey.

Just like that?
– He invited me and sent me the plane ticket. So I arrived at Prinknash Abbey, in Gloucestershire, to present my film *Pêche de Nuit*. And there was one person there to see the film: Houédard. He was devastated. That is how I first met Houédard, a poet still unknown even in England. He is a poet who decomposed classical poetry into a visual and graphic poetry of incomparable purity – a poet who I would compare with Mondrian in painting. For me, Houédard is of the same quality. Via Houédard I began to correspond with Edwin Morgan, John Sharkey and other English poets, and in *OU* 22 I published Morgan, Sharkey, Furnival, Finlay and Houédard. There was a whole British movement without equivalent today. At the same time I also knew Bob Cobbing, who ran Better Books in London, in Charing Cross Road, whom I had met through Stefan Themerson. Later, in 1968, when we fled from Paris to London, we stayed for four days with John Furnival, with John Sharkey for another four days, for a further four days with Richard Loncraine, and after that with Bob Cobbing.

Was it in London that you met Burroughs?
– Yes. In my 'Open letter to aphonic musicians', published in *OU* 33 in 1967, I wrote that 'we must quote William Burroughs, though we owe him nothing directly'. Burroughs replied, 'At last someone honest!' I was introduced to Burroughs by Antony Balch, who translated for us, and at our first meeting Burroughs greeted me and said, 'I'm glad that you're not a flatterer – you say what you think, and I prefer that'. William Burroughs said he was extremely interested in my research, and in 1969 when I organised the Festival of Ingatestine with my wife Jean, I invited Burroughs, Balch, Sommerville, Gysin and Claude Pélieu. There were about 600 people. We showed Themerson's and Balch's films, and other participants included Richard Orton, Hugh Davies, Bob Cobbing, John Furnival, Thomas A Clark, Jean-Claude Moineau and Dutch Radio.

1969 was also the year in which I first published *OU* in England from Ingatestone, with work by Dufrêne, Cobbing, Gette, Degottex and others in *OU* 34/35. Afterwards I published four other issues. *OU* was characterised by its records, of course, but there was no particular school of concrete, lettrist or visual poetry. I selected authors, irrespective of their generation, in terms of their independence.

Do you think that the creative climate has changed significantly since the early 70s, when you stopped publishing OU?

– I stopped publishing *OU* in 1974 for several reasons. Firstly, for lack of sufficiently interesting visual and sonic contributions. Secondly, those years marked a change in civilisation insofar as the last Dadaist artists were disappearing – such as Janco and others – along with those in Czechoslovakia. It was at that time I began to write my book on sound poetry in order to create an overview. My idea was to write 100 or so pages, but the subject was so huge that I finally wrote more than 300 pages.

At the same time, after 1974, tape cassettes began to replace records, and video art became increasingly widespread. By chance, a number of us – Bob Cobbing, Sten Hanson, François Dufrêne, Bernard Heidsieck, Ake Hodell, Gerhard Rühm, Bengt-Emil Johnson and myself – witnessed the first generation of video art at a Film Festival at Wilhelmsbad in Germany in 1971. Video did not seem very promising to us, but the present generation is far more enthusiastic about it. It is another art, another technique, another sensibility. Then, between 1969 and 1973 in Germany another development occurred which challenged the format of the review, the *Hörspiel* – or radio plays – produced in Köln by Klaus Schöning, and by the Atelier de Création Radiophonique in Paris. A review of *OU*'s stature would now have to combine visual contents with CDs and video cassettes, neither of which existed in the 70s.

All the same, other more or less experimental European reviews such as Julien Blaine's Doc(k)s*, Jean-François Bory's* Humidité *and Sarenco's* Lotta Poetica *had the distinction of offering independent alternatives to mainstream art and literature journals of the 70s and 80s.*

– Certainly. But what I do not understand, for example, is the reason why Blaine never used any issues of *Doc(k)s* in a unambiguously creative way, as a form of research. *Doc(k)s* has certainly published a lot of people, but it does not really have the spirit of research. Bory is a good friend, but his work often seems turned towards the past. He has published a book on the photographer Nadar – compared with his review *Humidité* it is a contrast like that between night and day. All of this often reminds me of early 20th-century painting. When in 1912 abstract painting began with Kupka, Mondrian, Kandinsky and Delauney, it was the continuing discovery of a first generation. The second generation – Herbin, Gorin, Soulages, Bazaine – was a generation which made works, but which no longer made discoveries. There is no longer any sense of revolution or innovation.

For example, the other day you compared one of my recent compositions with the sensibility of Turner's paintings. I replied that for me, Turner was the father – the creator – of Impressionism, in the sense that his work follows a very pure development from figuration into the decomposition of light and the dominance of light. One witnesses the same sort of development in Mondrian's painting. Well, when a generation is preceded by a presence like that, they have to explore new media. For the moment, the new media requiring research is video – a media lacking a sense of security insofar as it still lacks traditions.

In this interview I have been talking about my roots in the first half of the 20th century and my departure towards another dimension. The artistic missions of the first half of the 20th century and those of the second half have now been accomplished. It is now time to explore the art of the 21st century. This is the century of three technological revolutions: video, electroacoustic music and *poésie sonore* – sound poetry. In the case of music, for example, we need new instruments. In this respect the merit of Hugh Davies – to name but one such composer – is to invent new instruments corresponding to new sounds. The problem with Stockhausen, who is certainly more famous, is that he still uses the piano – an instrument made for the renaissance. Such instruments belong to the past.

You are not necessarily rejecting the whole of the past are you?

– No, no. One cannot reject the past, because one always needs it. But, in order to invent new electroacoustic music one needs new instruments. Otherwise, it is like wanting to equip an aeroplane with a wheelbarrow!

Presumably the computer is important too, as a means of orchestrating and accelerating new forms of composition?

– Yes, but in the case of computerised textual permutations and cut ups, I always find they lack the air of freshness and discovery of the earlier permutations of Oskar Schad in the 17th century, and those of Gertrude Stein and Brion Gysin. In the intuition of poetic languages, there is a richness and a human warmth that computerised language always seems to lack. To take another example, Christian Clozier and Françoise Barrière, who direct the International Festival of Experimental Music at Bourges, are both excellent composers. But their Groupe de Musique Expérimentale de Bourges – the GMEB – has immersed itself so completely within technological values that all compositional values have disappeared.

Discussing the compositional values of your audio-poèmes*, the American composer Kenneth Gaburo once remarked that despite your use of tape recording technology, your work is characterised by a peculiarly corporeal logic. This remark arose when I related something you had told me – that your work is all composed by memory, rather than from any specific score. Gaburo was very impressed by your mastery of what – in the context of his high tech studio – seemed relatively modest tape recording technology, and by your ability to retain what you would call a 'warm' corporeal logic in your work. Do you think you have achieved the kind of synthesis between technological and corporeal qualities that you have been striving for in your art?*

– No, I will never achieve it. But what astonishes me is that when I begin to make a composition I can remember absolutely every sound. My sonic memory is virtually infallible. I have no idea where it comes from, I simply do not know. Once I am working I remember everything. At the same time that my work is extremely improvised, it is also very, very carefully constructed.

What happens to this process in your collaborative pieces, such as your Voyage in California *with Larry Wendt?*

– When I collaborated with Larry, I recorded the first track, and then Larry recorded three or four other different tracks, at split second intervals, at the same time modifying the voice. In this respect *Voyage in California* is a real success, because it is the synthesis of

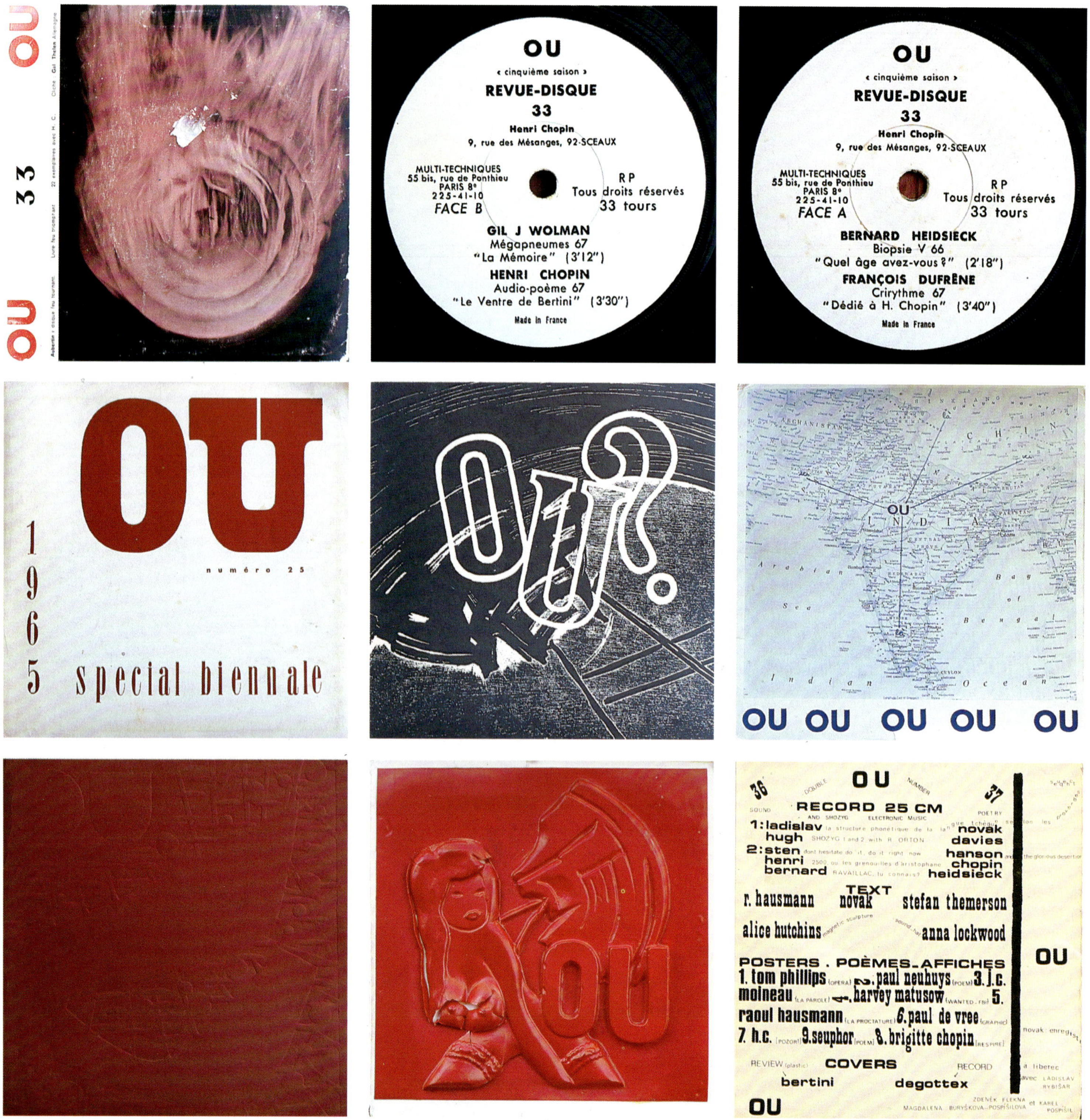

Covers and record discs, Revue-Disque OU, *1964-74*

Larry's technology and music and of my vocalic material – a synthesis between the computer and the voice. I have also collaborated in Sweden with Sten Hanson. Again, my voice is on one track, whilst on the other it is transformed by computer. It is a very fine work.

You have also collaborated with Bob Cobbing on Vive Rabelais!
– Yes, Bob and I improvised *Vive Rabelais!* together. This collaboration really brings out the wonderfully rich quality of his voice, it is a very nice collaboration.

What are your future projects? Do you have any other collaborations in mind?
– The possibilities before me are quite clear. First of all there are three directions I have mentioned: electroacoustic music, *poésie sonore* and the *Hörspiel*, three directions which imply new languages, which have nothing to do with Dickens or Balzac. Then there is another language which will perhaps introduce a cinematographic art: video. Then there are also the possibilities of digital composition – new technological possibilities. In this respect artists need to adapt their voices, sounds and images to these new media.

We are not only preceded by the first half of the 20th century, but by thousands of years of orality, writings and inscriptions, and we know that the arts are never static. But now we also have a number of absolutely new languages – for example, in order to computerise their language, the Japanese have been obliged to invent a second alphabet. The same thing has happened to Hebrew and Arabic. We already have a geometric, computerisable language. But what we still have not discovered are the ways in which this language will evolve. This is firstly because technology is evolving so rapidly, and secondly, because whereas computers only have 40 or so phonemes, we now know that we possess thousands of sonic values. We now know that the ear not only receives sounds, but also gives out sounds. All these discoveries were completely unknown when I began working with sound poetry – I was starting from very basic literary ideas. It is thanks to the new technologies that I have discovered all these new values. In the same way, future technologies will reveal the multiplicity of our auditory and visual cells – the eye, the ear and all our other senses. So while one cannot predict the future, it is certain that new departures have already been made, and that we cannot live without them. We cannot replace a TGV train with Stephenson's *Rocket*, instead we need more dynamic developments, surpassing the present.

All the same, one might well argue that new forms of dynamic transport should maintain the same comfort as their best earlier variants. In other words, there are new possibilities, but one might still wish to recuperate past values in some sort of positive synthesis.
– Well, in one of my books on the alphabet I propose precisely this sort of synthesis in the sense that one of my texts insists that typography should not be forgotten. These days in Paris typesetting is mechanical, typefaces are ugly and it is very difficult to locate a traditional typographer. As a result the manual and joyful aspects of typographic composition are becoming a thing of the past. In other words, one should not forget the artisans of the past in one's enthusiasm for digital technology. To do this would be to cut creativity from its roots. In other words, it is necessary to create a kind of synthesis, to go towards the future, while at the same time remaining aware of everything that has been written.

For example, I had the opportunity to see a number of incunabula books – pre-typographic books – in the Bibliothèque Nationale and I particularly admired a Giotto-like drawing in an 11th-century volume, accompanied by a remarkably accomplished inscription. These are the kinds of works which also serve to teach me. So if I work poetically in several ways, it is because I have the choice of writing, which is one possibility; of visual work, which is another possibility; the dimension of records, which is yet another possibility; the dimension of the tape recorder, which is another possibility; and the dimension of performance, which is yet another thing altogether to the tape or record.

It seems to me perhaps that the most profound dimension of your work is precisely that of performance. For me, it is in your performances that one sees Chopin in a truly integral dimension – not just the voice as recording, but all of the theatre of your body. Watching your performance in Geneva last year it seemed evident that this element of theatre was not simply a matter of banal gesture made to please the public.
– No, not at all.

Watching this performance I found it something that was almost painful to contemplate, because one could see a dimension of extreme effort – it was like watching someone doing completely exhausting work – a process of effort which produced this performance, and a performance that necessitated this effort. I found this very interesting, because this effect is not nearly so evident in your recordings.
– Well, what you heard on tape yesterday is the pure work. But at the same time, I can recompose this work in performance, in order to present it directly, not so much in terms of its composition but in terms of its existence as something emerging between the tape recorder, the loudspeakers and the dimension of physical presence.

Finally, do you think of yourself more as a composer than as a poet, or as something in between the two or combining the two?
– No. The thing that prevented me from studying music was my name. I am not joking. I was ashamed of going to a Conservatorium with the name Chopin. I was frightened that I would be mocked. But I have always been more attracted to music than to poetry – or rather, both have always attracted me. Radio had only just come into being when I was young and my parents did not own one. Back in 1932 or 33 when I was ten years old, I was walking past an open window in the street and suddenly I heard something I had never heard before – the music of Brahms! I immediately burst into floods of tears! Music has always interested me just as much as poetry. Perhaps this is the reason why I have always explored the sonic values of language.

Yours seems to be a curious destiny – to be halfway between poetry, music and art. It makes it difficult for those who wish to place your work in traditional categories.
– No. For me, the problem is that most people are completely unaware of the real quality of 20th-century creativity. Even in the

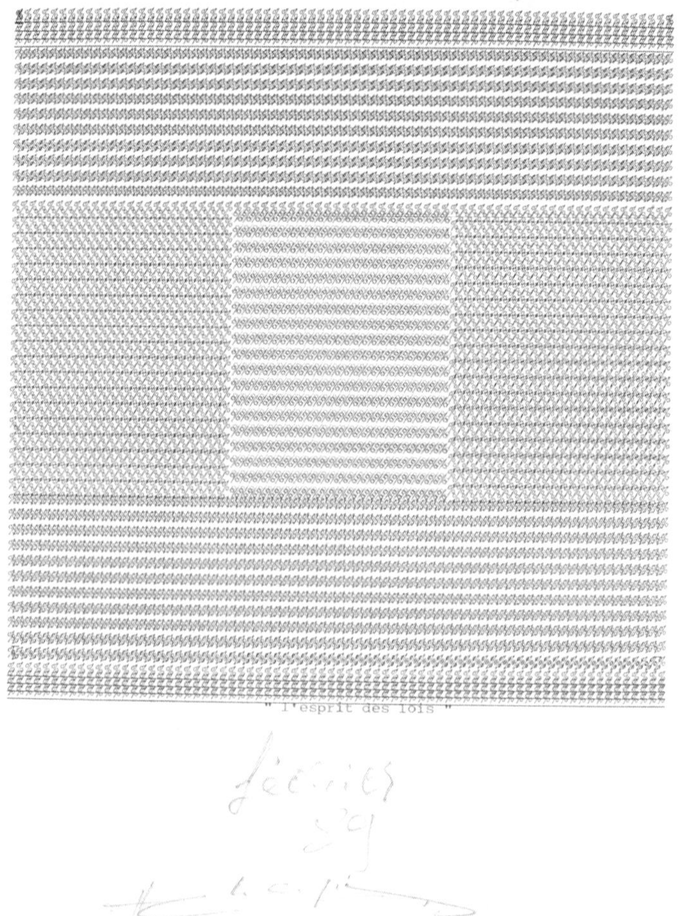
" l'esprit des lois "

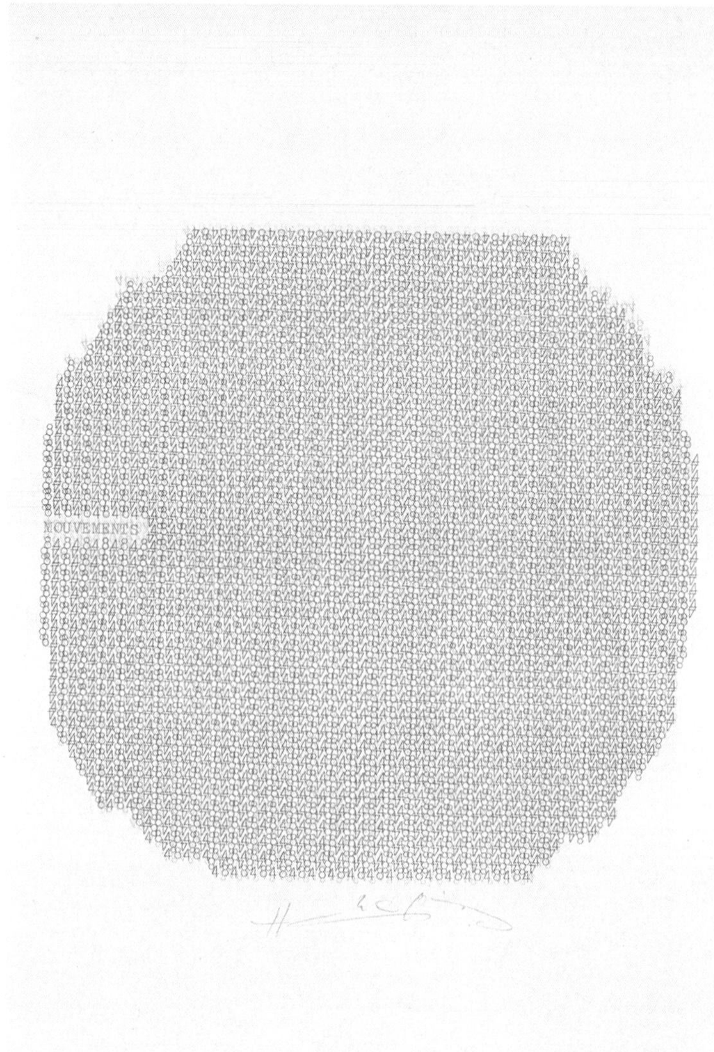
MOUVEMENTS

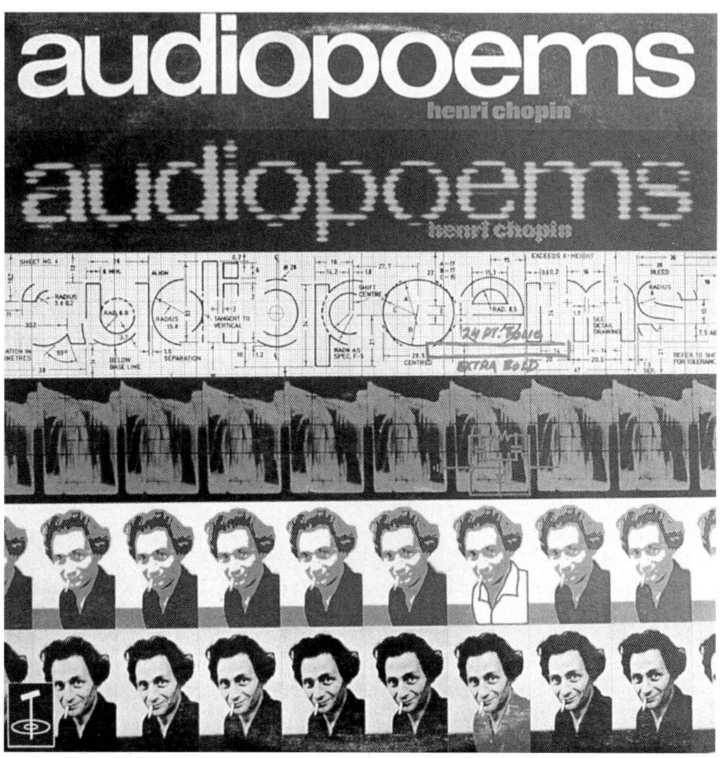
audiopoems
henri chopin
audiopoems
henri chopin
EXTRA BOLD

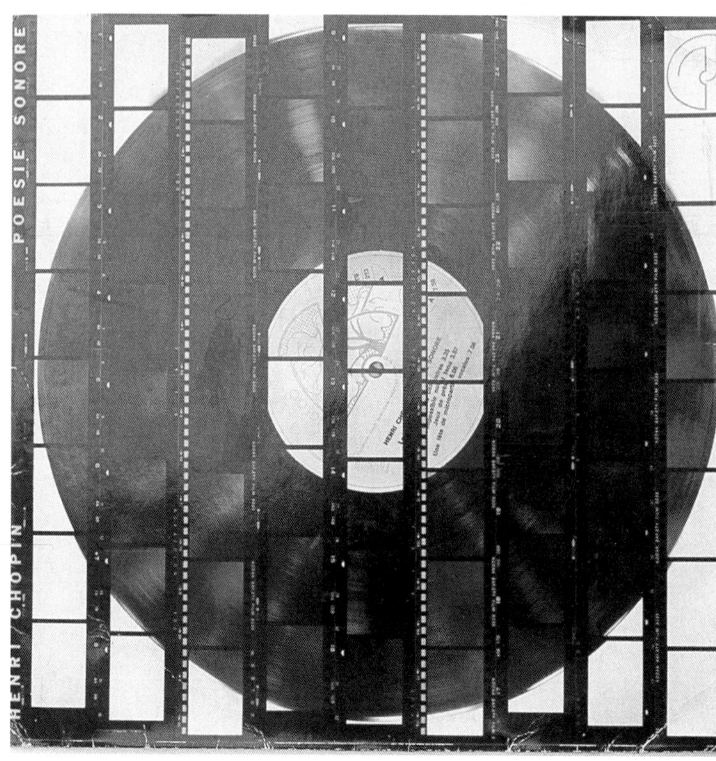
POESIE SONORE
HENRI CHOPIN

19th century, for example, Victor Hugo was perhaps a better graphic artist than a poet, Baudelaire was also both a very great graphic artist and poet, Paul Valéry was just as interested in drawing as in poetry. If we now turn to the Italian Futurists, for example, Luigi Russolo was a painter, composer and an inventer. Pierre Albert-Birot was a typographer, sculptor, poct and dramatist. Arp was the same – several disciplines. Seuphor, too. Throughout the 20th century, all of these categories have exploded. In other words, in response to the question of whether or not Chopin should be categorised as a composer or as a poet, the best critical solution seems to be to suggest that as a result of this research the frontier between poetry and music no longer exists.

Paris, 12 January 1992

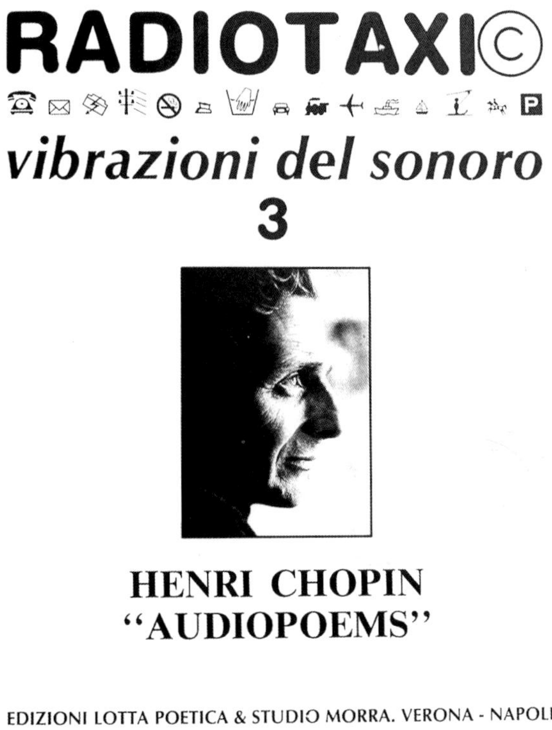

Audiopoems

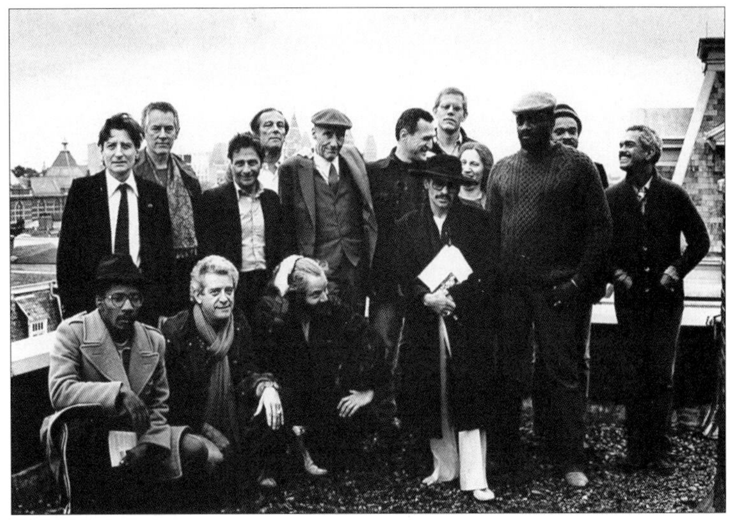

STANDING: Jackson MacLow, Michael McCluze, Henri Chopin, Bernard Heidsieck, William S Burroughs, John Giorno, Alurista, James Graverholz, Diane Di Prima, P Garvey, M Algarin; KNEELING: PK Johnson, Robert Cordier, Jean Jacques Lebel, Amsterdam, October 1981, Photo Françoise Janicot

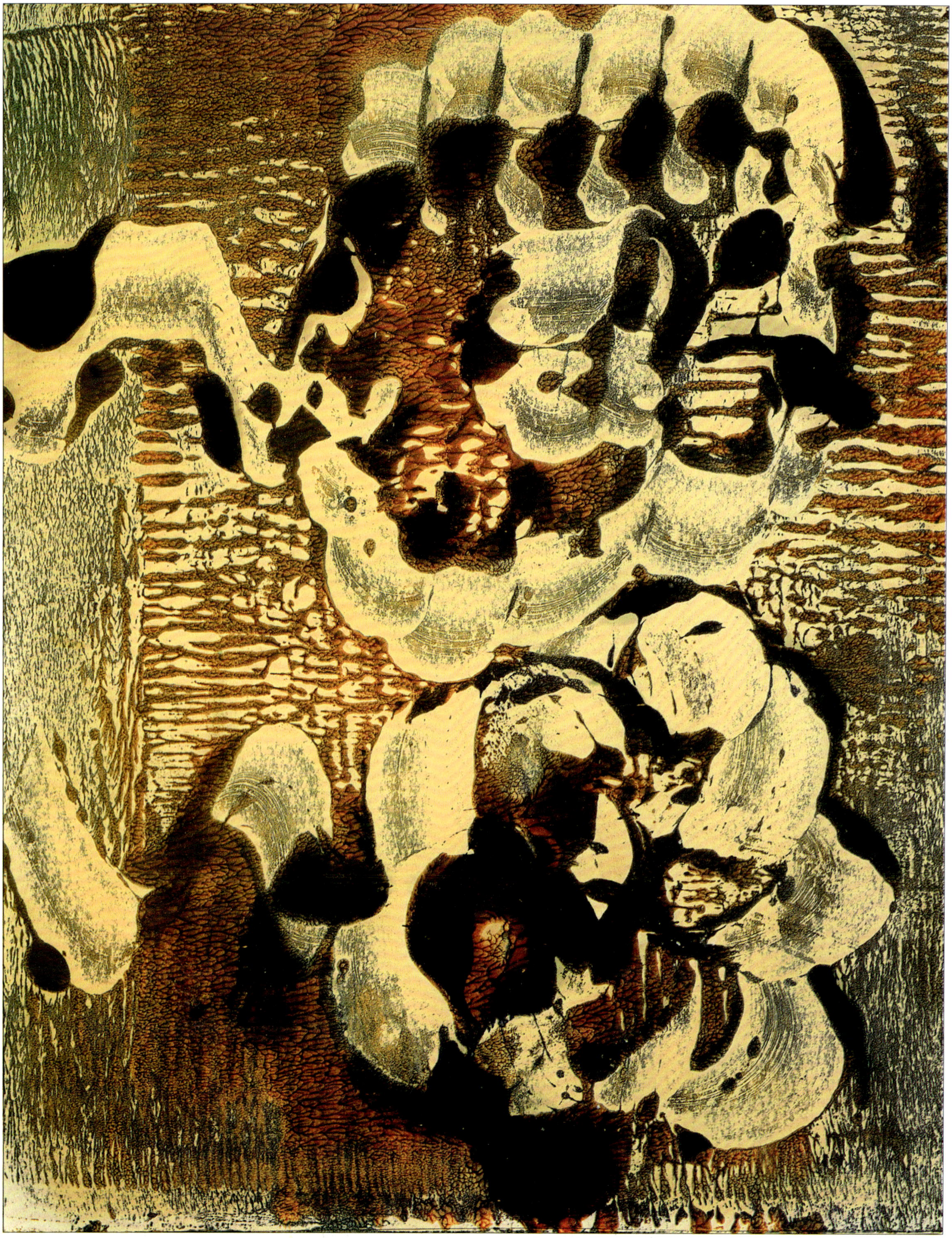

Finger painting, 1952

BOB COBBING

Interviewed by Nicholas Zurbrugg

Since the mid-1950s, Bob Cobbing's work as a sound poet, visual poet and publisher of Writer's Forum books has offered one of the liveliest and innovative contributions to the English poetic avant-garde. Hailed by the late Dom Silvester Houédard as 'the major sound poet in England' and applauded by French sound poet Henri Chopin as the author of richly burlesque antidotes to 'grave places, serious places . . . constipated places such as the White House, the Elysée, Peking and the Kremlin', Cobbing's verbal-visual experiments propel both language and its audience beyond the page and stage, 'bobbing you along', as the late French ultra-Lettriste poet François Dufrêne playfully puts it, 'into the extra-spatial extra-temporal, progressively sliding from sense to the nonsensical, the most genial of interlocutors'.

Nicholas Zurbrugg – *Bob, would you describe yourself primarily as a 'sound poet'?*
Bob Cobbing – I think 'sound poet' is as good as anything, although I am a visual poet as well, and also sometimes write semantic poetry which is only loosely connected with 'visual', 'concrete' or 'sound'.

What circumstances prompted your initial work with sound poetry and visual poetry?
– My father was a sign-writer and an amateur artist, quite a good one, and I started by doing paintings, as well as monotypes which I always visualised as scores for sound. Right from a very early age I had the idea that what you can see is also something you can hear, and the very first visual piece that I still put into my anthologies – a monotype done on an old Roneo duplicator in 1942 – was very much a visual piece which could be sounded, in fact we still sometimes sound it in performance. Then, when we started the Hendon Art Group, which later became known as Group H, quite a lot of people there were interested in the portrayal of sound in a visual way. Most of the stuff I was doing then was visual with a sound element to it.

Were you aware of earlier work in these fields by the Dadaists and the Futurists?
– No, I was pretty ignorant then, I was sort of stumbling along on my own, which is more or less what I have done all along, I suppose. I used to do things and then suddenly find out years later that other people had done similar things. Perhaps the advantage of this was it allowed me to approach things from a fairly independent direction.

Were you reading or 'sounding' your work at this time?
– No. At that time there really was not very much scope for poets to read their own work. If you got paid for anything at all, it was for reading somebody else's work. Nowadays you would not dare to so, you have to read your own work all the time, but back then all the performances I did were really of other people's work.

When did you first perform your own sound poems? Wasn't one of your first sound poems Are your children safe in the sea*?*
– Yes, that was quite an early one, but it was composed with a tape-recorder, and then broadcast. I cannot remember it ever being performed live in public. Group H had a writing group, and we used to read things there, but there was no scope really at that time for public performances. It was not really until 1964, when I read my *ABC in Sound* as part of a series of readings at the Institute of Contemporary Art, that Anthony Thwaite became very enthusiastic about my work, and got onto George MacBeth who produced my first BBC broadcast, the BBC Electronic Workshop version of the *ABC in Sound*. That was really the beginning for me.

Did this collaboration with the BBC's Electronic Workshop represent a major step forward, or were you already working with the tape-recorder?
– I was already using the tape-recorder in a fairly crude and primitive way. I never regarded the tape-recorder simply as a reproduction of the human voice – I always thought of it as something more than that, as something creative. I worked quite a lot with Anna Lockwood from New Zealand – who now calls herself Annea Lockwood. We made quite a lot of tapes on the floor of my living room with fairly primitive equipment. The BBC Electronic Workshop had far better equipment, but they were a bit more conservative in how they used it. The engineers had their own ideas about how things should go, George MacBeth had his ideas, and of course I had quite different ideas too, so it was very much a three-way tussle. I think that the BBC's *ABC in Sound* was a bit timid in its approach and a bit rigid in places. I would have preferred a bolder, more spontaneous approach perhaps.

Did this production lead to other BBC collaborations?
– Not really, no. But people phoned me up and offered readings, and I decided I might as well try to earn my living from poetry. It was that broadcast that led to my going abroad to festivals. George MacBeth was rather proud of it and he used to take the tape to various conferences on the Continent. I was first invited to Sweden in 1968, and then went to Amsterdam and other places. So George was doing this propaganda for me, playing the tape to radio stations all over the world, and my career took off.

Had you already met many of the European sound and visual poets that you met in Sweden?
– I had corresponded with quite a number of them. Dom Silvester Houédard – to whom I had sent a copy of my *ABC in Sound* in

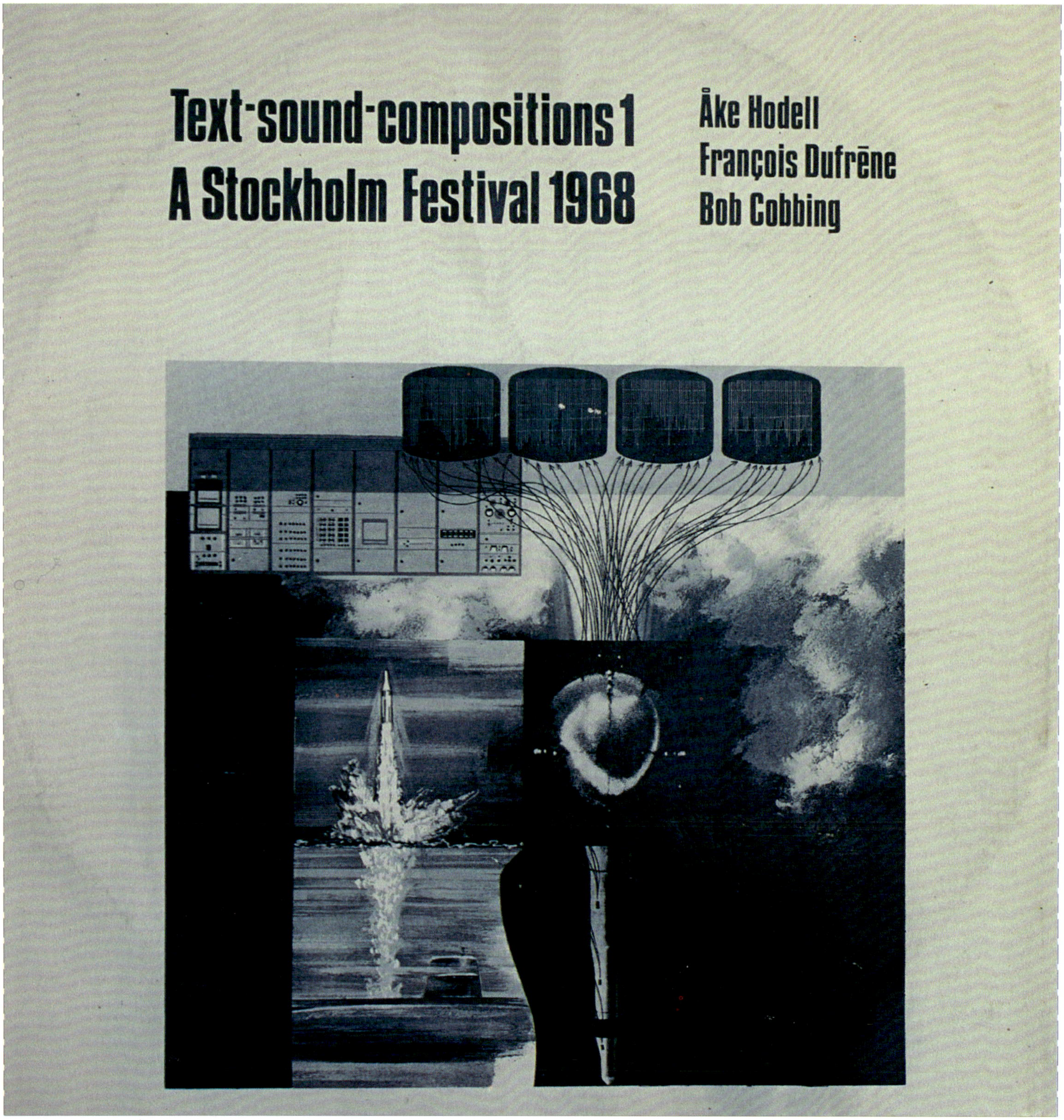
Text-sound-compositions 1
A Stockholm Festival 1968
Åke Hodell
François Dufrêne
Bob Cobbing

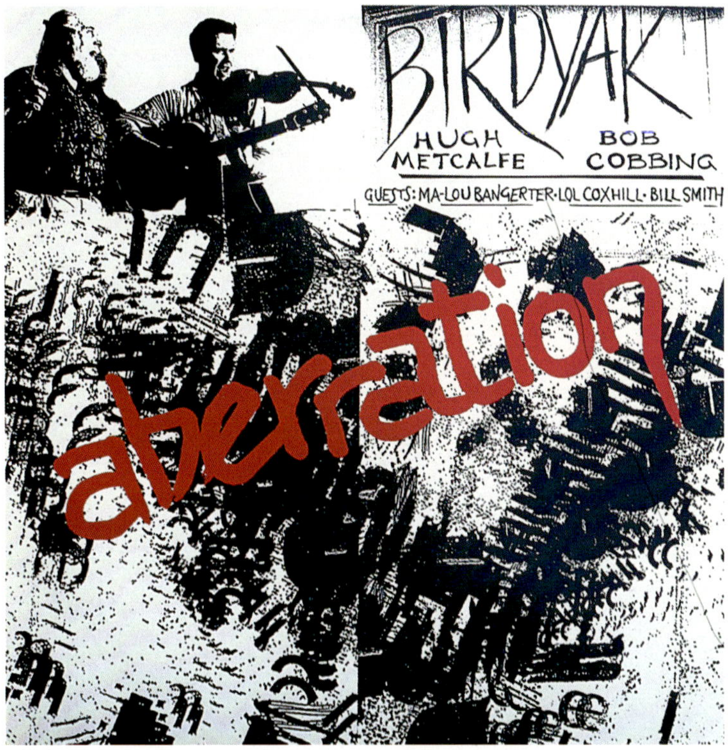
BIRDYAK
HUGH METCALFE
BOB COBBING
GUESTS: MA-LOU BANGERTER · LOL COXHILL · BILL SMITH
aberration

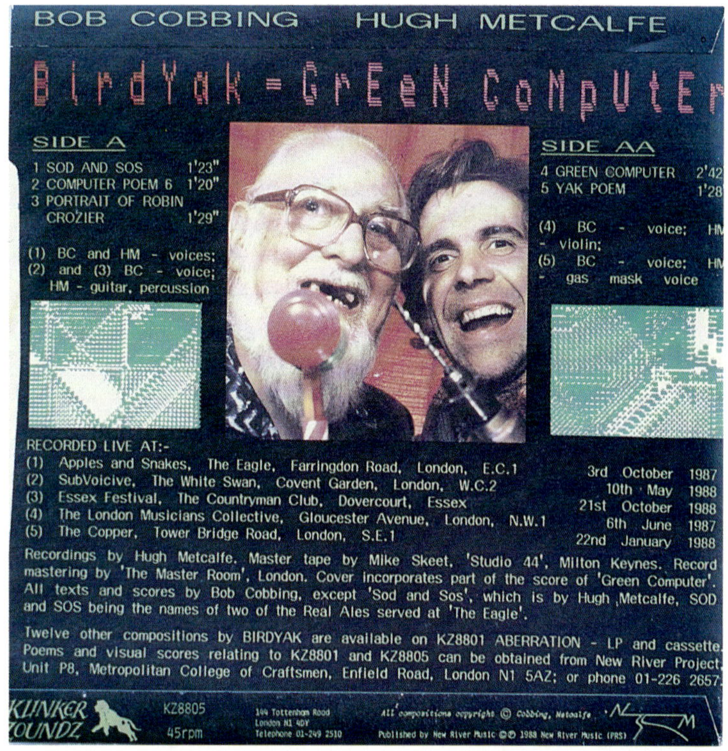
BOB COBBING HUGH METCALFE
BirdYak = GrEeN CoMpUtEr
SIDE A
1 SOD AND SOS 1'23"
2 COMPUTER POEM 6 1'20"
3 PORTRAIT OF ROBIN CROZIER 1'29"
(1) BC and HM - voices; (2) and (3) BC - voice; HM - guitar, percussion
SIDE AA
4 GREEN COMPUTER 2'42
5 YAK POEM 1'28
(4) BC - voice; HM - violin;
(5) BC - voice; HM - gas mask voice
RECORDED LIVE AT:-
(1) Apples and Snakes, The Eagle, Farringdon Road, London, E.C.1 3rd October 1987
(2) SubVoicive, The White Swan, Covent Garden, London, W.C.2 10th May 1988
(3) Essex Festival, The Countryman Club, Dovercourt, Essex 21st October 1988
(4) The London Musicians Collective, Gloucester Avenue, London, N.W.1 6th June 1987
(5) The Copper, Tower Bridge Road, London, S.E.1 22nd January 1988
Recordings by Hugh Metcalfe. Master tape by Mike Skeet, 'Studio 44', Milton Keynes. Record mastering by 'The Master Room', London. Cover incorporates part of the score of 'Green Computer'. All texts and scores by Bob Cobbing, except 'Sod and Sos', which is by Hugh Metcalfe, SOD and SOS being the names of two of the Real Ales served at 'The Eagle'.
Twelve other compositions by BIRDYAK are available on KZ8801 ABERRATION - LP and cassette. Poems and visual scores relating to KZ8801 and KZ8805 can be obtained from New River Project, Unit P8, Metropolitan College of Craftsmen, Enfield Road, London N1 5AZ; or phone 01-226 2657.
KLINKER ZOUNDZ
KZ8805
45rpm
144 Tottenham Road
London N1 4DY
Telephone 01-249 2510
All compositions copyright © Cobbing, Metcalfe
Published by New River Music 1988 New River Music (PRS)

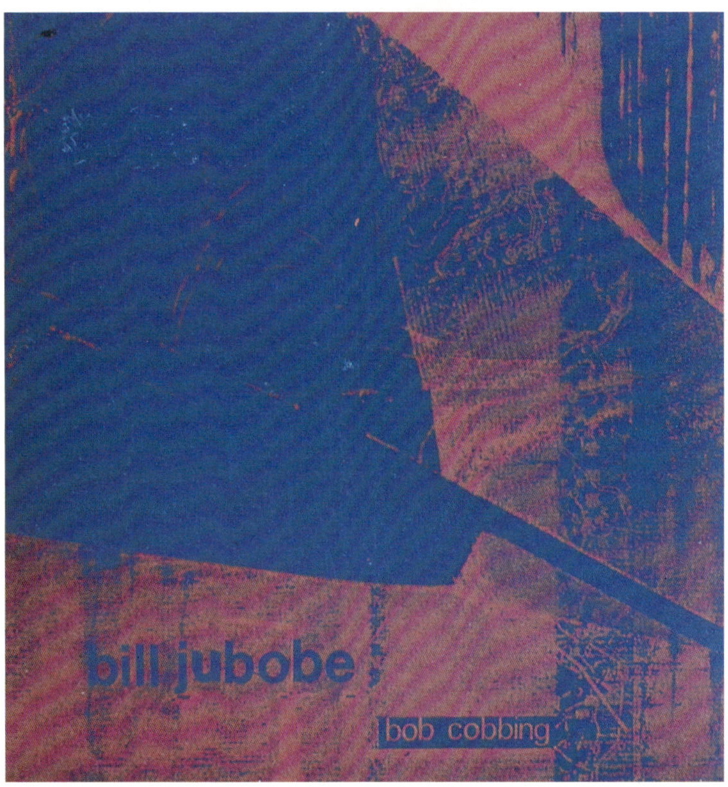
bill jubobe
bob cobbing

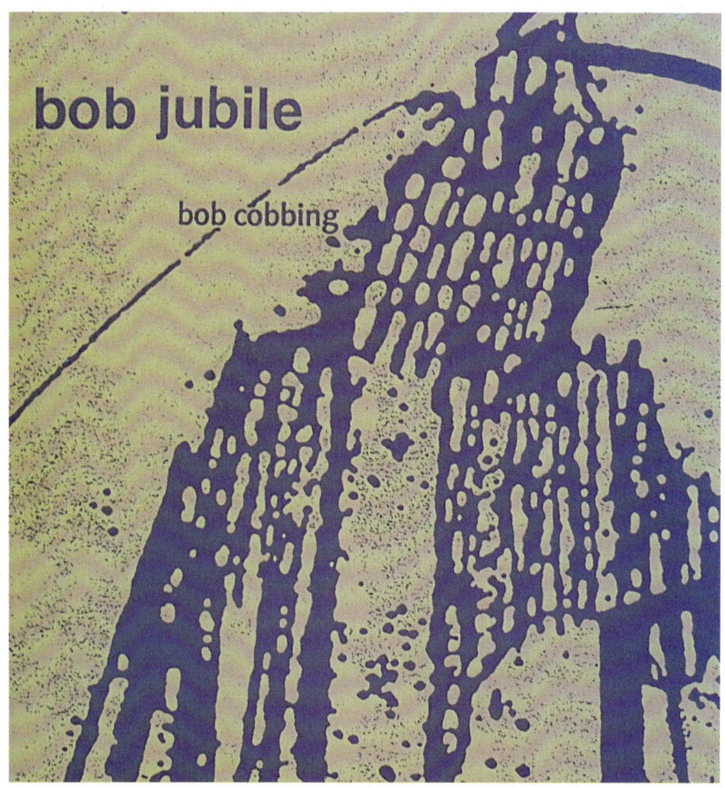
bob jubile
bob cobbing

printed form – again carried out propaganda for me and put me in touch with poets all over thc world. He had just about the biggest address book ever, I think, and put me in touch with people like the Austrian poet Ernst Jandl.

Writer's Forum published a joint LP with Jandl.
– Yes, with myself on one side and Jandl on the other. At that time we worked in a very similar style and did quite a number of live readings together. The Swedes, by contrast, were very much geared to taped performances, with the audience sitting in the dark with the speakers in all four corners of the room. Concerts like that would go on for hours, but that was not my idea of fun. I preferred the live performance to the taped performance and it took me quite a long time to persuade the Swedes to let me go up on stage and perform live, which is what eventually happened.

Your 'whisper piece', Whississippi, *which you presented at the Fifth Fylkingen Sound Poetry Festival in April 1969, seems to combine this kind of spontaneous live performance with subsequent studio editing.*
– Yes. I had done the visual version of the piece especially for Sweden, and when I was met at the airport by Kerstin Lundberg, a girl who worked at Swedish Radio, I said to her, 'I've got to do this piece tomorrow and I need another voice – a female voice – would you be interested?' And she said, 'I've never done anything like this in my life before, but yes, I'll have a go'. Next morning I just handed her these five cards, and said, 'This is what we're going to perform'. She said, 'How?', and I said, 'Well, don't worry about how, just do it – it's much more important just to get stuck into it, rather than to talk about it, it's very much a direct response to the bits and pieces in front of you'. And she performed marvellously. It was a very interesting experience, because I did not know her and she did not know me, yet we found that by responding to each other's voices we were gradually getting to know each other – there was a tremendous feeling of getting familiar with the other person.

This collaborative impulse seems central to your performance work.
– Yes, I like to perform with other people, because I think that most of the work I do is too complex to be performed by one person. If you regard it as a musical score, it is a score for an ensemble rather than a single voice. I like performing with other people – other poets or musicians or dancers or what you will. One of the most satisfactory performances of my work was at a teacher training college up in Liverpool with a group of trainee dance teachers. I provided the initial voice but got them joining me on the vocals and then interpreting the shape of the poem in movement. I also did another quite exciting performance with dancers in Hampstead, using both my voice on tape and my live voice.

Do you like mixing taped and live performance?
– I have more or less discarded tape. Almost everything I perform now is live and completely improvised, but at one time I used to play a tape and then perform live to it and get other people to join in. For example, for *Marvo Movies Natter*, a soundtrack for Jeff Keen's film *Marvo Movies*, I got several people together, and we each chose something different to read, and then all read simultaneously. It is interesting how the rhythm and the form of the thing developed from this process of several people reading several completely different texts.

Would you say that what interests you most are performances which develop this kind of unexpected form, interweaving different elements?
– Yes, I never start with any intention, either when I am doing the visual score or in performance. It should be completely open, it is something which happens, rather than being dictated. The text does not dictate – the text stimulates or allows performance. I used to call my texts 'song signals' – signals for song. They are meant to be completely open, so that when they are performed with different people, different aspects emerge.

I think you wrote once that you could imagine a poet spending their entire life creating different versions of one poem.
– Of course, as soon as you do a second poem, you have lost that opportunity! I lost it fairly early. But certainly, I think one could become 'the poet of one poem', with infinite variations visually, and infinite variations in performance.

Henri Chopin's review OU *34 has a record of both* Marvo Movies Natter *and another collaboration –* Spontaneous Appealinair Contemprate Apollinaire, *with the voice of François Dufrêne. When did you first begin to meet French poets such as Dufrêne and Chopin?*
– I met François Dufrêne on the first trip to Sweden in 1968. Both he and Bernard Heidsieck were invited to Stockholm on that occasion. But Dufrêne could speak no English or Swedish and as I could speak a little Swedish and French, I found myself interpreting between the French and the Swedes. This led to Dufrêne and myself doing several taped pieces where we were using the two languages, French and English, making all sorts of mistakes and producing very interesting wrong sounds out of the languages! Some of them were quite hilarious.

What did you think of Dufrêne's Crirythmes*?*
– I thought they were tremendous, to stand up solo with a microphone and come out with such sounds was really tremendous. By contrast, I found some of the other earlier Lettriste poets too tied down by intention and too lacking in spontaneity and organic development.

Did you find your work closer in spirit to Henri Chopin's more abstract electronic improvisations and compositions?
– Yes. I think as far as abstract compositions go Henri Chopin's best work is superb. But I think I have always had the two influences behind me: the abstract tradition of work like Dufrêne's and Chopin's, and the more verbal tradition of James Joyce, of Kerouac's *Old Angel Midnight*, Gertrude Stein, and people like that. I have definitely got those two strands going in my work I think – I can do fairly straight verbal pieces and completely abstract pieces.

What did you like best about the work of Joyce, Kerouac and Stein?
– Well, the sheer sound quality of them. Kerouac's *Old Angel Midnight*, for example, is sheer be-bop jazz in words.

What about the work of more recent American and Canadian poets – would you say that there are any significant differences between European and American approaches to sound poetry?

– I think American poets are more hung up on words than European poets. I think European poets have much more of a concept of 'total' poetry, rather than of something word-based. We obviously use words as well, but the words are part of it rather than the whole thing.

How do you respond to poets like the Californian poet/composer Larry Wendt, who use new kinds of 'handy tech' high technology?

– Well, Larry works with primitive electronic equipment of his own making, rather like the English composer Hugh Davies, for instance. I do not take to it all that much because it seems to me it does not really make very much of a public performance. I prefer the live approach.

I remember I once saw you perform sometime in the late 60s with a group called 'The Australian Dancers', none of whom were Australian, and none of whom danced! Maybe that sort of approach best exemplifies the way your open-ended aesthetic mixes different kinds of performance?

– Yes, anything went. Most of it was quite spontaneous. We had texts, which we more or less completely abandoned, and just let things develop. Yes, it is this sort of anarchic approach I like. I am interested in an amalgam of visual with sound with movement, with music, in a more total approach than other kinds of poetry.

It is very much a body art, both in terms of the vigour that goes into the making of the visual score, and the vigour that goes into the performance which is using the voice, which is using the whole body, which is as much dance as it is virtually anything else. My sound work has got a vigour and thrust to it, and so when I am making the score on the page it is the same muscular, physical bodily movement that goes into it. When I am making my scores on the photocopier, by manipulating things on the plate while the machine is operating, it is that vigour of movement which gives the result which allows the vigour of voice and vigour of bodily movement when I come to perform it. It is all one, really.

London, 26 January 1992

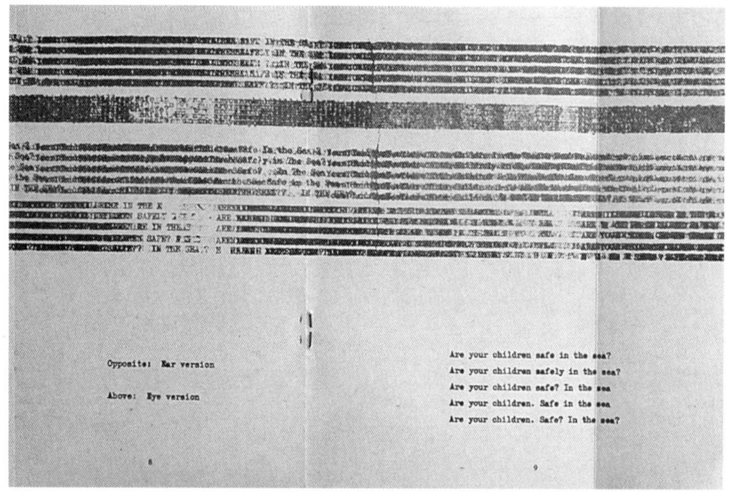

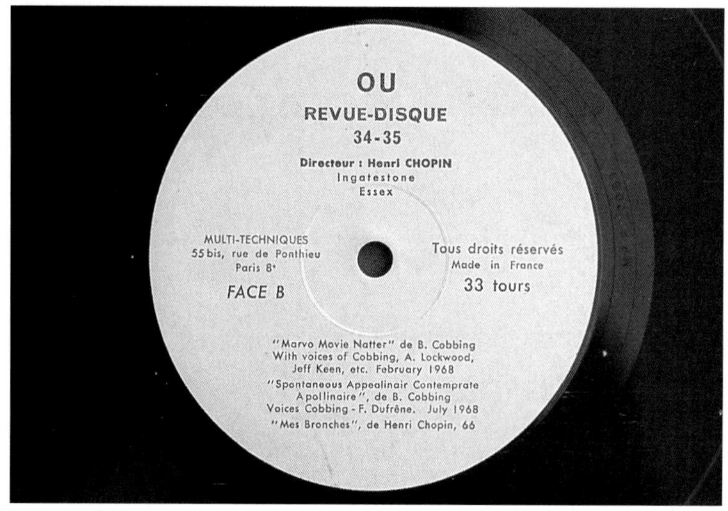

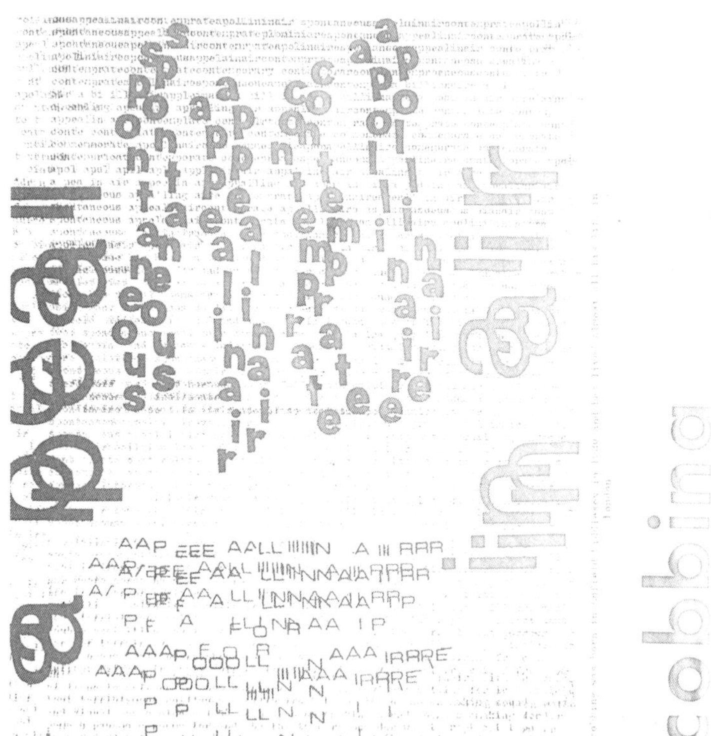

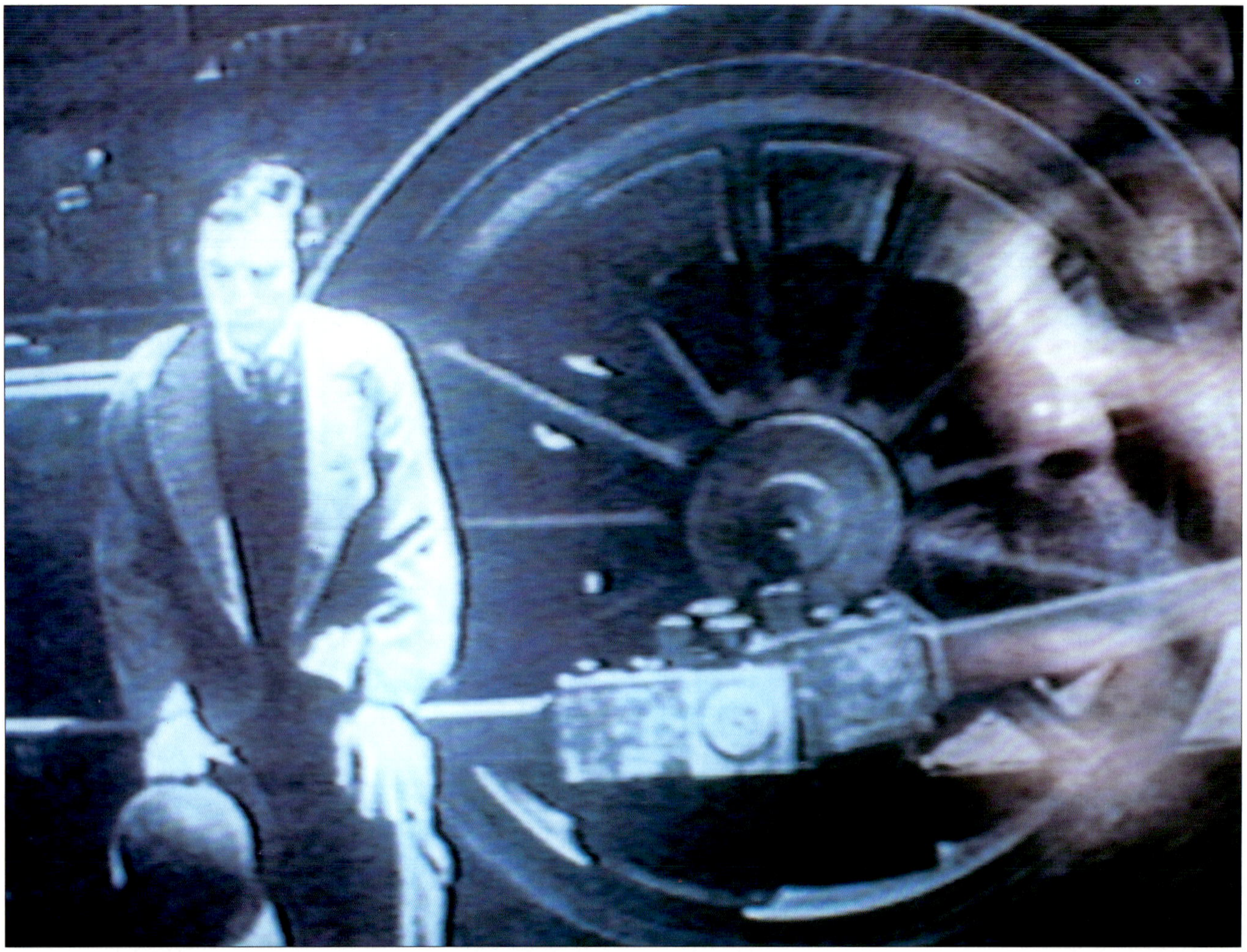

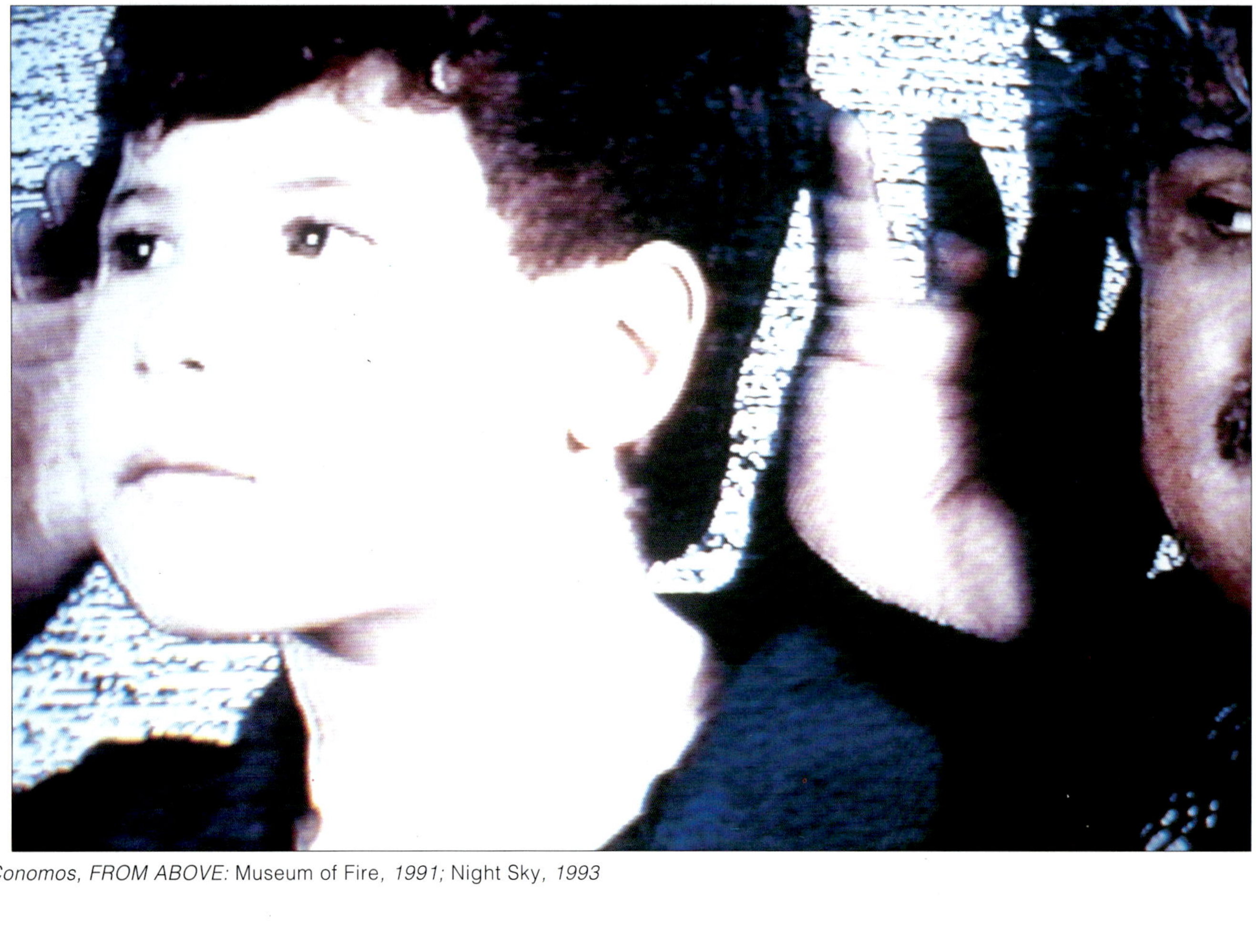

John Conomos, FROM ABOVE: Museum of Fire, *1991;* Night Sky, *1993*

THE MOVEMENT OF SHADOWS

VIDEO AS ELECTRONIC WRITING

John Conomos

In the last 20 years certain artists have used video (especially its collage/montage techniques of representation) as a form of electronic writing. Commentators such as Raymond Bellour have perceptively written about video's 'writerly attributes' as a highly elastic time-based medium of representation production. Arguably, certain artists like Jean-Luc Godard, Robert Cahen, Jean-Paul Fargier, Chris Marker, Steve Fagin, Thierry Kuntzel and Irit Batsry, to name a few, have in their respective videotapes articulated a Mallarméan-inspired approach to electronic image-making.

In other words, these artists have created experimental videos that suggest the significant idea of video as 'video-stylo' writing (following Alexandre Astruc's concept of the 'camera-style' form of film making) in Post-Modern techno-creativity. This is a highly self-questioning, non-conclusive kind of electronic writing that is uncertain of its own authority; that stops and starts in an intermittent narrative fashion, weaving a trans-generic hybrid and mobile kind of audio-visual writing. Videography is markedly indebted to Montaigne's articulation of the literary essay form and also to autobiography and the self-portrait. Making videos, as Fagin once reminded us, is a form of crossing generic boundaries without the imperative of holding onto a passport. And in so doing, these artists have in their respective ways acted as 'go-betweens' (Serge Daney) in keeping a sustained and informed dialogue between cinema, literature, the visual arts and the new electronic media.

What follows is a brief, speculative look at Godard's and Marker's video works in the context of the metaphor of cinema and video as writing and how this metaphor also animates my own video practice as a post-colonial subject living in Australia. The discursive qualities of the video medium have allowed many artists to experiment with image, music, sound, text and performance to construct intimate, anti-hierarchical and heterogeneous works that speak of border-crossing aesthetics and new polycultural agendas. To use video collage as an elliptical fragmentary mode of image and sound writing that exemplifies a 'Northwest Passage' aesthetic (Serres) highlights a transmedia view of cultural production that criticises the dualistic constraints of modernism and official culture. Making a video attempts to capture the polyphonic indeterminacy of the new essay form (Nietzsche, Adorno and Barthes).

Informing Godard's oeuvre is the key notion of image-making as writing. No other European film and videomaker is so obsessed with the idea of cinema/video as writing and so inextricably intertwined with the fate of the image. In Godard's case his form of 'video-stylo' writing (an ideal anticipated since the cinema's beginning – Artaud, Cocteau, Epstein, and as mentioned earlier, Astruc) permits him to transcribe rigorously and subtly his inner thoughts and feelings onto the video signal. It is a highly subjective, introspective form of audio-visual writing that clearly conveys the risks in crossing the threshold of the sayable. Godard's concept of writing video is interested in formulating new fictions, new strategies of presenting information, new means of addressing the viewer.

At the centre of Godard's videotapes is collage as a dominant critical and textual technique to problematise the myths of cinema and to create new hypotheses and fleeting hunches about this particular medium, and moreover, to critique the discussive dimensions and materiality of images and sounds as they re-ground themselves in the lived experience of everyday life. Yet to focus on Godard's videos in the belief that they form a cohesive category in themselves divorced from the filmmaker's prolific films (irrespective of the decade we care to cite) is illusory. To speak of Godard's videos is by definition to evoke a rhizomatic Godard. Equally, to speak of cohesive 'periods' in Godard's work is also illusory, believing the intricate intertestuality and referentiality of his multifaceted oeuvre.

Since the appearance of *Ici et ailleurs*, a watershed film in 1974, Godard had broadened his interrogation of the image by experimenting with new electronic systems of image and sound that redefine representation in reference to bodies, speech, time and space. During the last 20 years Godard has taken us across a new forbidden zone between film and video – a new territory of imaginative possibilities, of 'in-between' forms, gestures and spaces (Bellour) which is based on the artist's inventive, open-ended enterprise of attempting (*essaying* in the Montaignian sense), as Godard once put it, 'to see not this or that, but only to see if there is something to see'. Godard's fecund ability to locate new images and sounds in the 'in-between' spaces of cinema, video and photography suggests a highly plural form of audio-visual writing which is contributing to the underlying concerns and methods of the hybrid intertextuality characterising today's rapidly developing computer-inflected new media. With Godard's major videos like *Scenario du film Passion* (1982), *Soft and Hard* (1986) – both tapes made in collaboration with Ann-Marie Mieville – and *Puissance de la parole/The Power of Words* (1988), we are on the threshold of new anti-binary forms of electronic and digital mass communication – the so-called new non-analogical systems of representation, spatialisation and temporality.

Godard's approach to video as writing that is essentially 'dedicated to the present' (Daney) signifies new modes of seeing and hearing, new modalities of composition and decomposition, of accelerating and slowing down the image, of creating new strategies of positioning and *mise-en-scène*. It also represents, as Philippe Dubois recently argued, a whole way of being and thinking, a permanent state of matter. Video is a way of writing electronically with images and sound, about image and sound, and of posing generally ethical, historical and theoretical questions about art, culture and society. It represents a way of breathing through, and being intimately associated with images always within one's reach.

Video, for Godard, is the only medium which allows him – in his decentred questioning search to locate new sites in the image – 'writing with and in images' (Dubois). Godard's unceasing wish to see and hear his films and videos typifies an oblique off-centred kind of image writing that values the wisdom of Montaigne's words: 'The world is but a perennial movement. All things in it are in constant motion . . . I cannot keep my subject still . . . I do not portray being, I portray passing'. This is incarnated, for example, in *Scenario du film Passion* where Godard suggests that images are meant to render the invisible visible. Godard's stirring studio discussion which takes place in front of his large TV screen ('the white beach') in *Scenario* constitutes a grand search for the function and reality of today's images predicated on the dictum '*voir-receyoir*' (see-receive). Godard is the film/video-author who needs to create cinema and video as a continuous dialogue, a theatre of memory, infusing the image with language, with quotations.

Video collage (especially in terms of its organic and 'musical' aspects) for Godard suggest the opportunity to write electronically – thereby transforming images – to compose and decompose images and sounds, to use the video medium as a site for writing live. Godard's deployment of collage in his work is structured around his obsession to harness the image to language, and according to Bellour, this has so far taken the form of four different modalities.

From Godard's shorts in the 50s until his more recent videotapes, we encounter the ubiquitous presence of books as heralding the artist's concern to make art which is indebted more to language and writing than to music and painting. The second modality takes the form of quotations issuing from characters and books like fragmentary traces pregnant with meaning, veiling and also unveiling the image. The third modality consists of privileging the text over the image. Ads, signs, graffiti are often foregrounded in his works like Cubist collage elements. Phrases and words in so many of his works – in the credit sequences of Godard's films in his first period, to the many films and videotapes from his second, from *Ici et ailleurs* to *Historie(s) du cienma* – are splashed across the image, 'composing and decomposing the image (Bellour), thereby making the screen look like a writing tablet. Then there are the voices of his characters and the quoted books, and most significantly, Godard's own voice addressing the spectator. This is perhaps the most famous textual trope of Godard's art: the *mis-en-scène* of direct address – Godard's self-reflexive voice questioning the work at hand, its fictionality, and cultural and production features. In a word, to cite Edward Said, its 'wordly' circumstances.

Someone else who (like Godard) uses video technology as a camera-pen or quill to create and think live, to interrogate the image (often archival), history, politics, time and memory is Chris Marker. Marker's futurist enigmatic work – his films, travel books, imaginary film scripts, videos, installations, photographs and travel essays – constitute a highly subjective voyage across the world and its Borgesian labyrinthine features of faces, landscapes, objects and animals in memory, time and space. He wanders the world recording his impressions as a furtive lyrical *flâneur* reporting his poetic meditative image – sound letters that are indebted to Montaigne as much as to Vertov – chronicling life as a vertigo of space and time linked by the insane impossibility and unreliability of memory. For Marker, fact and fiction intermingle in so many different ways as do images, sounds and words; he is one of cinema's most elusive explorers seeing it as complex hypnotic kingdom of shadows (evoking the apt title of Part One of his homage to his friend the Russian filmmaker Alexander Medvedkin called *The Last Bolshevik*, 1993). By stepping aside and looking at his themes from the margins, so to speak, Marker's early 'essay films' like *Dimanche à Pekin* (1955), *Lettre de Siberie* (9157) and his only fiction film to date made of still photographs, the science-fiction short *La Jetée* (1962); and his more personal epistolary works like *Sunless* (1982), *AK* (1985) and *The Last Bolshevik* constitute one of the more elaborate haunting examples of film/video-stylo creativity as 'autobiographical documentary' in contemporary media.

What distinguishes Marker's work from his contemporaries is his playful, erudite and literary approach to the paradoxical nature of the image and time's hallucinatory labyrinth. Marker's oeuvre (including his more current 'multimedia' works like the installation *Zapping Zone* (1990) envinces not only a growing concern with computer-based media, but more significantly, it italicises the contradictory qualities of the image: its absence and its presence, its distance and its proximity, its reality and its virtuality. The image in its solitude, as memory, haunts us beyond our grasp.

Hence Marker quotes George Steiner's following words as an epigram in *The Last Bolshevik*: 'it is not the literal past that rules us: it is images of the past'. The six posthumous 'audio-visual' letters that form this work trace Medvedkin's life as 'the last Bolshevik filmmaker'. Characteristically, however, it is Marker's distinctive mixed genre kind of audio-visual writing with its focus on a pliable mixture of reportage, autobiographical confession (echoing Philippe Lejeune's concept of the *autobiographical pact* without any visible traces of Marker's presence – unlike Godard – in his own videowork) and historical essay that displays the open-ended, meandering textuality of the essay genre. Marker's typical emphasis of creating a visual writing that is always on the *move* is captured by his supple ability to freeze the image as he does in *Sunless* or in the opening preamble of *The Last Bolshevik* where we see Medvedkin beg Marker to write to him just a few words – just enough to fill in the space between Medvedkin's two foregrounded fingers.

Marker's oeuvre is notable for its hybrid indifference to the material specificities of media and in this sense it evokes Godard's reply to the late Ed Emswhiller (who asked Godard why he did not bother to pursue technological questions in his video practice): 'Video, film, writing – it's all the same to me'. Above all, Marker's interest in audio-visual writing stems from his speculative interests in making the spectator see and hear afresh and essentially doubt the reality of the proliferating images that shape our everyday lives. It is Marker's distinctive gaze of irony and engagement, empathy and criticism, that makes his work (across all media) so absorbing to encounter.

Finally, my own videos (tapes and installations) are primarily concerned with the notion of video autobiography as a form of electronic writing that is informed by Astruc's camera-stylo aesthetics as much as it is by ideas of cultural mistranslation, post-colonial dislocation and transmigratory spaces. In recent videos like *Museum of Fire* (1991), *Night Sky* (1993), a three-channel video and neon installation, and my forthcoming videotape *Autumn Song*, I am concerned with the project of continuing the idea of video collage as electronic writing as defined in the context of cinematic modernity and the new media arts.

As the son of Greek-Australian migrant parents reared in a a milk bar in a working class suburb in Sydney, I experienced the need to scramble the prevailing cultural and linguistic codes quickly in order to make some 'sense' of the Hericalitean flux of antagonistic values which surrounded me. Yet, as we know, this is a lifelong enterprise worthy of the surreal logic of the Marx Brothers (who feature in *Night Sky*). In my work I like to weave references (specifically by quotes, intertitles and certain props in my improvisatory performances) to past visual artists, videomakers, filmmakers, writers and thinkers as an 'antidote' to the underlying institutionalised amnesia that seems to be impacting on electronic media's history.

Night Sky is a baroque self-portrait posing self-reflexive questions about the contradictions, tensions and transgressive silences of my own polycultural being and past in post-war Australia and the expressive possibilities of the medium of video. It is equally concerned with the idea of video as cinema, video as electronic writing. (Hence, the six blue neon words in their fractured orthographic state as an expression of Greek-Australian speech and the calligraphic flexibility of neon as a writing medium). Born virtually under a Claude Neon milk bar sign, I was always fascinated with the idea of cinema and video as writing; the spectre of film and video as a form of writing has always haunted me (Cocteau, Godard, Marker and Welles).

Godard's and Marker's far-reaching essay videos are anchored in the metaphor of writing as defined within the Post-Modernist traditions of cinema, literature and the visual arts. Video as electronic writing represents a deconstructive reading of representation itself and is at the centre of both artists' highly autobiographical inflected work (as in mine). Transforming Astruc's notion of cinema as camera-stylo, both Godard and Marker have illustrated a profound authorial and intertextual capacity to excavate new sites in the image to write their moving multilayered meditations on image making.

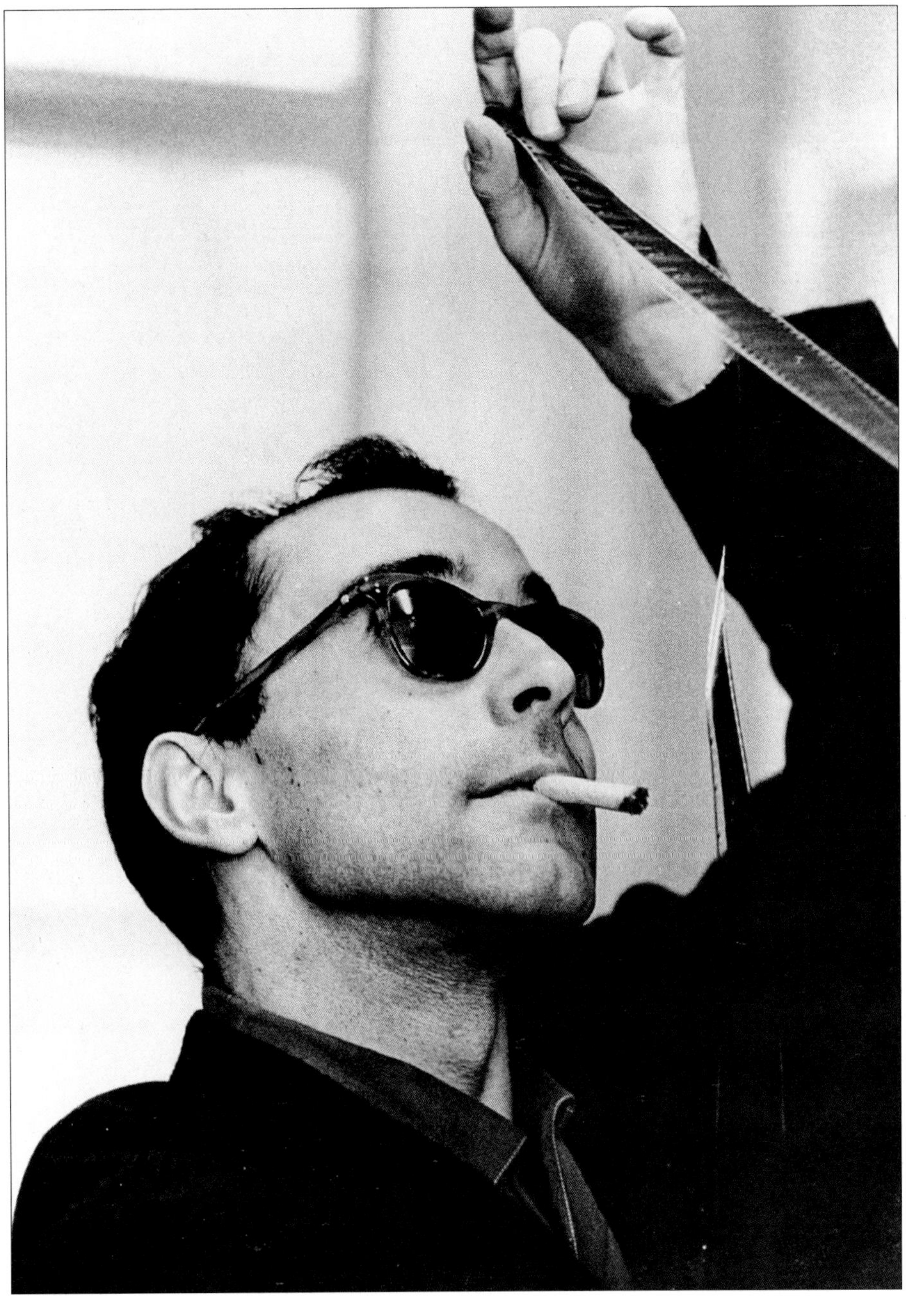

Jean-Luc Godard

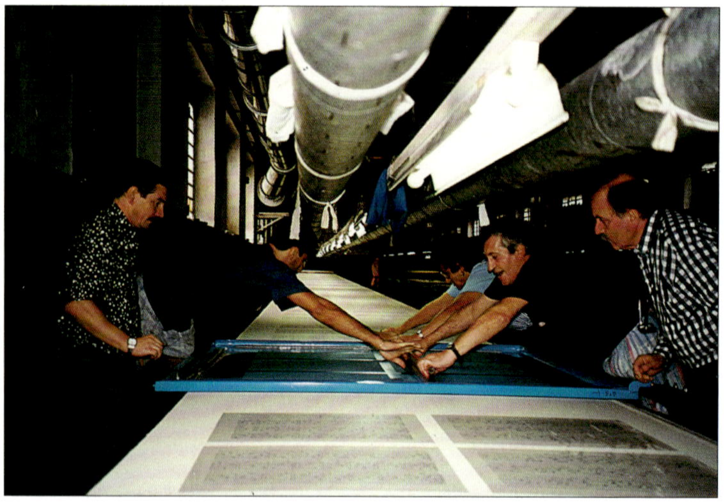

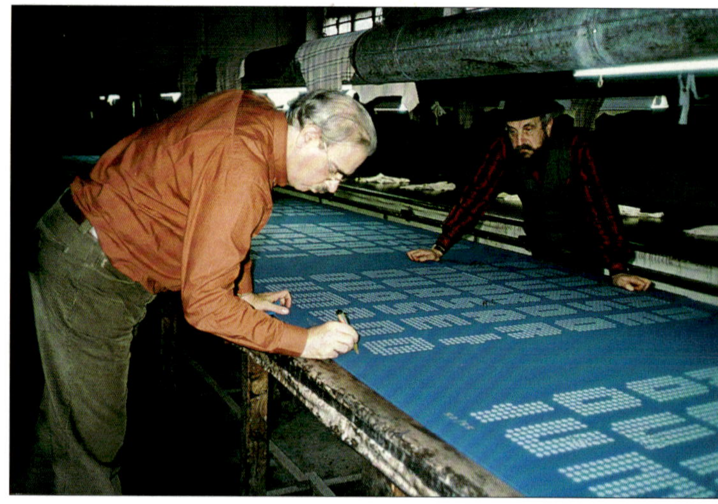

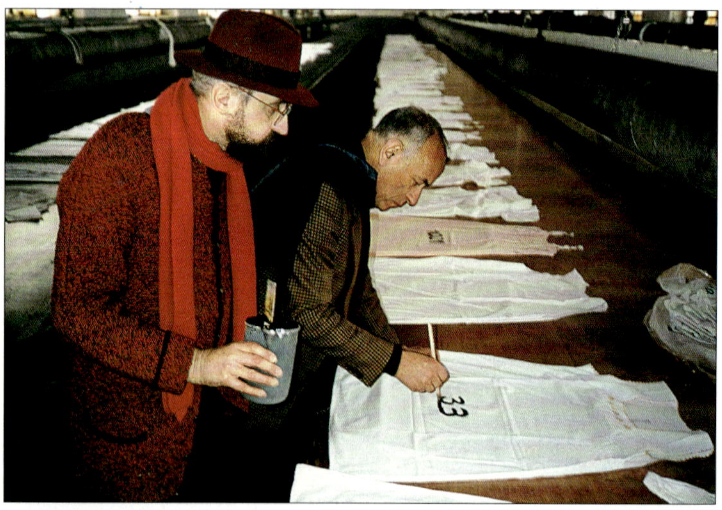

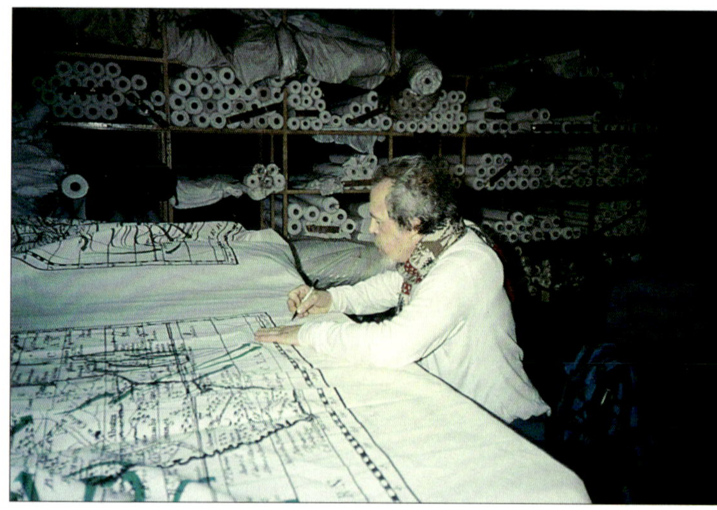

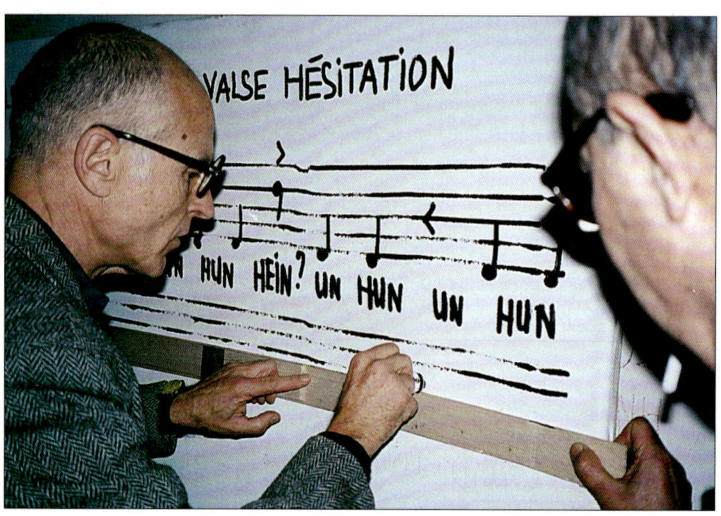

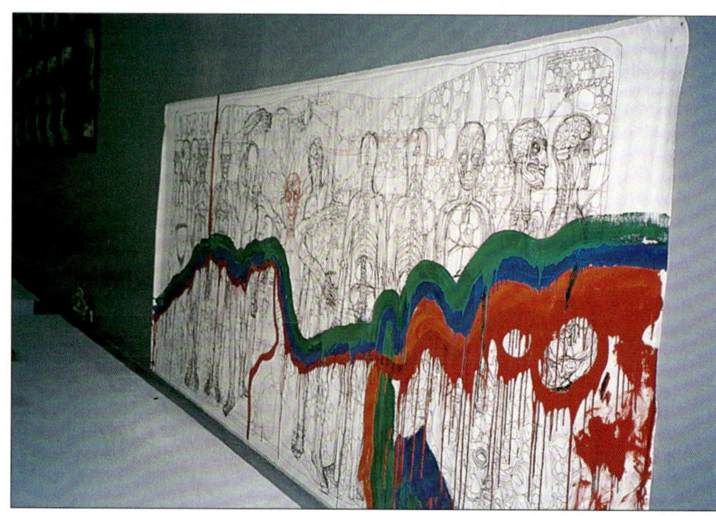

FROM ABOVE, L to R: Alvin Lucier, 1991; Francesco Conz with Augusto de Campos, 1991; Francesco Conz with Eugen Gomringer, 1991; Dick Higgins signing Africa, *1991; Jean Dupuy painting* Hesitation Walz, *1991; Herman Nitsch,* The Last Supper, *1991. Photographs courtesy Francesco Conz*

MULTIPLYING THE TEXT

FRANCESCO CONZ

Interviewed by Nicholas Zurbrugg

For the past 25 years Editions Francesco Conz have published some of the most innovative verbal/visual multiples. Collaborating with – and championing – the frequently neglected veterans of Viennese Actionism, Fluxus, Lettrism, sound poetry and concrete poetry, and the transatlantic new music avant-gardes, Francesco Conz's editions are distinguished above all by their exploration of highly portable large-scale textile screenprints, ranging in size, as Conz observes, 'from modest up to large' – and one might add, 'very large', capable of transforming 'an ordinary house' – and one might add, 'an ordinary gallery' – into a space of 'Art, Poetry and Wonder'. In the following interview, Francesco Conz discusses his projects in terms of his photo documentation of some of the artists, poets and composers who worked at his Verona studio in 1991.

Nicholas Zurbrugg – *Francesco, how did you begin Editions Francesco Conz?*

Francesco Conz – Having travelled in Europe for five years, learning different languages, I initially worked as an industrialist, manufacturing furniture. Coming from a rich bourgeois family I had no idea what art was – it was something inside me like a volcano which could not erupt, or which only erupted little by little in terms of my overwhelming need to discover more about the real creativity of our time. I decided to start an art gallery just to have the chance to meet people, coming as I did from rather a forlorn part of the province of Padua, a very typical old-fashioned Italian region.

So in the 70s I said to myself, 'If I open a gallery in Venice, I will certainly meet people', so I abandoned my factory and opened the 'Galleria di Arte Multiplicata'. Since the very beginning I had the idea of art as multiple pieces – something that I could exhibit in shows organised simultaneously in different parts of the world. Venice was not really the best place for this gallery, and at the time I tended to show relatively commercial art – the work of Miro, and Arman's multiples – which left me feeling that I still had not made any real contact with artists themselves, something that I wanted at any price. I had no real pleasure in just buying and selling art and felt convinced that I had to find something else.

Then in 1972 or 73 I took a plane to a small art fair in Berlin where I met somebody who said, 'Why don't you visit artists like Joe Jones and Günter Brus, who are in Berlin?' And so I met Joe Jones, and that is what started the story. Joe Jones was in a very bad shape, so I said to him, 'Joe, why don't you come to Italy – maybe you'd have a more healthy life?', because in the meantime I had rented a palace in Asolo, where property was much cheaper than Venice. So Joe came to Asolo, and it was Joe in a way who introduced me to Fluxus, while Brus gave me the address of Herman Nitsch and showed me Nitsch's works, which I liked immensely. Many more meetings followed. I visited Nitsch with the poet and composer Gerhard Rühm and then met artists like Geoff Hendricks, Carolee Schneemann, Alison Knowles; poets like Emmett Williams, Dick Higgins, Robert Lax and John Giorno; and composers like Robert Ashley, Philip Corner and John Cage.

Of course, these were all multimedia artists, working with painting, drawing, writing, music, plays, books. Eric Andersen commented that for him art is not really one work of art but all of one's works of art gathered together. In other words, rather than producing the kind of conventional individual works which I think of as handicraft, all of these multimedia artists, who are real children of their epoch – 1995, not 1925 – continually work right across the media. I only publish this kind of work.

Can we discuss these artists in terms of some of your projects for a typical year – say 1991? – by reference to your photo documentation of their visits to Verona? Could we begin with Alison Knowles' February visit to work on her multiple Italian Dress in a Box*?*

– This project began when Alison and I went to a second-hand store selling beautiful old-fashioned fabrics and dresses. Alison said that she had never seen such luxurious, 50-year-old fabrics, and recalled that she had always wanted to make an object out of a dress in a box. So I said, 'Alison, why don't you use these dresses to make an edition?' So she selected a number of old Italian dresses, we then found boxes in a number of different sizes, and she made the labels for each work by hand. It is an object that you feel but cannot open – if you open it you break the magic – it is to do with the fragility of the object, of a kind of secret object.

One of your next visitors was the pioneer concrete poet, Eugen Gomringer.

– Yes, following several visits to Gomringer in Germany, he came to Verona to make an edition of 100 nightshirts – a series of works with vowels on the front, and with different sentences on the back. We also republished his poems of the sixties along with more recent poems, in order to make a travelling show of his poems. Because while poets like Gomringer have books and small prints, they have very few large-scale artworks. All of my collaborations with artists try to explore possibilities. I try to draw them out of their holes, to say, 'Come to Italy, let's have dinner, let's have a party, let's go to the factory, let's take your work in a new direction!'

Is this the sort of thing that happened when the Brazilian concrete poets Augusto and Haraldo de Campos came to Italy?

– Yes – when he came to the factory in Como, Augusto de Campos was able to make precisely the kind of work that he had aspired to in the 50s, when they were using photosensitive canvas. And that was not all! On the way to Como, Haraldo remarked how the publicity texts on the sides of certain vehicles were almost like visual poems, so I said, 'Why don't you do the same on my car?', and having stopped outside an art supplies shop, said to Haraldo, 'Please, make what I suggested'. He was so surprised and asked, 'Are you serious?' and I said, 'Yes, I'm serious'. So both he and Augusto made a huge concrete poetry piece on my car, which is now stored in my archive!

Dick Higgins seems to have followed the de Campos brothers.
– Yes, I have worked on many projects with Dick Higgins, combining images and words. On this occasion he worked with a number of 19th-century maps of Africa – the kinds with images of cannibals and head hunters – blowing up one of the maps as the background for a musical composition based upon a cluster of arrows. These were published as hand-printed silkscreen prints, one metre 80 square, in a small factory specialising in high quality, 30-colour fabrics for Gucci, Cardin and so on – a process which ties in with the Fluxus idea of producing portable, industrially printed multiples.

Another American poet, Robert Lax, seems to have visited at the same time as the American poet and artist Emmett Williams.
– Yes, Lax was here at the same time as Emmett Williams, and we did a series of five prints based on his handwritten abstract colour poems. His poetry seems to me so essential, so near to life. He is like a guru or a saint, living a monk-like existence on the island of Patmos. And like the medieval monks he creates beautiful things – photography, poetry, visual works.

The same is true of Emmett Williams in a different way. It's such a pleasure to work with such an intelligent man. Just as Lax left America to live in Greece, Williams withdrew from a position at Harvard University, where he felt he was maybe too involved in academia, in order to become a more independent creator. He has done fantastic graphic works, alphabets, labyrinths and all kinds of typographical compositions.

What was Herman Nitsch doing when you photographed him at work in Verona?
He was overpainting one of his graphics, a three metre long version of *The Last Supper*. It is one of the most incredible graphics that he has printed. Again, Nitsch is a multimedia artist working with theatre, philosophy, music and performance: a man who has been redirecting his art in all kinds of directions. Herman Nitsch, Robert Lax, Emmett Williams, Dick Higgins, Alison Knowles, Philip Corner and John Cage are all the same – they all put creativity first, before all commercial considerations. They do not put the market first, they do not have time to care about the market.

Jean Dupuy – who was also working in Verona – is another artist who withdrew when he felt he was being trapped in New York's commercial gallery system. He gave up making art in this way and became associated with Macunias and Fluxus. At the time he was preparing his *Hesitation Waltz* – a piece of music based upon anagrammatic graphics which he painted after first drawing them upon fabric. As you can see, my house is a meeting point for artists and poets from Europe and North and South America, like Dupuy, the de Campos brothers and Dick Higgins.

The American composer Alvin Lucier also visited in order to

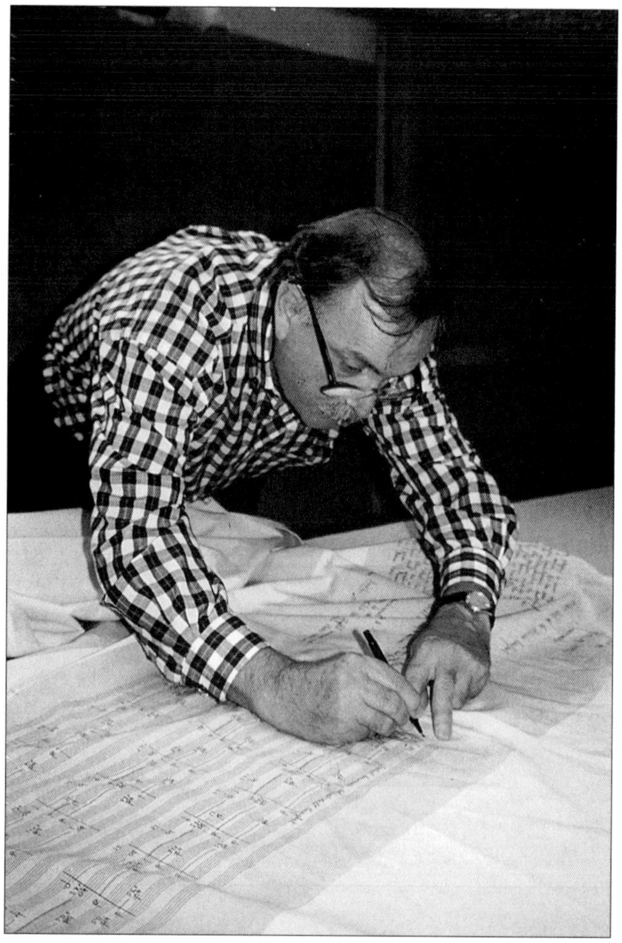

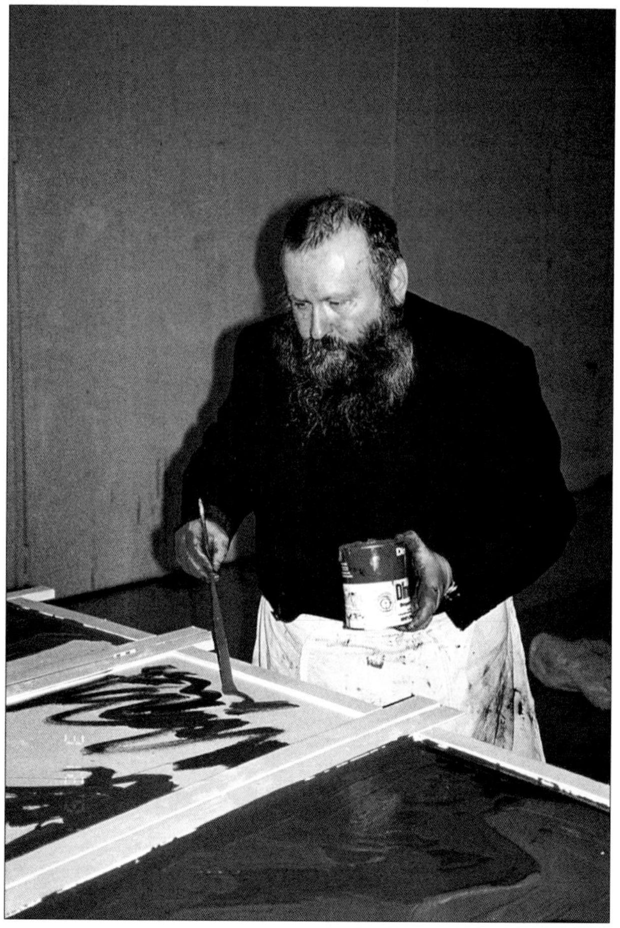

FROM L to R: Alvin Lucier, 1991; Herman Nitsch over painting The Last Supper, *1991*

prepare the graphics for prints of his scores on fabric – it is what Cage predicted, the score becomes a visual work. Once again, an artist is given the chance to work on the kind of scale they have always wanted to explore. Lucier worked in the factory in Como preparing a score of about one metre 30 by one metre. Everything was done in total collaboration with the artist – Lucier was very much aware of what he wanted, of what proportions and what colours he wanted to use.

You also have another very memorable sequence of photographs of Robert Lax's subsequent collaborations and meetings at your house with Emmett Williams. Why do you think Lax's abstract poems are still relatively unknown?
– Because he does not care to go to see people to promote his work, whereas other artists promote themselves brutally. In other words, while the over-promotion of art and the subsequent disappearance of over-promoted art is part of the capitalist system, the soul of true creativity is part of the system of passion – a kind of creativity that remains integral, that remains '*vrai*'. You cannot find a second example of someone like Robert Lax, with his intelligence, his choices, his ways of doing, his ways of thinking, his way of talking to people, his way of creating art – you cannot find a second one, he is unique.

So in a sense your photographs show meetings of exceptional artists in simple circumstances? On the one hand your photographs are a celebration of a particular quality of aesthetic imagination, insofar as artists like Lax work right across the media. But as you have suggested, your photos are also a celebration of a particular kind of spiritual or existential decision, insofar as these are also all artists committed to refining their integrity.
– Exactly. They do not need to sit on thrones – they can sit on chairs, very simply. People who are very weak in their work have to sit on thrones, but these people can sit on the stairs because their work stands up for itself. That is the point. What remains is a style of life, where art integrates life, and where the work of art is never finished. Even after their death it is not finished, because many artists have left projects that have not been developed yet and they have to be developed. Art has to interact with life, and with all the sequences of new technological developments that we are going through.

In other words, one might say that what you have been doing is facilitating a kind of laboratory situation in which poets and artists and composers came to your 'laboratory', collaborating with your 'technicians', meeting one another and sharing each other's ideas?
– Yes, when you share ideas you get something else, you get a sort of criticism of your work and you see what other artists are doing. And you see things in an intimate way, you do not see things already finished on the wall, but you say, 'What have you been doing lately?' 'What is your opinion about art?' 'Where are we going?'

In this respect your project of photographing these artists offers a way of 'multiplying' traces of these important collaborative meetings?
– Yes, and I have so much to do – I have to put some order into my archive of photographs, to keep on photographing, and perhaps to have the pleasure of seeing some of these photographs exhibited. Maybe such living documentation becomes 'a work of art'. I see such photographs as a way of exploring the intimacy of art – not the posed formality of exhibition openings – but moments of intimacy when the artist is producing, discussing, eating or drinking. All this is a part of life.

Verona, 7 January 1995

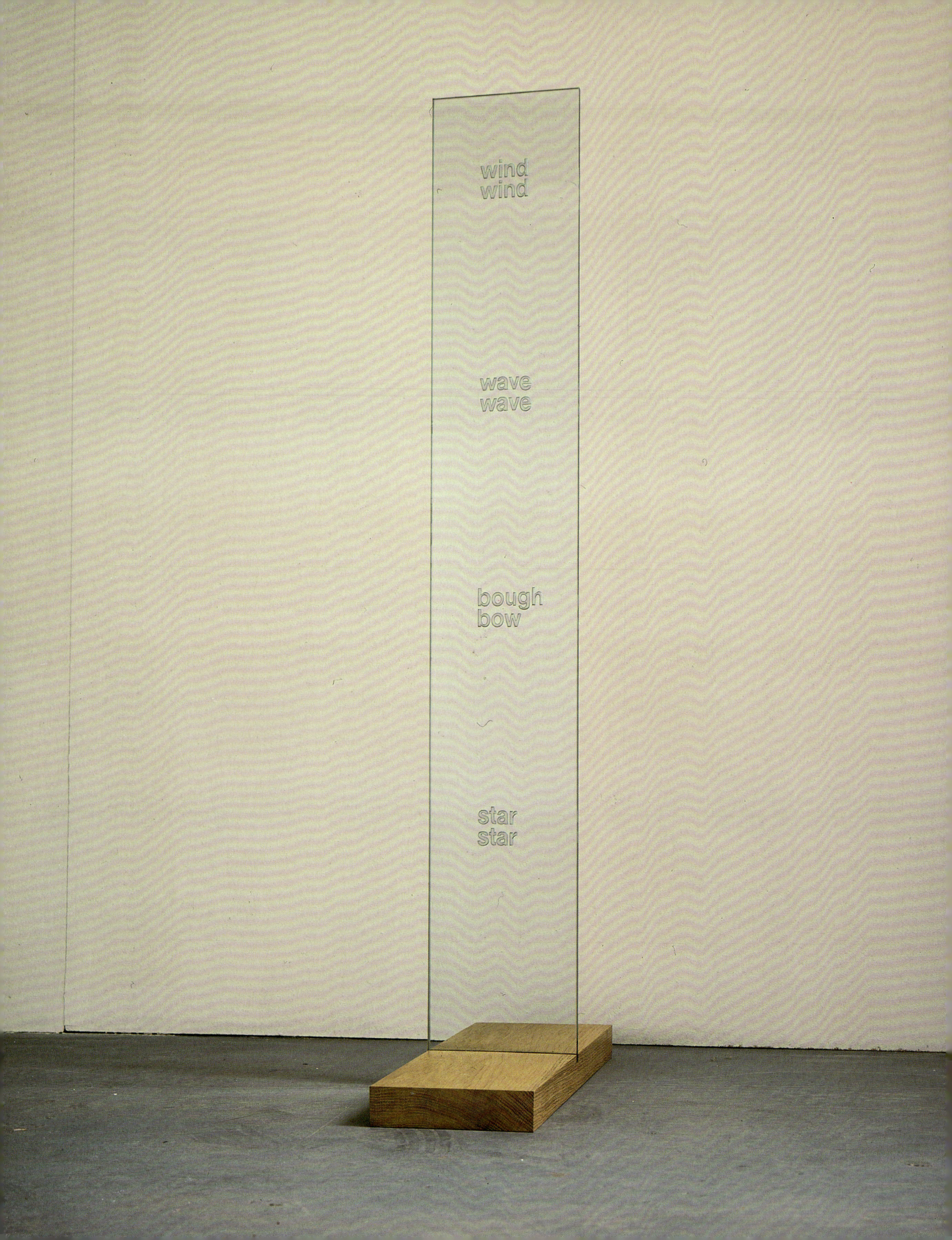
wind
wind
wave
wave
bough
bow
star
star

IAN HAMILTON FINLAY

Interviewed by Nicholas Zurbrugg

Nicholas Zurbrugg – *Perhaps I could begin by asking you how you first began to write visual or concrete poetry, as opposed to linear verse?*

Ian Hamilton Finlay – I have to say that I do not think concrete poetry and visual poetry are the same thing at all. I could produce for you – not of my own, necessarily – a lot of concrete poems which have very, very little visual element. In Gomringer's poetry for instance, there is very little visual element, but it is still a very, very pure example of concrete poetry. It has always been a worry to me that these two genres have been confused, and I think a lot of the exhibitions we used to have in the days when such exhibitions were fashionable, in the late 60s, were really spoiled by not distinguishing between the genres.

How would you distinguish between the two?

– Well, it is partly a metaphysical question, I mean, there is some mystery involved, but I suppose I would say that in concrete poetry the noun is the hero, and not the adjective. In concrete poetry, language, of course, moves from left to right and has a velocity, but by some talent, instinct or capacity on the part of the writer, it manages to cancel that. If one takes the Brazilian poets' concept of the poem as an object – or as being an object – as a metaphor, it is really very exact. It means something quite different from making the poems into objects on glass or something like that. The genuine concrete poem has an object-like aspect to it. Different philosophical approaches have considered language as a kind of being, or a kind of entity, which in different ages has had very different possibilities and actualities. I suppose concrete poetry really was an international phenomenon, and who knows how it arose, and who knows whither it has gone? But it definitely had a unique kind of being or identity.

How did you first find out about it? Was it through contact with Gomringer and with the Brazilians?

– Well, that came afterwards. It began with the very strange experience in the way I was putting words together in my early poems – which at that time were considered very unconventional – this way of putting words together suddenly ceased to have any kind of validity for me. And I found this very disconcerting. At first I could not understand it at all, I really could not understand what was happening. I used to say to other Scottish poets, 'There's a crisis of syntax', and received very strange looks. Anyway, I came to the point where I just could not write any more, and at that point I began to make all sorts of toys out of cardboard and wood. They were literally objects, but they had a certain poetical presence – I regarded them as a kind of stopgap. It was at this point that Edwin Morgan drew my attention to a letter in the *TLS* by EM de Melo E Castro, about this collection of concrete poetry. I was very, very sceptical to begin with, because I did not like avant-garde art. But when I actually saw it, I was delighted, and I realised it was just what in my little naive, home-made, Scottish way, I had been thinking about. And there it was – it was really quite amazing! So I had the experience, so to speak, before I met examples of it.

What anthology was this?

– I think it was produced by the Portuguese, but it included Brazilian poets. I remember that you could write to this address in the *TLS*. There were the de Campos brothers, and one or two other people who were not really part of that group, but it was very exciting.

Presumably that encouraged you to work more confidently.

– Yes, that was a great help to me. But of course, this is an aspect of my character or nature – that I usually have the experience before I can explain it to myself. For instance, when I discovered emblems – obviously there is a relation between emblems and concrete poetry, partly because of the brevity – I had this kind of incoherent experience of the form before I read Gombrich's essay on the subject. What the Gombrich essay did was what the Portuguese anthology did – it elucidated forms which I had previously experienced incoherently. For me tradition has always played this clarifying role. I see that other people regard tradition as a very dead thing, which is against their own development or expression, but I have always found tradition to be absolutely liberating. But I can see that sometimes writers do not have these primitive experiences that I have had, and maybe if I had been in a culture that was more of the world at that time, I would not have had to go through this incoherent stage. But I do not really believe that. I think it is part of my nature to discover such things for myself.

At the same time did you feel a certain impatience with other prevalent trends, such as beat poetry?

– Yes, at the time I became very dogmatic and Presbyterian. I did not approve of non-concrete poetry. I thought a more Catholic attitude was reprehensible. It was virtually a moral question to me.

Have you mellowed?

– Yes, I have mellowed, I have mellowed – there is nothing like being battered for mellowing one! Now I feel that I can write in different genres. But I do not really have much control over it. I still sometimes write concrete poems, but I cannot say to myself, 'Now I'm going to write a concrete poem'. I can only do what the thing inside me allows me to do, and very often, I would like to be doing something other than it allows me to do, but I have to follow it – I do not have any choice. But theoretically, I no longer consider it absolutely immoral to write non-concrete poetry.

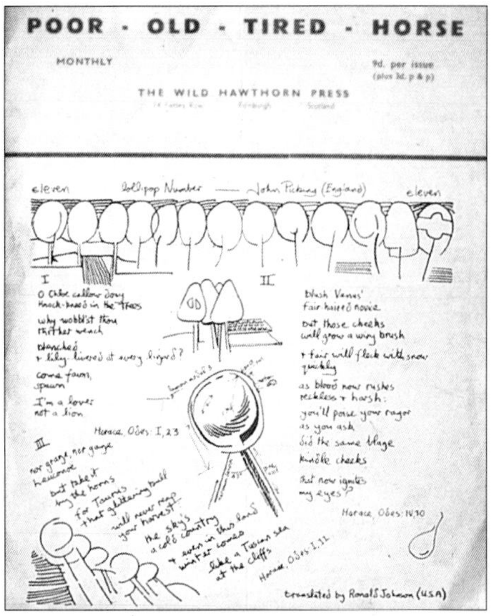

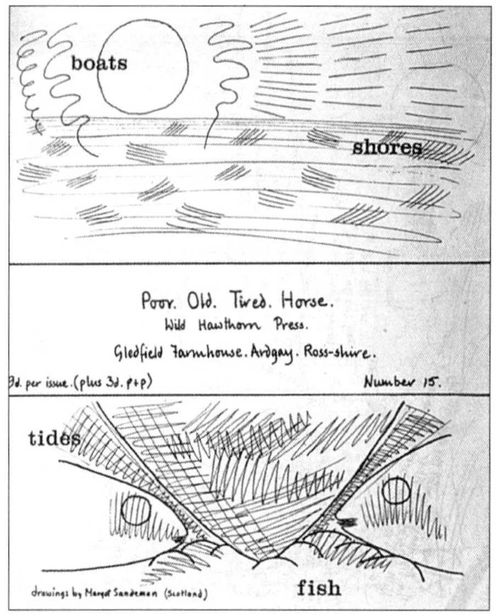

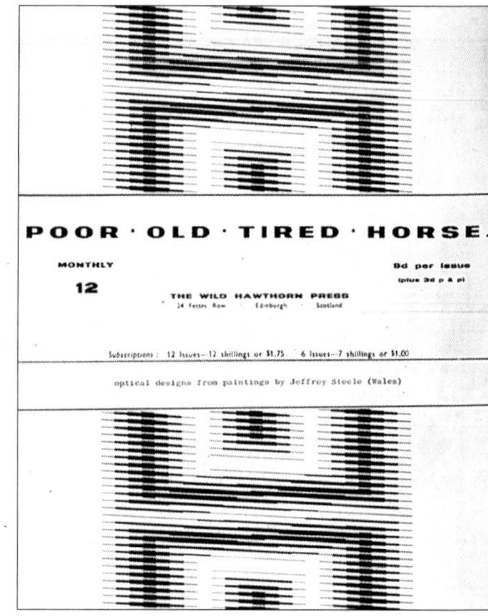

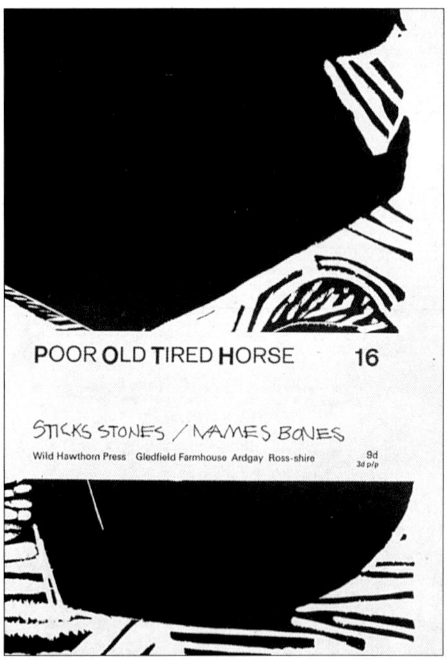

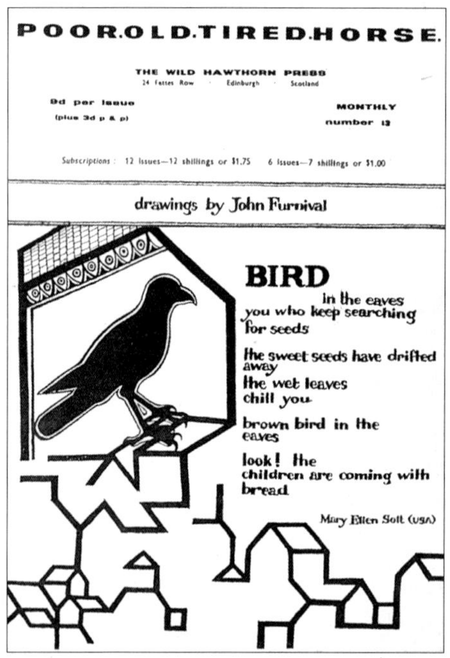

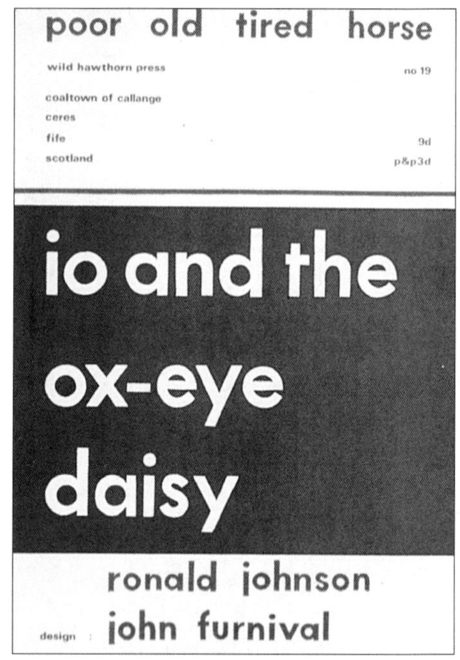

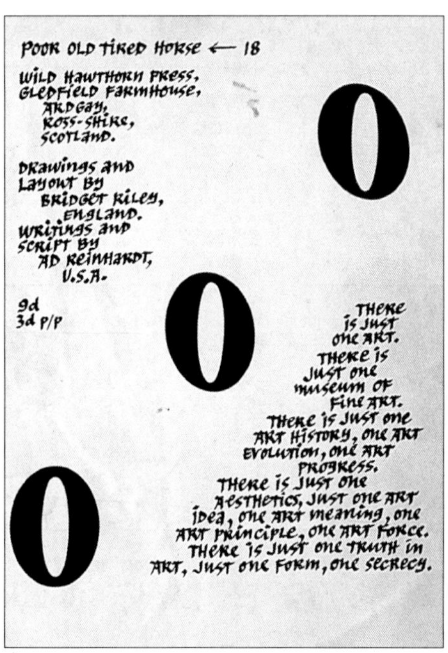

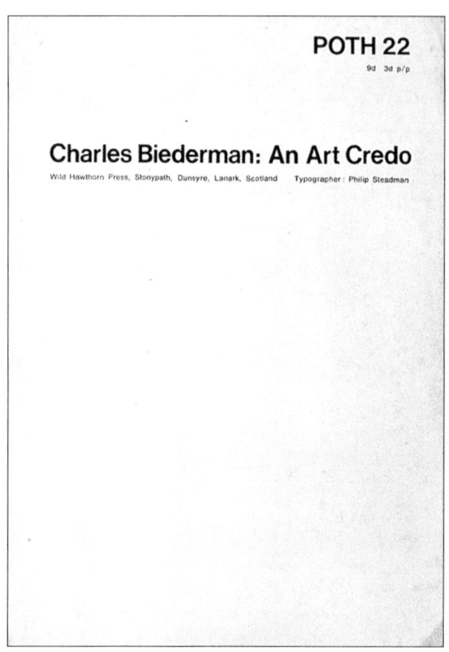

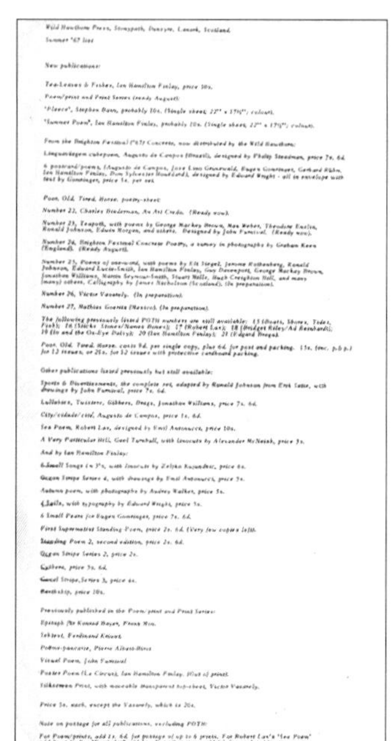

PREVIOUS PAGE: Wind, Wind, *1990, glass; ABOVE:* Poor Old Tired Horse

Have you changed your opinion of Joseph Beuys? The last time we spoke, you suggested he should have been publicly executed for producing such untidy work.

– No, no, I absolutely deplore Beuys. One of the great mysteries to me – and when I say 'mystery' I mean it in a pure sense – is that my work is considered by many people to be very dangerous and worrying, and yet I consider large areas of modern art to be very dangerous and worrying. I cannot understand how these people consider my art to be dangerous and worrying, when there must be countless people like Beuys or – well, everybody, really. I mean there is hardly anybody that I much approve of on moral grounds. I consider Beuys outrageous – I remember one image of an exhibition space that had been converted from a church, and he filled this space with huge incoherent lumps of stone. I considered this to be absolutely outrageous – really, it was like the sack of Rome to me. I would have had the man who perpetrated it guillotined very cheerfully! It was really an outrage.

Wasn't Beuys simply being very insensitive to the exhibition context?

– Or else he was being deliberately sacrilegious and blasphemous, or barbaric or whatever.

Perhaps Beuys was trying to use metaphors in his own manner – in an extreme manner.

– I suppose he probably was, but I cannot see this work as being other than totally reprehensible and an affront to the traditions of civilisation and culture and everything that I instinctively hold dear.

Could one say that one of the prime impulses of your work is to translate and comment upon traditions and to rephrase them in contemporary terms?

– Well, I do not think of it in that way, I do not really think of tradition as something separate or as something past. I do not really have this experience of it being something that is over – it is something that is very present. The thing that I think of most when I work is purity. When I fail, which is almost all of the time, and make things that are impure, I feel very pained, and then I set out and start again. But the thing that most concerns me is purity. So, when, for instance, I had that exhibition at the ICA last year, and one of the English critics wrote that I was 'the most decadent major artist in Britain', I was really quite amazed. I do not expect that a critic should like my work, but that they should describe it as decadent seems quite extraordinary. I mean, I do not remember whether Bacon was still alive at that time or not, but to call me decadent in a country that produced Bacon is ridiculous.

Can you remember why this critic thought your work was decadent?

– No, he did not explain. The critics wrote extraordinary things. Another critic from one of the leading papers wrote that I was Scottish and on good terms with the enemies of England – Germany, Italy and France, or something extraordinary. I could not believe that such things could be written in serious papers. Another wrote that I was Scottish and belonged to a subject nation – I wrote to the Race Relations Board, but they told me there was nothing I could do about it. Why I was being singled out for this was a bit hard for me to understand. There seemed to be more to it than that – the fact that I was Scottish was only being used to express some other kind of dissatisfaction with my work, which obviously struck them as being impure in a worrying way. I really do not understand it, because, not to say my soul, but my main preoccupation is with purity – except when I do things which are deliberately comical or light-hearted or bizarre, but even then I would not do anything I considered to be impure. It was the same when I edited *Poor Old Tired Horse* – I would not publish poems about drugs or anything like that, and people got angry, almost considering it a disgrace that I would not do so!

I remember reading an issue of Tarasque *which included a statement recommending that poems should be about certain flowers and certain non-alcoholic beverages, such as tea. I do not know whether you said that or whether it was written by someone else.*

– Yes, this could probably be mine! Obviously, I have extended my subject matter a bit since then, but I quite sympathise with the viewpoint, only now I do not exclude guillotines with such severity!

Considered at a general level, it seems ironic that whereas your focus was a very careful, cautious, and restrained focus, while certain French concrete poets such as Julien Blaine and Jean-François Bory tried to be very revolutionary in their thematics and imagery, the subversive impact of their work more or less fizzled in the early seventies, while your recent work with different levels of verbal-visual metaphor has had the most surprising impact on France in recent times. I am referring to the uproar over your OSSO installation, and the French government's cynical cancellation of your commissioned garden project for the Bicentennial of the French Revolution.

– Yes, but here you are talking about a phenomenon – it is a sickness or madness in that culture, one which extended to London also, and I consider it an aberration there too – a reaction which is not morally serious. As for Julien Blaine's and Bory's work of the late 60s, you could not really think that they were very revolutionary. If Saint-Just and Robespierre are revolutionaries, then these people are not.

In that regard, would you say that one of your aspirations, or one of your impulses, is to be revolutionary, without perhaps being programmatically so?

– Yes, of course, in several different senses, but most obviously because I live in a secular – or a completely secularised – society that I absolutely abhor, and therefore I want everything to be radically changed. That is not to say that I want complete revolution. I am not interested in revolution in a destructive, anarchic way, but as something that would advance very coherently and forcefully some concept of goodness, which I quite understand is not this age's idea of revolution. But then, of course, this age does not understand Saint-Just or Robespierre. There has probably never been an age that is less likely to understand them than this age.

Are there any other artists who you feel to be fellow-workers in terms of your values?

– Sadly, no.

Would the artists you admire more be artists of the early twentieth century?

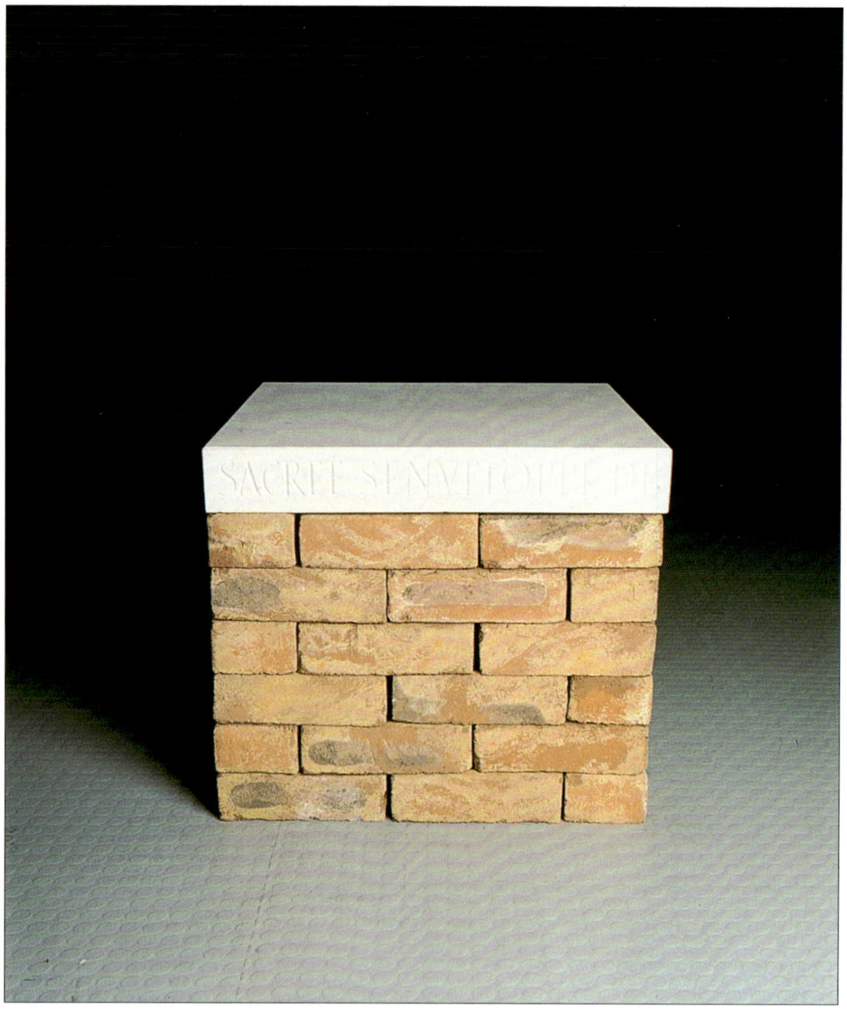

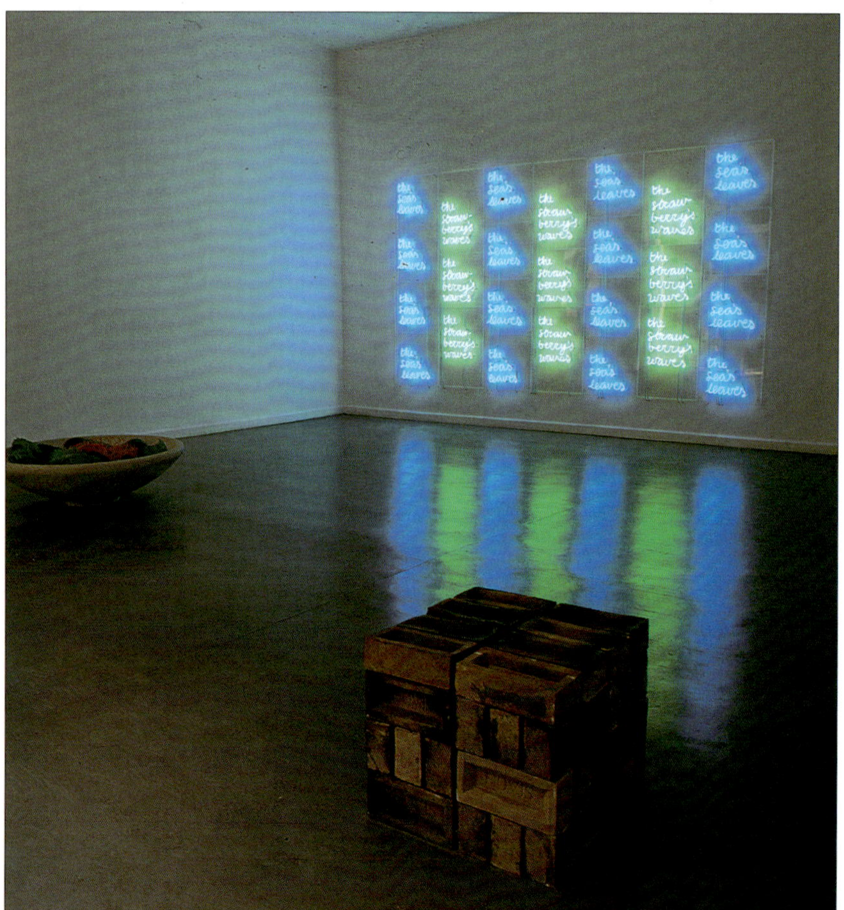

FROM ABOVE: Inscribed Altar Stone, *1987, stone and bricks, 47x54x54cm;* Idylls, *1990, installation shot*

– Yes, of course. I like Gris very much, I like Braque very much, I like Léger, I like Metzinger – I like all the artists who found some vision of order. And then of course from the past I like David, I like Puvis de Chavannes, I like the brothers Le Nain, I like Corot very, very much – all of those people whose work seems to be moral and sound.

It is strange isn't it, that a lot of cultural theory today seems characterised by moral abdication. The French theorist, Félix Guattari, comments that we are living in an age which has virtually abdicated ethical or aesthetic responsibility.
– Yes, of course, I am completely old-fashioned in this respect – I belong to another age altogether. I feel completely alienated from the culture that surrounds me. I mean not only plebeian culture, but high culture as well – I absolutely deplore it.

And yet it seems to me that your work has been very influential or inspirational for several generations of younger artists.
– Well, I do not know. I read in the *TLS* that there is going to be an exhibition about the 60s in British Art. I do not suppose that I am in this exhibition. I suppose my work has been influential, but in another way I have remained very much an outsider, especially in Britain. And I suppose I always will – it is my fate. I mean, every time I begin to become a wee bit accepted, something happens, and then I am an outsider again.

What do you think it is that makes you suddenly become an outsider again?
– Something that worries people. I do not play their game.

In a sense, I have the utmost admiration for people who can virtually preserve themselves from being permanently inside this or that establishment or regime. I was talking to the New York video artist, Nam June Paik, and he said that he has probably had three different styles in his work, whereas most artists develop one style and leave it at that, or perhaps develop two styles. He felt that because his work has been outside the mainstream, and he has been poor for so long, he has had the opportunity to develop three phases, as it were. Perhaps someone like John Cage permanently explored different possibilities – and that is perhaps the sign of considerable independence.
– Maybe it's something that you don't have a choice over? I have always – from a child – been on the outside, and never been, as it were, allowed. I remember an occasion when I was about twenty-five or something, and this artist came to stay the weekend, and said, 'We have in the National Gallery of Scotland this very good Gauguin'. And I thought this was a very nice phrase, 'We have'. So the next time I was with people, I thought, 'I'll say this, "We have"', and everybody stopped talking and said, 'What do you mean, "We have"?' I never tried 'We' again. 'They have'. That was a little lesson.

My sense would be that it is perhaps a two-fold issue. Perhaps what you are doing in terms of multimedia work, or exploring different media, takes people by surprise, so that they are never quite sure how to catalogue or box it – the formal inventiveness or your sensitivity to the potential relationship between materials takes people by surprise. But perhaps your work has a moral seriousness which also takes people by surprise, because you are not simply recycling a comforting formula or recipe.
– Yes, and also it has an interest in the world, which is a surprise too, because so many people involved with the world of culture do not know very much about the world, and have no interest in it at all. The thing is that people do not recognise the moral aspect of my work. They just do not recognise it, and this astounds me – I just do not know what to do about it. As for this question about multimedia, I never think about my work in such terms. In one sense I think that the lines that lie between different media should be very, very sharply drawn, and adhered to. And when I am told that I belong to this sort of multimedia thing it really surprises me. I suppose that there is a certain truth in it, but in another way, it is not true. I am very clear as to what the nature of the convention that I am employing is, and so on and so on. I think it is maybe just that my range of interests is perhaps a wee bit larger. Most artists do not have gardens, for instance, and probably if they did, they would make a rigid separation between their art and their garden. I see no reason to do this, because everything is a possibility. I think that my particular gift, insofar as I have one – and I am very modest about it – is for relating different areas together in a lyrical manner. And maybe this alarms people. People used to say about the *Garden Temple*, 'Have you got the Arts Council's permission to do this?' It is the same in the avant-garde – there is a general feeling that you have to gain permission to do what you do, and of course most of what passes for avant-garde or innovative or whatever is not innovative at all. Quite the opposite – I have said often enough that the avant-garde is just the State art of today.

Do you have any other feelings about the avant garde?
– I really do not have any other feelings about the avant-garde, except that it bores at me, and that it has nothing to do with me, and it's mostly impure and should be suppressed and censored in any civilised society.

That sounds a little draconian! I wonder if the avant-garde is not simply in a state of immaturity, in the sense that artists are gesturing in new directions, and just do not seem to get it very right. Perhaps their mission is often immature, so they do not have a lot to say.
– Very often they are just messing about – they are not really evoking some vision, they are just messing about. I mean, they are living in a society which is too tolerant!

This sounds a bit like Trotsky – I think Trotsky said that experimental art should remain in the studio, and remain unphotographed, until the artwork had become practical or finished.
– But the whole idea of experimental art is totally absurd, because science is experimental, but art is not experimental. I mean, to experiment is fundamentally flippant in art – it is just nothing to do with it. No other age has got on with experimental art – experimental art belongs to societies where people get subsistence grants from the State and things like that – it is the art of the Welfare State.

There might be some Welfare State avant-gardism, but it seems to me one might use the adjective avant-garde more positively to describe the way the sort of publications that you have always

published – and magazines like Poor Old Tired Horse *– took people by surprise because of their vision.*
– Yes, but that was only because of their ignorance and their closedness. If you look at *Poor Old Tired Horse* now, it really seems a good, solid publication. There are very few poems that have died. It really seems very, very good – there is a much higher standard of poetry then you would get in the *PN Review* or the *TLS*. And this was because it was not in any way intending to be subversive or whatever. It was considered, of course, to be so. I remember at the time the English poet Ian Hamilton wrote a review of Creeley and other poets, and talked about 'someone called Creeley' – this was the general attitude of the day. And so to publish Creeley and Celan was considered very contentious of me. But it was not. This was just a good thing that was going on, and it was really just sensible to publish it – and that is what it looks like now. It does not look like something that set out to shock, and that was never part of its intention. Though, of course, it did publish some very light-hearted poems by people like Pete Brown, but I would do that again, today, unhesitatingly.

Well, as you know, I have published Stereo Headphones, *a magazine which at one time you said 'belonged on the compost heap'.*
– Yes, well, it was probably full of decadent, immoral things.

But for all that, my attitude would be that publishing magazines is rather like climbing mountains – with the difference that it is not 'because it's there' but 'because it's not *there'. What one is doing reflects a compulsion to put something onto the page, or wherever, because one feels that something like that deserves to be there.*
– Yes, it is an intention to be sensible.

That is not trying to shock people by putting on a red nose.
– No. But of course, some magazines obviously do set out to be avant-garde.

Perhaps there is also a more positive form of avant-gardism, in the sense of advanced publishing. Although thematic contents might be totally traditional, there might be some formal aspects which are a little bit advanced for the general sensibility. Poor Old Tired Horse *might be one such publication, and perhaps another one might be Henri Chopin's review* OU, *which, simply because it had LP records of sound poets, made something new available. And certainly now, looking back at* OU *as well, you either like the work or you do not, but it seems perfectly sensible and of its time.*
– Yes, this is what I am saying – whether it is true of *OU* or not is another matter – but the intention is to be sensible and to make things available. Very often these magazines are doing what the larger presses ought to be doing now, but are not, because they are too dim to do it. That is what it amounts to.

Perhaps instead of saying that the avant-garde is trying to do something extraordinary – and funnily enough Chopin suggests the same thing, when he says, 'I'm not avant-garde. I'm just an artist working in my own period' – one might say that the average productivity is so banal, so mediocre, that what passes for the normal is in fact pretty catastrophic. So that from the point of view of those used to the catastrophe, anything that has got a little bit going for it, in terms of authenticity and integrity, seems outrageous.
– Yes – but for this reason I do not find it very helpful to distinguish things as being avant-garde or non-avant-garde. It does not really seem to me to be useful. For example, I got a letter this morning from a Scottish man of letters who is going to be doing a book on gardens, and he asked very, very politely, if he could come and see my garden because he wants to discuss it in the book. And I remember when the first book about my garden was published twenty years ago, how he sneered at it, really sneered at it. And why? Pure ignorance – only ignorance. He thought that any upright stone with wording on it must be a tombstone. He just had no notion of the western tradition of gardening, or he would have seen that my garden fitted into it perfectly. But now he has grown up, and is a bit more educated, or something like that, and wants to put my garden in his book. But my garden was not avant-garde! It was they who were retrogressive, or just ignorant, or whatever. At no time has my garden been avant-garde – not as far as I am concerned. And as I say, I do not really see this word as being particularly helpful.

I find it helpful, but I am probably looking from another perspective, which is that of the cultural cartographer or critic. From my point of view, if people seem to argue that British poetry equals Ted Hughes, Philip Larkin and other such poets, and if their work seems to be the only standard, certain other kinds of writing are being neglected.
– Absolutely, but it does not really follow that the other things are avant-garde.

Well, perhaps one might define the term more clearly in terms of Walter Benjamin's suggestion that avant-garde creativity, such as some of the dadaists' works, anticipated possibilities which only became realised later, in an era of changed technological options. And so you might say that Hausmann and Schwitters had rather simple phonetic poems, but that now, with the availability of the tape recorder, all manner of tape recorded creativity can happen – some of it as traditional as Chekov or whatever you like, and some of it a horrible noise not far removed from pop music, perhaps. But to that extent, there may be some artists – and publishers as well – who sense that it is not good enough to continue rowing the same boat at the same pace as everyone else, and that something needs to be added.
– I do not see it like that. It is the same boat, but people cannot see the possibilities in such and such a thing. It occurred to me that concrete poetry has – as it were – reanimated the possibilities of the inscription, almost accidentally, so that it then becomes sensible to return to a tradition that seemed to be finished. It is just a question of having the openness or the intelligence or whatever to recognise a possibility which is there. Its newness is not what occurs to one. Its validity is what occurs to one.

I think you are right, particularly with regard to concrete poetry and the inscription. Perhaps with something like sound poetry, the newness of technology becomes a little bit more significant. Burroughs said somewhere that he was amazed that a lot of writers would not work with tape recorders and seemed frightened of technology.
– Yes, but to be frightened of working with a tape recorder seems to

me to be absolutely just absurd. I mean, what would there be to be frightened of? Everybody has one.

I think one of the key words in what you have just said is the notion of 'reanimation'. Obviously a fairly superficial sense of the avant-garde implies a belief that the past is dead, and that some new-fangle thing is aspiring to replace everything. The notion of re-animation seems important, in the sense that it implies that in certain eras, certain past traditions have been forgotten and certain kinds of creative potential have been forgotten, and then people find bridges, unexpected bridges, that turn out not to be so unexpected.
– Oh yes, and then something happens over here that nobody thinks has any relation to what is happening there, and then it turns out that it does. The question of whether such relations are avant-garde or not is not really an issue – it is not important. Certainly, in my own case, I do not think that my work provokes hostility because it is avant-garde. But of course, it does provoke hostility sometimes because of the sheer ignorance of people.

In a sense, I suppose that perhaps what you are saying is that the category of the avant-garde is at worst a trivialising category.
– Yes, trivialising is the thing, because it is much more trivial to be avant-garde, than to be sensible or perceptive.

Are you very familiar with the work of New York feminist language artists such as Barbara Kruger or Jenny Holzer? One of the things that they say is that they are trying to work with the mass media, and that they are competing with advertising, making works for four-seconds' contemplation.
– I am not very familiar with them, but I have seen their work in magazines. I have done things for those machines – the LED message machines – because they are a lovely possibility. They are a very exciting medium, and at the same time they are quite quaintly old-fashioned, because they are like nothing so much as embroidery – all the little dots are like stitching in samplers. But it seems to me that the sentences that they have written for these machines are not particularly great. I feel that if they had read more in the great tradition of the aphorism, they could do it a bit better.

Well, to put it very simply, your work seems to be multi-dimensional at a number of levels, evoking several things at once, so that you are not simply giving a sort of superficial flat statement, such as 'Four legs good, two legs bad'.
– No, of course. But there is a place for that too. It is quite nice to do something simple. It is just a pity that they do not use these machines in a better way. But certainly, if I could afford one, I would not hesitate to do more work with them.

Do you feel frustrated at not having the kind of financial backing that such artists have, in the sense that they have been able to place huge public texts in places like Times Square?
– Yes, I do feel frustrated in general about not having the money to do the things that I want to do, but of course, sometimes I just do it anyway.

You have made an increasing number of installation pieces for

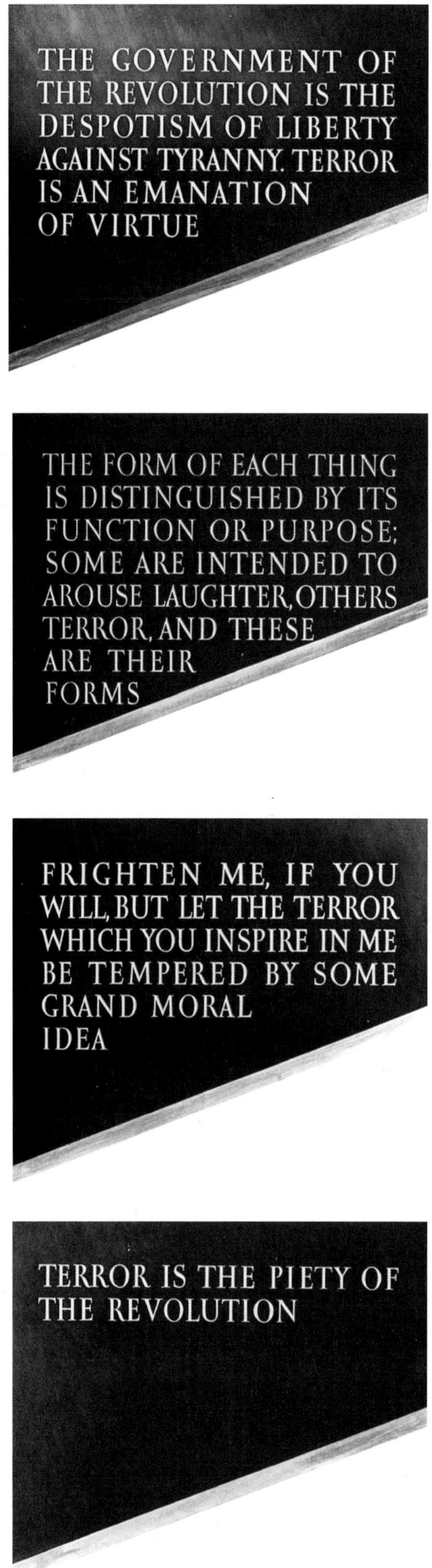

Four Guillotine Blades, *1987, stone – each 69x80x2cm, red lettering*

international exhibitions, such as A View to the Temple *in Documenta, and* Adorno's Hut *in the Sydney Biennale. Does this constitute a new chapter in your work?*

– Well, not really, because I came to it from gardening – this is the thing. I did not come to it through thinking about installations, but made in the garden what people would consider to be installations. When I had exhibitions before, I used to think of the rooms as things that you could put a lot of different works in. But now I like to think of the room as an entity, and plan the whole room, so that even if there are a lot of different works, they are really part of a room. I do no longer like the idea of rooms that are full of different things. Each room has to have a theme and a unity, and whether this is done with a lot of works or just one work does not matter to me. I suppose that this relates in a way also to theatre or to drama. I suppose that a lot of my battles with the Strathclyde Region could also be thought of as a form of drama. And the things I am doing for an exhibition in Munich in November – proposals for buildings in Munich – are also quite dramatic.

What buildings are these?

– They are the remains of two temples that were built in the Nazi period to house bronze coffins containing the remains of the Nazis who were killed in the Putsch in 1923 – they are two identical little temples. At the end of the war, the Americans blew them up, because of their associations, but incredibly, they only blew up the upper parts – the columns and the roof – leaving the plinths, which are really about ten or twelve feet high, with very solid stone steps. I find it quite extraordinary that they left them! The plinths remained, and over the years, wild flowers and trees seeded themselves into them, and now very large trees grow out of them – like a Casper David Friedrich painting or something – and lots of wild flowers which are all enumerated and, I think, actually protected. I discovered quite recently that a competition was held for architects to design buildings that would replace them, which produced a very, very bitter public controversy. Some people wanted the buildings totally removed, some people wanted the ruins kept – and I suppose they were divided between those who wanted them kept for sentimental reasons, and those who wanted them kept as a warning. And then the Green Party wanted the ruins kept, because of the wild flowers! I could not believe it – it was like something that I would invent!

So I made two proposals for the Ayran temples, which both involved rebuilding the original buildings. In one of them the bronze coffins which were placed under the open part of the roof, under the sky, would be replaced by bronze plaques which would bear the names of all the wild flowers which had to be destroyed in order to rebuild the temples. Anyway, this was one of the ideas. Then there is this other very big building, the Haus der Kunst, where they had big exhibitions of approved Nazi art – the building remains just the same, only it is now called the Haus der Kunst, rather than the Haus der Deutscher Kunst. I took my idea for this building from a book on Speer by another architect, Leon Krier, in which he said that there is more fuss about a single colonnade of classical columns than about all the tanks which roll off the assembly line of Krupps which of course still manufacture NATO's panzers. Anyway, at the Haus der Kunst, at both the front and back, there are really wonderful colonnades – so the proposal is for each column to have a red and black arm-band saying 'Verbotten', 'Forbidden', 'Verbotten', 'Forbidden' – as though the columns were all absolutely censored. It is just to make people realise the absurdity of throwing out a whole architectural tradition – the whole Western architectural tradition – because of a regime which lasted ten years or whatever. This, with the red and the black, is very, very dramatic. Whether they will actually do it I do not know, and I do not really mind, because it is just a proposal. This is the sort of thing I like now – these interventions in actual history.

Of course, this for me has very real meaning. Two years ago I was invited, along with three other artists, to make proposals for the street adjoining the European Patents Office in Munich. I proposed this very simplified triumphal arch, with the inscription 'Neo-classicism builds elegiac as well as triumphal arches'. The city of Munich approved my project very much, very enthusiastically, but the Patents Office, which had a committee made up of people from all over Europe, refused my work on the incredible grounds that it was too dangerous to build a triumphal arch, even one that is elegiac! The Munich people were very nice about it, and very sad, and apologised to me, but I thought this incredible. This is a pseudo-problem – one of the problems used to cover up real problems. One of the things about our age is that it very much prefers to fight yesterday's battles and not today's battles. And so you get things in Britain like the Anti-Nazi League and so on, which is fairly absurd.

Aren't there neo-Nazi movements in parts of London, for example?

– They are minuscule, minuscule. One of the features of the Anti-Nazi League is that when it has rallies they cause chaos – they smash up people's cars – they cause incredible violence. And nobody sees the absolute absurdity of this. I mean, it is patently clear that a revival of Nazism is not a problem that is facing Britain today. Or it is like this awful Frenchman who attacked me, and went on and on about the Holocaust and so on. But he said absolutely nothing about Serbia – about what is going on there – nothing! When I tried to explain that you cannot isolate the Holocaust from history – that you cannot see it as a one-off phenomenon or something, and that no matter the scale or scope, you must see it as a part of human history, he said, No, that this was unique, and that what is happening in Bosnia at the moment is inconsequential. I mean, this is a way of avoiding responsibility and feeling very, very moral.

Maybe it is a question of there being two focuses – the immediate memory and the long term perspective. I suppose that both parties would feel that to over-emphasise one or the other would be equally erroneous.

– It is not like this – in attacks on me, it is quite clear that it was an argument that was used to destroy my work.

That reminds me of a remark that the American poet Jackson MacLow made when discussing Post-Modern culture and the so-called crisis of language, and Adorno's statement, 'No poetry after Auschwitz'. MacLow commented that Adorno's remark was not simply a diagnosis, but almost an imperative, insisting, 'Thou shalt not write after Auschwitz', in the sense that this would imply slandering or belittling the recent past. MacLow's conclusion was that while the Romans similarly put vast quantities of people to the sword, poetry still went on.

– Exactly, exactly. People show a lamentable ignorance of human history.

To sum things up, could one say that your work is concerned very much with large historical perspectives, without being inhibited by contemporary obsessions – by restrictive obsessions? That is putting things rather programmatically.

– Yes, but this is the case. Every age imagines itself to be free, and every age has a set of taboos which it fails to recognise precisely because they are its own – and they are only recognised 50 years later, or something. But one must work purely, and not in terms of the passions or prejudices of the present moment. You know, you must rise above that, completely. When I was in Germany, at the end of the War, all the girls used to say to me very, very seriously, 'Oh! If only you'd been here in the Hitler time! That was so happy!' And undoubtedly, they believed it! I mean, our age has got to understand how it is going to be looked at later on, when it will be seen clearly what taboos it has. We now understand that the Victorians had this great taboo about sex, and say 'ha !ha !ha!', but we do not see that we have a similar taboo about power, or however you like to define it. There is a definite taboo now, so that certain subjects cannot be approached in a rational manner.

But the nature of the universe does not change. Sex did not vanish because the Victorians could not discuss it, and power will not vanish – or the possibility or potentiality of power will not vanish – because we cannot discuss it. I mean, these things have to be recognised, identified and dealt with in a rational manner. But you cannot do that as long as you regard them as too dangerous to identify. And damn it, one should not be bullied into accepting this nonsense about being 'politically correct', and all that, which is obviously an enormously inhibiting force. One recognises at once that these people are not 'politically correct' because they wish to be morally good or something, but because they wish to be on good terms with the people around them. One has feel that it is possible to be very serious about art – it is a very serious subject, and it can be trivialised into PC.

Where does that leave the artist who is serious, given that critics are probably going to be prejudiced, and readers might well be ignorant?

– You have to bear it , you have to just not be afraid of it. You have to bear it, it is not comfy, but there it is. And you can get some comfort out of thinking that 'No, you're not alone'. A number of people in the past have had to put up with the same thing, but always, of course, for a different reason. But I cannot deplore it enough. I mean, any kind of bullying seems to me to me utterly deplorable, and so much bullying goes on now in the name of morality.

Little Sparta, Dunsyre, 5 May 1993

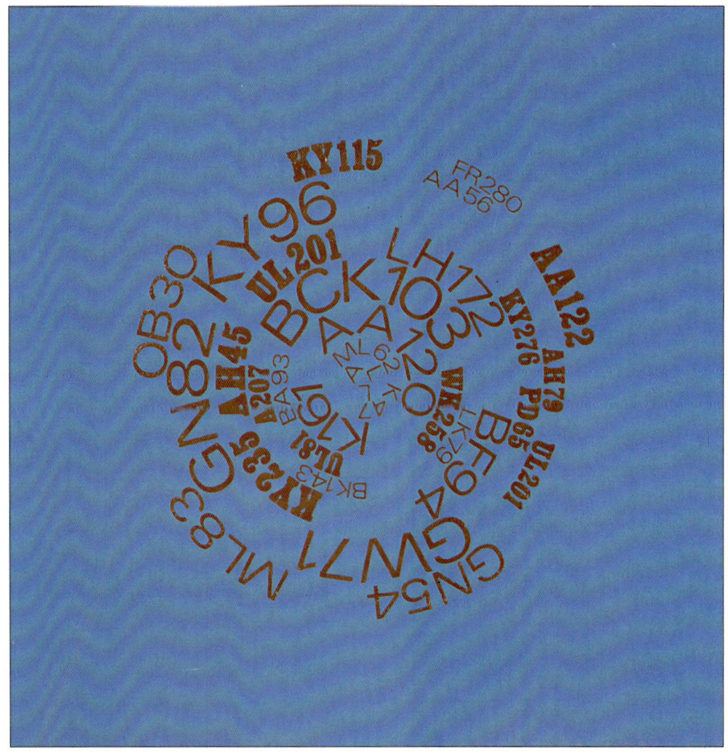

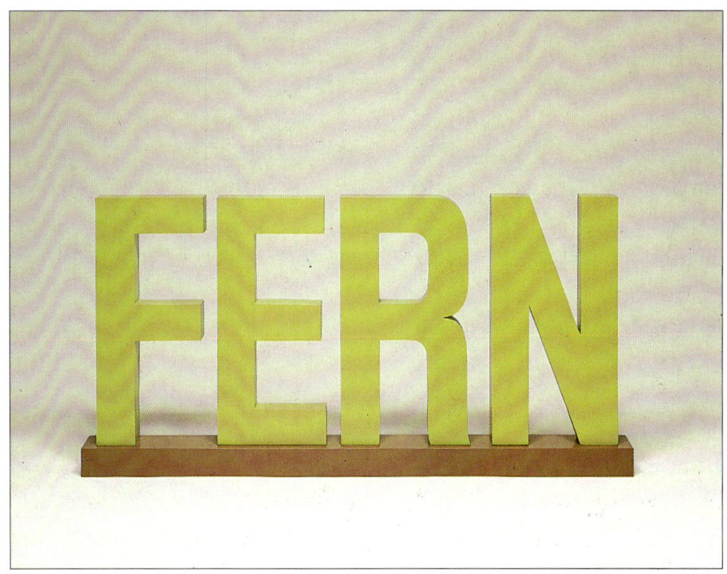

FROM ABOVE: Sea Poppy I, *1966, with Alistair Cant, silkscreen, 55.5x43cm, Tarasque Press;* Fern *(fishing boat: BF205), 1977, collaboration with Peter Grant, painted wood, 48x99x9cm*

LANGUAGE AND CULTURE IN THE INFORMATION AGE

Ken Friedman

Symbolic Interaction and the Physical World

The technology of the information age clarifies the relationship between symbols and the physical world, generating a broader understanding of how symbolic interaction transforms the way we see and live in the world around us. Some effects are as immediate and visible as the dramatic transformation of work in the industrial nations. Even though knowledge has always been the working medium of research, education and communication, until recently the physical output of these professions took precedence over symbolic output. It was easy to see the technological artefacts born of research, to walk into a room full of students or buy a newspaper. These were the obvious products of the less visible information structures that shaped them and managed their development. These functions have been made visible by the new information technology. As a result, we are redefining our understanding of information.

The management of symbols does more than define our apprehension of the physical domain; it enters into it and we recognise symbolic control as the key to managing the physical domain. Ancient and modern examples of the subtle interaction between symbols and the physical world offer perspective on language and culture in the information age.

Money as an Early Example of an Information Artefact

Money has usually been represented by physical artefacts but money has never been physical. Information technology makes it obvious that most of the world's money is represented by the flow of information among financial institutions such as banks, credit card companies and national treasuries. It is less clear to many that this has always been the case. Money is not seashells, stones, gold bars or bank notes. It is an abstract form of information established by convention to represent the flow of energy. The energy begins as physical labour or material goods. The medium of exchange is abstracted and distilled, a convention that makes it easy for farmer, physician, computer programmer or publisher to exchange goods and services. Money is a message used to make the exchange of value possible by storing the information value of labour or of physical objects. The distilled and abstract energy in money becomes physical again when it is applied to the world of services and goods.

Let us now consider the confusion surrounding the most reified form of money – gold. Gold is not money. It is, rather, a convention used to represent money, which is itself an information construct. Like seashells or bank notes, gold is a second-order abstraction used to represent and store money. In many parts of the world, convention allows us to translate the information stored in gold into physical goods, but the physical material of gold itself has few uses. If you are dying of thirst and hunger on a desert island, a pint of water and a loaf of bread are worth more than a kilogram of gold.

Gold is physically stable and the fact that it has had few technical uses until recently made it a useful medium for the representation of wealth. It has had few purposes other than the storage of value. Because of its physical stability and relative uselessness, gold has been less prone to physical manipulation or fluctuation than national currencies on paper or coin.

Gold holds its value by agreement rather than physical logic. While people in different nations and cultures rarely agree on the value of currency for more than short periods, they seem to agree on the long-term value of gold. Gold has become a conventional embodiment of wealth. This is true of money in all its forms. What is new in our time is the growing recognition of money as a form of information, recognition of the fact that money is an abstract, distilled medium.

The odd quandary of money and the durable reification of gold raises fascinating questions about wealth in the information age. Precisely because money is symbolic, its meaning and value are subject to interpretation. In a world defined by symbols, a person with nothing more than a pint of water and a loaf of bread will soon be in trouble. Someone with a kilo of gold will do well. Even though gold is as purely symbolic as digits, pieces of paper or seashells, millions of people around the world collect gold in a physical form. This is a case in which the relationship between symbols and the things they represent is as problematic as ever.

Information into Object

The weight of history and emotion is less powerful in other areas. In these fields, information is transforming the physical world and people seem more ready to accept the transformative value of information. Industries that were once considered primarily physical now embody and transact information; consider the mass manufactured automobile, one of the tools that defined the 20th century.

No single industry was more physical in substance and impact than the making of cars. That is no longer the case. More and more of what now goes into a car is information. Information and information management represent an increasingly greater proportion of the value of a new car. Information technology is used to plan and design cars. It helps automobile companies to build them and it makes them more useful.

Today's car is more a computerised tool than a block of metal. Cars last longer and work better than before. Tomorrow's car will last longer still and it will be recycled when its usefulness is complete. The future car may finally resemble a computer around which interchangeable plug-and-play modules permit physical variation and functional transformation. The key element in the car may be a kind of software, an operating system that allows two kinds of transformation. One kind of transformation will allow the performance of the car to change without changing the hardware. The other will allow the exchange of damaged or obsolete hardware without changing the performance.

The inventions and technology that we create – the symbols that we use to manage our world – shape the world in which we live. The shape of the world in turn transforms the symbolic tools through which we grasp and express culture. These ideas and issues are not new, but as multiple forces interact in complex ways to shape increasingly complex systems, the complex world to which they are giving birth is very new indeed.

The New World

Language, culture and technology are three of the great human creations. They are so inextricably bound up in our nature as human beings that they define what it is to be human. They shape our world and they shape the lives we lead within it.

We easily notice individual languages, local cultures and specific technologies but the larger background functions of language, culture and technology are so central to human consciousness that they tend to become invisible.

Human beings are perceptual and behavioural animals. Human perception and behaviour have redefined the human species, moving it beyond the natural environment into which the physical species was born. The language, culture and technology that we create become the human patterning mechanisms that create us. They are linked in a series of behavioural and perceptual feedback loops. In the course of transforming ourselves, we redefine and change the world around us, often physically.

The ways in which we grasp and understand reality is the basis of our ability to shape a future that does not yet exist. The result is a series of physical effects which shape our cultures while shaping the physical world around us. The process of shaping the world has many effects: good, bad and neutral; intellectual, social and physical. Culture, in the broadest sense, defines the way we comprehend our world and shapes the way we give expression to what we comprehend. Language gives voice to our comprehension and shapes the culture.

We have not always been clear about the ways in which our technology shapes our culture. The mechanical clock was originally created to inform people of the proper times for prayer, but the functions of time were soon linked to the flow of commerce. Noon once came when the sun was directly overhead, hundreds of different noon-times flowing into one another in a world of endlessly shifting time zones. Just as navigation depended on an accurate mechanical clock, the development of dependable scheduled railroads required accurate, coordinated time zones. Today, computers and everything that flows from them depend on timing devices unimaginable in a world where the original clock was a bell that called people to prayer from their daily tasks.

How will the new information technology affect language and culture? It is too early to predict accurately, but it is possible to speculate. The occasionally random workings of technology yield what chaos specialists call strange attractors. The keyboard on which we type, for example, was created specifically because human typists were far faster than the machines on which they first worked. The QWERTY keyboard was designed to deliberately slow the speed of typists on early mechanical typewriters prone to jammed keys. Today, that same keyboard is recognised as the source of typing mistakes, information errors and physical repetition injuries that could easily be reduced by the far more effective DVORAK keyboard. The keyboard behaviour of the information age, however, is still locked into a pattern shaped over a century ago by the primitive mechanical typewriter that was nevertheless an important information technology in its time. So, too, the emergence of important information technologies may affect our language and culture to lock us into behavioural patterns that will seem equally primitive a century from now – or even in a decade's time.

Thoughts on the Future of Language and Culture

In speculating on the future of language and culture in the information age, one must consider the development of visible trajectories while imagining the ways in which trends may be deflected as forces that now seem minor come into play as major factors.

In the 1920s, America was a nation with a vast number of regional accents and dialects. The coming of radio began a shift from regional dialects to regional accents of a standard American-English. Television has nearly completed that transformation with broadcast standard becoming the most influential accent. Specialised regional vocabulary nearly vanished.

In recent years, however, dialects have returned. These have not been the dialects of regions, but the dialects of sub-cultures. Computer freaks, engineering professors, gang-bangers, MTV watchers, bond traders, MacDonald's managers have all had their separate ways of speaking. These meet in some forms of common discourse, but drift apart again in the workplace. Language is a tool for shaping public space and a weapon used to divide spaces among competing publics.

I suspect that language has several futures. English has become the dominant language of business and science and thus the main language of the Internet. This broadens the reach of standard English while in some ways reducing its local inflection and thus its emotional value. It seems to me that English will become everyone's second language to an ever greater degree while becoming the native language of ever fewer people. I can imagine a world in which few of us in English-based nations will speak English as our native language. There is a resurgence of original languages in many areas – of Spanish in Texas and California, of Gaelic in Ireland. Other major languages once spread through conquest and commerce are faring the same: this is visible in the resurgence of Catalan and Basque in Catalonia, native dialects in Francophone Africa, etc.

At the same time, an astonishing number of young people in the industrial nations speak fluent English in addition to their native tongues. In Norway, for example, the population is characterised by extensive travel and a heavy international diet of books, television and film. The generations that grew up before television and in the early television era speak excellent English with an accent. The television generation is different. It is often impossible to tell where a young Norwegian comes from. More precisely, it is easy to place a young English-speaking Norwegian as a native of Chicago or East London until they speak Norwegian with the dialect of their own part of Norway.

This is a clear trend. The question is how it will work? Will regional dialects blossom again in England and America to the extent that standard English itself becomes a second language in the English-speaking nations? Will small nations or remote nations such as Jamaica or Australia remain the last nations where a common English is spoken by the entire population?

Another conjecture is even more interesting. More and more people who speak excellent English but who do not write English are coming to communicate in writing on Internet. They must make themselves clearly understood across language boundaries and cultural barriers. I wonder if it might be possible for Internet to bring about the development of a good writing style in a way that good writing was never before necessary among groups with a common – if fractionated – version of English.

Needs-based Communication

The information age and the growth of international communication is creating a series of new needs in every area from scholarship and science to commerce and entertainment. For the last several years, I have been studying simple paralinguistic communication elements – how phone numbers are written and phrased, how stationery is structured, etc – that serve to make international communication easier or more difficult. I have isolated over 80 items now, and while I find common agreement for the value of any one element across wide groups, I find that very few groups manage all 80 elements well. That is, any one organisation or individual handles ten or 20 specific elements in a manner that is most widely functional on a worldwide basis, but few organisations or individuals handle all (or even many) of the elements well.

On the Internet, I observe a growing culture of individuals who share information and teach each other. For example, while you can buy books on using the Internet in most bookstores, the two best books are also available free on Internet itself. So, too, members of different lists and information groups coach each other, share information, explain language and grammar or communication techniques. Will this lead to a growth of better communication elements? If it does, how will it be reflected in language?

Similar issues are emerging in science and scholarship. Tens of millions of documents are now available on Internet, but the way in which they are organised is so problematic that it is difficult, if not impossible, to find many of the documents you need at any moment. Documents will require more than titles in the future; they will require a good series of key words, a good index notation, and a good abstract. The time will come when all of these items will be a necessary adjunct to any serious article. Scholars will recognise that sharing the results of their research requires a good abstract. In an era of 'compare with' and 'also see' citations, a good abstract is as valuable as, and perhaps more important than, the original article.

So, too, the need to share information across boundaries and even among professions and disciplines will require common bibliographic standards. Right now, there are a dozen or so major styles and many minor styles of bibliography. Some styles accepted in certain universities are actually obsolete, created for an era when a handful of books were printed in any city in any given year. Working across fields makes the use of common bibliographic standards imperative. At The Nordic Centre for Innovation – a research institute shared by the Norwegian School of Management, Lund University and the University of Art and Design Helsinki – we recommend a common standard for our authors and scholars and for their publications. I suspect that as authors find the standard congenial and comprehensible, they will seek to apply it elsewhere. This same process must be taking place in other places around the world. As international information commerce becomes broader, instantaneous and standardised, with the need to shift from format to format, document to document, this will be a growing need. How will it be handled?

The Unknown Internet

Much too much has been made of the visual properties of the Internet. The fact is that our technology is not good enough to make visual communication effective in many of the applications we require. Consider the home page on the World Wide Web: a densely illustrated home page takes a long time to download and build up for many people. Intelligent Web sites, therefore, use clear, simple illustrations, recognising that a good home page is an effective transit point. The effort of an interesting page must be spent in shaping a page that is informative and easy to use.

In the past, expensive technology and lavish illustration was used as an index of institutional power and excellence. This is no longer the case. One major American university is known and has always been known for its lavish publications. The entry point to their Web Site has been designed by looking at that heritage, and their home page takes several long, annoying minutes to download. When it finally appears on the screen, it is nothing more than a fancy illustration. The image is a dense, beautiful bookshelf standing in a rich, wood-and-leather study portrayed in deep sepia and dark brown, possibly meant to emulate a professor's office or the private study of a wealthy industrialist. The bookshelf is nothing more than the table of contents for the home page, with words representing the departments or units open to inspection printed on the spines of the books. The experience was an exercise in miscommunication, an information site offering me information with no content while consuming time I should have been able to spend porting direct to my destination. Even worse, due to the transaction in which I was engaged, I was forced to wait for the image to download. I was not impressed; I was astonished that an organisation so famous and powerful, so skilled in its public communication for so long, should be so thoughtless and inept.

Right now, much of what happens in visual art resembles that experience. I feel that these experiences – art on the Internet – are interesting experiments. They are primarily failures, as so many genuine experiments tend to be in their early phases. These failed experiments teach us what not to do, and they teach us how to refine and clarify our search. The problem is that too many artists refuse to learn from their own experiments. That is, they are not engaged in experimental art, but in novel art that wears the guise of experimentation. I applaud many of the artistic experiments developed for the Internet, but my primary interest in the Internet is communication, language and culture. While information technology may make radically new art forms available to us in the future, I am generally not interested in using Internet to see work that would not interest me in person or in a book. That fact that something is on Internet usually does not improve it.

This issue finds its parallel in the search of so many designers for a set of pictograms that will supposedly shape a universal symbol language. The idea is based on a notion that has no basis in the function of human behaviour. Symbols, as much as language, are rooted in culture. They are established by convention in the same way that the meanings of money and gold are established.

We can surely recognise that the glyph on a door in a restaurant is a human being. Beyond that, meanings can be very strange indeed. In a culture where men wear kilts and never pants, for example, the glyphs that Europeans take to represent 'women' and 'men' might have the same meanings or different meanings on some other criterion. In a context – once common in many parts of the world – in which men and women share the same bathroom, two doors would make no sense. To some people, a standing man might represent a place of prayer or learning or law. It is silly to imagine that we can shape a universal pictorial grammar.

In considering the future of language and culture in the information age, we must, therefore, consider the issues of language and culture in three ways. One is contextual. We must consider the places, ways and means in which information will be used. One is processual. We must consider how people interface with and address the equipment we use to transmit information. One is definitional. We must simply recognise that language and culture are matters of convention, of definition. In the information age, the need to work across so many borders and boundaries while reaching common understanding will mean an increasing difference between possibility and probability. There are differences between what we can do and what we ought to do in communicating, and only thoughtful, cross-cultural sensitivity will provide a good context for what we actually do.

All circuits are open. Because so much is possible, we must choose ever more carefully how we work with one another as we shape the language and the culture of the information age. We shape our tools and our tools shape us. Never before in human history have we had such clear and conscious opportunities to shape our tools.

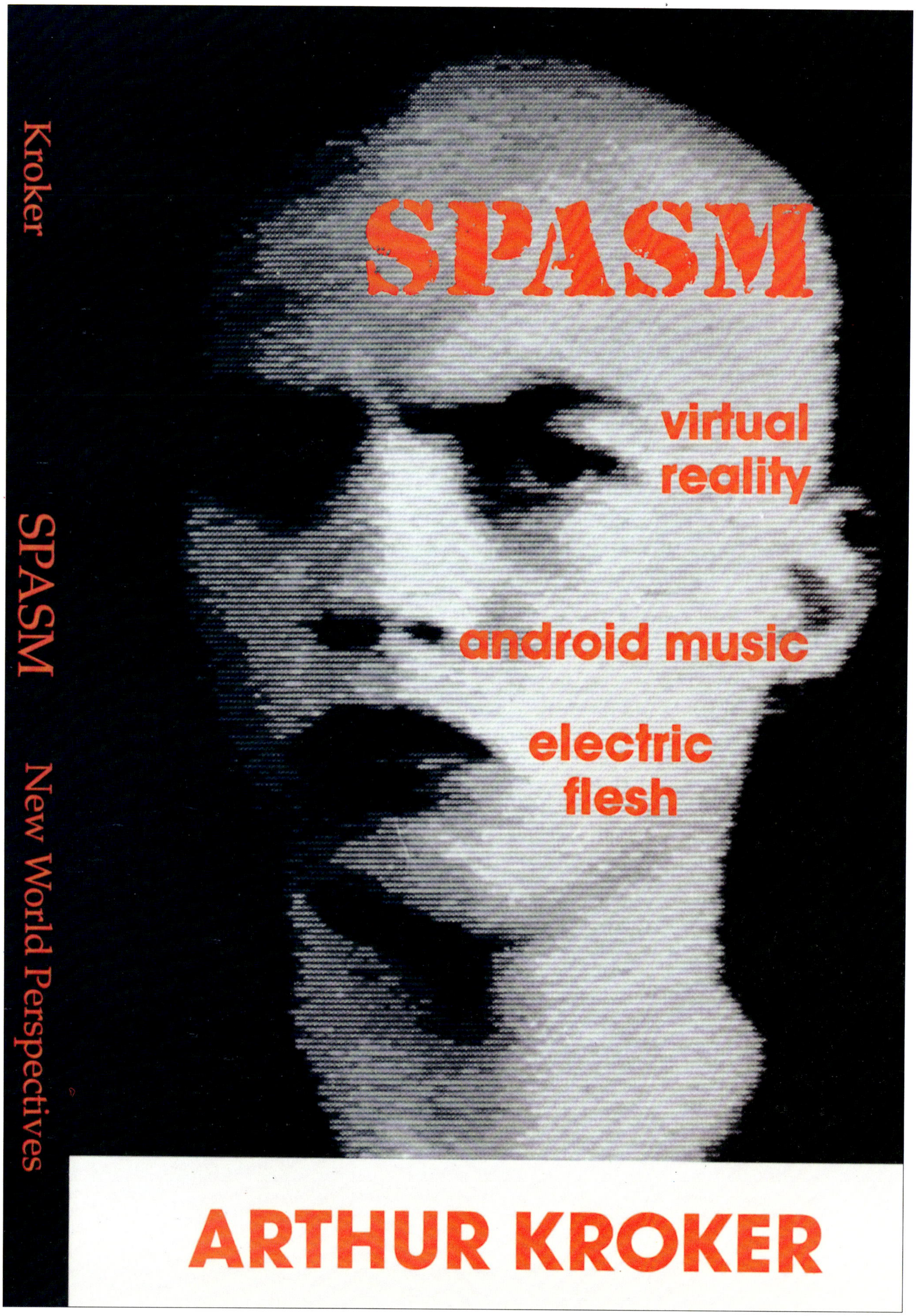

Book cover for Spasm *by Arthur Kroker, design by Marilouise Kroker*

IN THE SHADOW OF McLUHAN

Gary Genosko

Many Canadian intellectuals and cultural workers concerned with information technologies dwell in the shadow of Marshall McLuhan, regardless of whether they intentionally seek out the cool shade or are momentarily escaping the hot sun. Today, a new generation is coming of age in the information environment whose emergence McLuhan predicted. While an older generation is busily maintaining McLuhan's legacy through personal reminiscences and long overdue institutional recognition, this new generation is recoding McLuhan's ideas and texts in pop music, alternative theatre and the new electronic discourses of the cybersphere.

Claims of misinterpretation are regularly fired from both generations across their respective screens. In between these extremes, in what McLuhan called the resonant interval of tactile interfaces, new contacts and connections are being made between academics, artists and businesspersons that shadow things to come. These intergenerational struggles are staged in two divergent streams of Canadian work on McLuhan whose leading practitioners are the Director of the McLuhan Program in Culture and Technology at the University of Toronto, Derrick de Kerckhove, and at Concordia University in Montreál, the political scientist and performer of theory as fiction, Arthur Kroker.

The Situationist Guy Debord once wrote of McLuhan that he was 'the spectacle's first apologist, who had seemed to be the most convinced imbecile of the century'.[1] Debord also noted that even a global village idiot like McLuhan eventually recognised that mass media cannot deliver on their promises of freedom and accessibility. Generations of critiques of McLuhan's techno-optimism have demonstrated the negative consequences of freedom from fragmentary specialism (un- and under-employment) and freedom to be involved in the planetary social process through new technologies (pseudo-freedoms of consumption, pay-per-play). It is important not to lose this critical perspective in today's heady reflux of McLuhanism.

Less an idiot than an intellectual jester in the humanist tradition of Erasmus's folly, Joyce's wit, and Rabelais's bawdiness, McLuhan played the clown in order to infiltrate specialist discourses and satirise them in a mode he called 'anti-environmental'. While McLuhan may have lacked the sense of folly as a philosophical vocation, by playing the clown he was also playing at being an artist. He chose eclecticism over the effort to synthesise. He used the probe, the pun, the blast, and the mosaic method instead of integrative strategies. He was a media artist who created the new form that Donald Theall dubbed the *essai concrète* with its 'collide-oscopic' principles of typographic play, surrealistic juxtaposition of images, and unfortunately, heavy doses of technological mystification.[2]

McLuhan began to reflect on the role of the artist in relation to the media in the early 1950s. He wrote that 'the artist arrests his cognitions by recognition. He then reverses the process and embodies in an exterior work the drama of apprehension. The stages of apprehension, reversed and embedded in new matter, enable us to contemplate, purge and dominate the drama of cognition, the dance of existence'.[3] The artist thus exteriorises the process of recognition, metamorphosing it into a work made available for the cathartic contemplation of the audience.

By 1967, McLuhan believed it was the artist, like the amateur and the drop-out (now recast as a networker), who could see that the emperor 'ain't got nothin' on'. The artist was a kind of social irritant who created anti-environments that brought to consciousness the active, but largely invisible, sensorial changes and dislocations effected by technologies. In *The Medium is the Massage* McLuhan wrote: 'Anti-environments, or counter-situations made by artists, provide means of direct attention and enable us to see and understand more clearly'.[4] When Glenn Gould dropped out of the concert circuit in 1964, and abandoned live performances, for the recording studio, he created a counter-situation which foregrounded the importance he invested in recording technology. A performance could be created out of splices and montages of different takes. This counter-situation simultaneously exploded the notion of a performance's integrity and repetitiveness.

Under the direction of De Kerckhove, the McLuhan Program has become an interface of academics, artists and business people all working with interactive new media. The Virtual Reality Artists Access Program (VRAAP), headed by Graham Smith, provides virtual reality tools such as David Rokeby' s Mac-based *Very Nervous System* which renders sonorous bodily movement. The importance of artist-engineers like Smith and Rokeby was recognised by Gould in 1968 when he heralded the collaborative effort of engineer Walter Carlos and musicologist Benjamin Folkman on the recording *Switched-On Bach*.[5] Just as, today, the Moog synthesiser seems like a relic, in the future, contemporary VR technology may also seem like a museum piece. De Kerckhove has recently curated an exhibition of 'TechnoArt' at the Ontario Science Centre (OSC) around the theme of interactivity which calls into question the traditional exhibition and its distancing mechanisms. Indeed, the OSC's mandate is to provide a tactile environment. Many of the installations at TechnoArt, including those of Rokeby, Nancy Paterson's ride in the virtual countryside *Bicycle TV*, and Hiroyuki Moriwaki's electric mirror *Rayo-Graphy*, put the participant's body to work in the virtual environments created by each piece.

The VRAAP also has a high-resolution video conferencing system (PictureTel's System 4000) which makes possible virtual seminars bringing together academics and performers across vast spaces and time zones. Taking as a cue Nam June Paik's experiments in what he called 'satellite art', such as the New Year's Day 1984 simultaneous broadcast of *Good Morning, Mr Orwell* from Paris, New

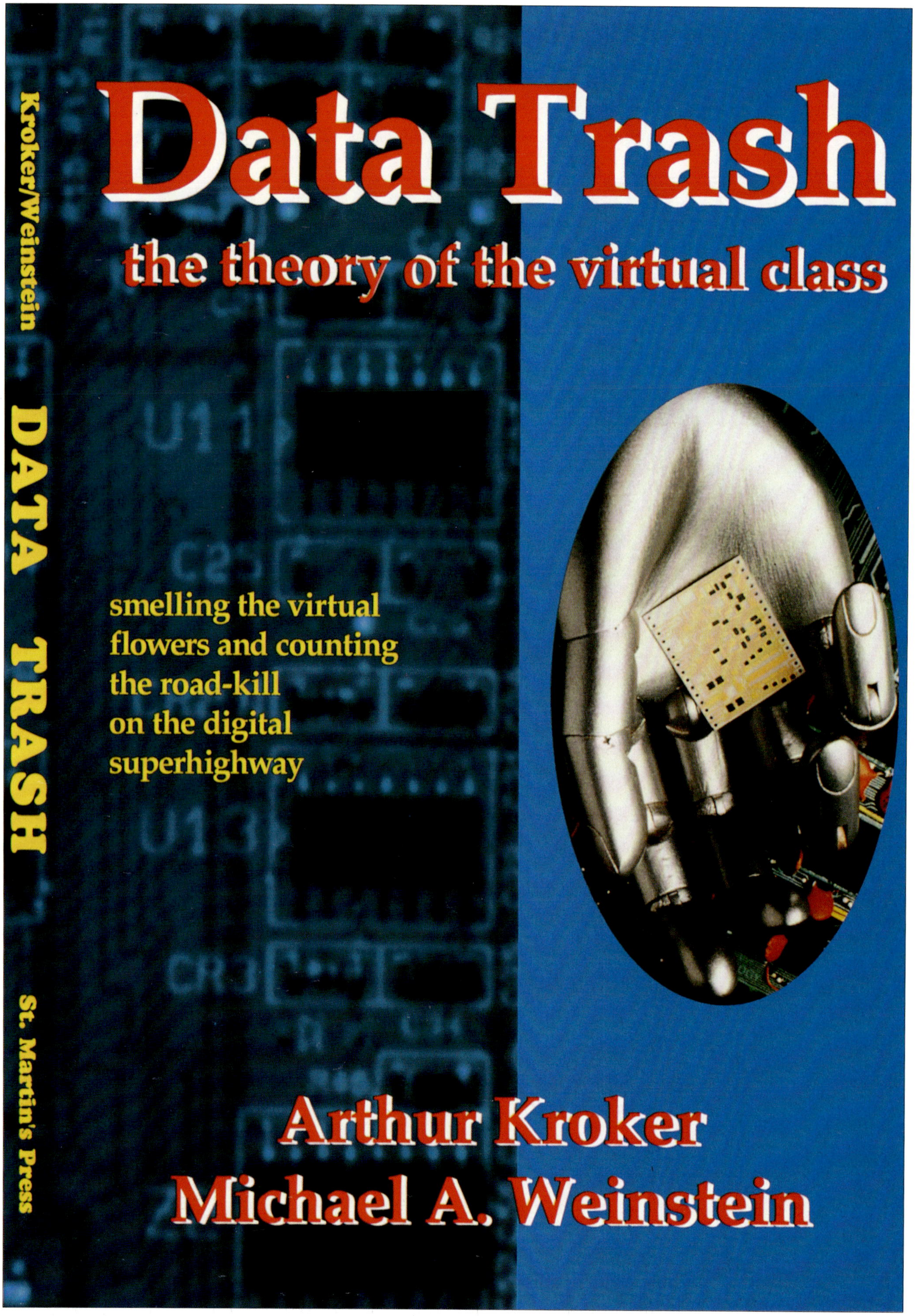

Book cover for Data Trash: the theory of the virtual class *by Arthur Kroker and Michael A Weinstein, design by Marilouise Kroker*

York and San Francisco,[6] De Kerckhove has orchestrated several ground-breaking transatlantic contacts. The artistic exploration of interactivity at a distance and the emergence of new spatial sensibilities through the medium of video conferencing has, in the projects with which De Kerckhove has been involved since 1986, exposed by trial and error many bugs and, on occasion, fallen back on faxes and telephones and E-mail.

For technical reasons the 'trans' doesn't always come off. Trans-interactivity is conceived of as a kind of intimacy at a distance, a dialogue of bodies interacting in a virtual tactile space. Many of the performances designed for *Les Transinteractifs*, a transatlantic colloquium in Paris at the Canadian Cultural Centre and in Toronto at the OSC in 1988, emphasised telepathic communication: Christian Sevette's *Le toucher transatlantique* would have allowed members of both audiences to bring together two pieces of Michelangelo's *The Creation of Man* in an act of divine inspiration; in *Le baiser transatlantique*, Orlan proposed to project on a screen the profiles of two persons from each city, turned toward one another, whose lips would meet in a kiss as they continued to speak French and English respectively.[7] More recently, the Program has organised transatlantic and inter-urban Canadian video conferences of the more traditional academic sort such as the 'World Series on Culture and Technology' between the Program and leading cultural theorists of various host countries. These are now a staple of its formidable battery of electronic pedagogical tools. Fifteen years after McLuhan's death, the lethargic academic community at the University of Toronto finally opened a Marshall McLuhan Studies Room in the Faculty of Information Studies. This opening coincides with the release by the media giant Southam of the *Understanding McLuhan* CD-ROM.

The Canadian political scientist Arthur Kroker remains at the forefront of the performance of advanced theoretical speculation. Kroker almost single-handedly brought McLuhan into Post-Modern focus through his influential journal *The Canadian Journal of Political and Social Theory* and in the pages of the provocative books issued by his publishing house New World Perspectives, especially his *Technology and the Canadian Mind: Innis/McLuhan/Grant*, in which he concluded that McLuhan's fate was to be an 'intellectual servomechanism' of the technoscape he so brilliantly described.[8] The CJPST has been superseded by an electronic journal *C Theory*.

In the mid 1980s Kroker began issuing supplementary materials such as cassettes (including spoken texts and music such as 'Mutant Madonna', and more recently the recombinant experiment in sound called *Spasm*, a CD which features the sounds of virtual reality, that is, processed samples of sound). Also engaging in multi-media theoretical performances Kroker recently completed a European tour in support of the *Data Trash* book with his partner, the designer Marilouise Kroker, and Montreal based composer Steve Gibson, who provided an ambient soundscape for the spoken performances. The video work of the Krokers includes the *Body Program*, a panicky romp through virtual America, made in collaboration with Stefaan Decostere for Belgium TV.

If the impulse of trans-interactivity is the creative interface between the human body and the virtual environment, then Kroker's gesture moves in the opposite direction: the natural body has become obsolete at the hands of new technologies. The so-called panic body – and, more recently, the body in a spasm of contradictory feelings – is defined by the hyper-exteriorisation of its organs and viruses and the hyper-interiorisation of designer subjectivities.[9] Kroker takes McLuhan's thesis of the 'outering' of human senses by technology and turns it into an emptying into the technoscape and then a reverse 'invasion' of the media environment. In his terms, the information highway is paved with human flesh and littered with fresh road kill run over by the corporate behemoths who are trying to run the road. As catchy as a Kroker buzz phrase can be, he never loses sight of the class struggles being waged over the conditions of access and the social choices implied by new technologies.[10]

The projects of De Kerckhove and Kroker represent two wildly divergent facets of the Canadian academic imagination stirring in the shadow of McLuhan. While the academic imagination is in the process of outering itself in novel ways, one would need to look outside the academy to such notable writers working in Vancouver such as William Gibson (see Robert Longo's film version of Gibson's story *Johnny Mnemonic* as an instance of the incorporation of what was once subcultural) and Douglas Coupland (recall that his novel *Generation X* was part of the first major pop sociological phenomenon of the 90s, before the Internet; his latest book is *Microserfs*) in order to find technological, indeed, sociological 'fictions' with really widespread currency. For what was once fictional is now the social.

Notes

1 Guy Debord, *Comments on The Society of the Spectacle*, trans M Imrie Verso, London, 1990, p33.

2 See Donald Theall, *The Medium is the Rear-View Mirror: Understanding McLuhan*, McGill-Queen's University Press, Montreal, 1971.

3 McLuhan, 'Notes on the Media as Art Forms', *Explorations* 2, April 1954: 7.

4 McLuhan and Quentin Fiore, *The Medium is the Massage: An Inventory of Effects*, Bantam Books, New York, 1967, p68.

5 Glenn Gould, 'The Record of the Decade', in *The Glenn Gould Reader*, ed Tim Page, Lester & Orpen Dennys, Toronto, 1984, pp429-34.

6 See Nam June Paik, 'La Vie, Satellites, One Meeting – One Life', *Video Culture*, ed John G Hanhardt, Visual Studies Workshop, Rochester, 1986, pp219-22.

7 See De Kerckhove, 'Ratés dans les grandes largeurs', *Les Transinteractifs* Espace SNVB, Paris, 1990, p15ff.

8 Kroker, *Technology and the Canadian Mind*, New World Perspectives, Montréal, 1984, p86.

9 Kroker, 'Body Digest', *CJPST* 11/1-2 (1987): iii.

10 See Kroker and Michael A Weinstein, *Data Trash*, New World Perspectives, Montreal, 1994.

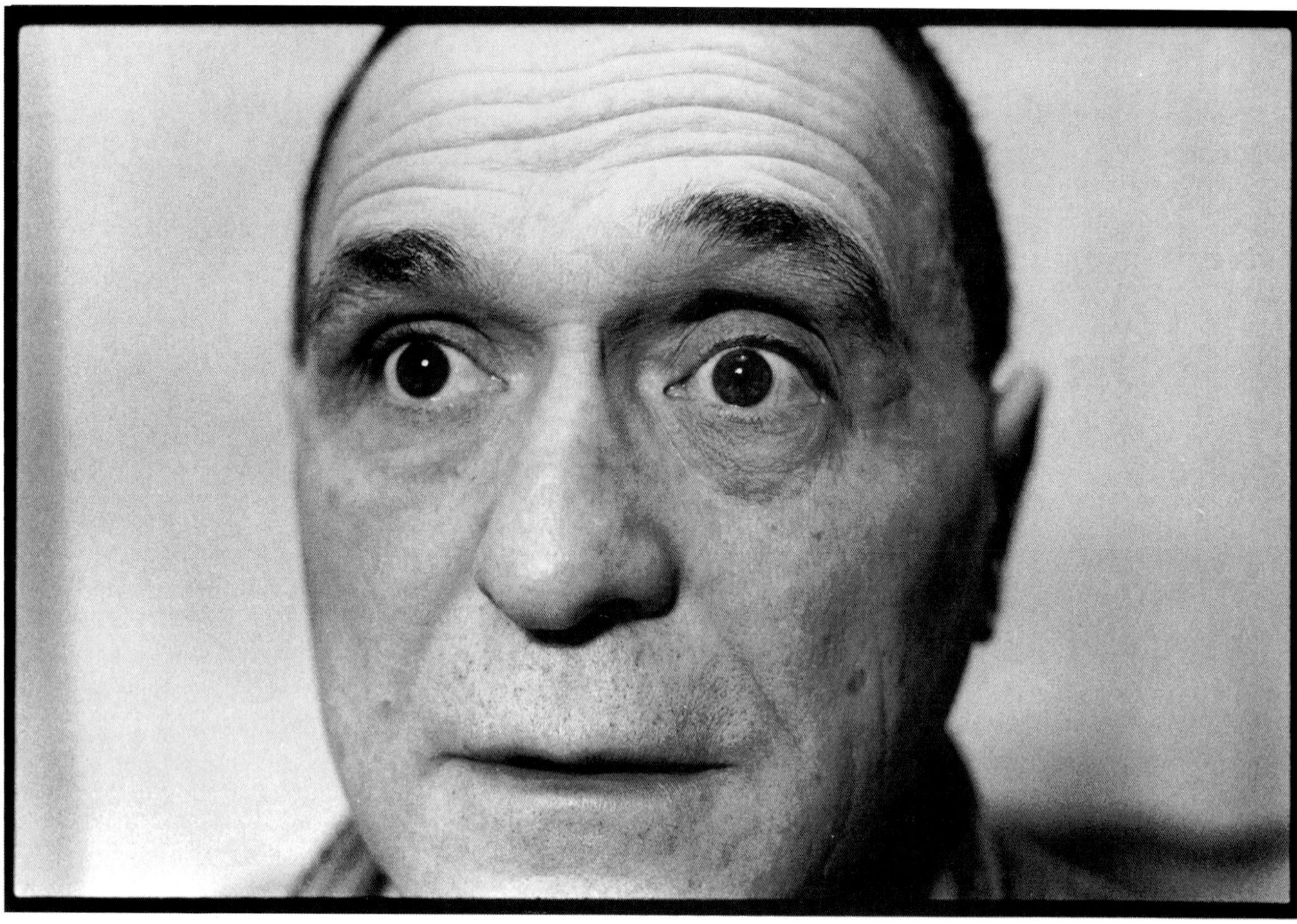

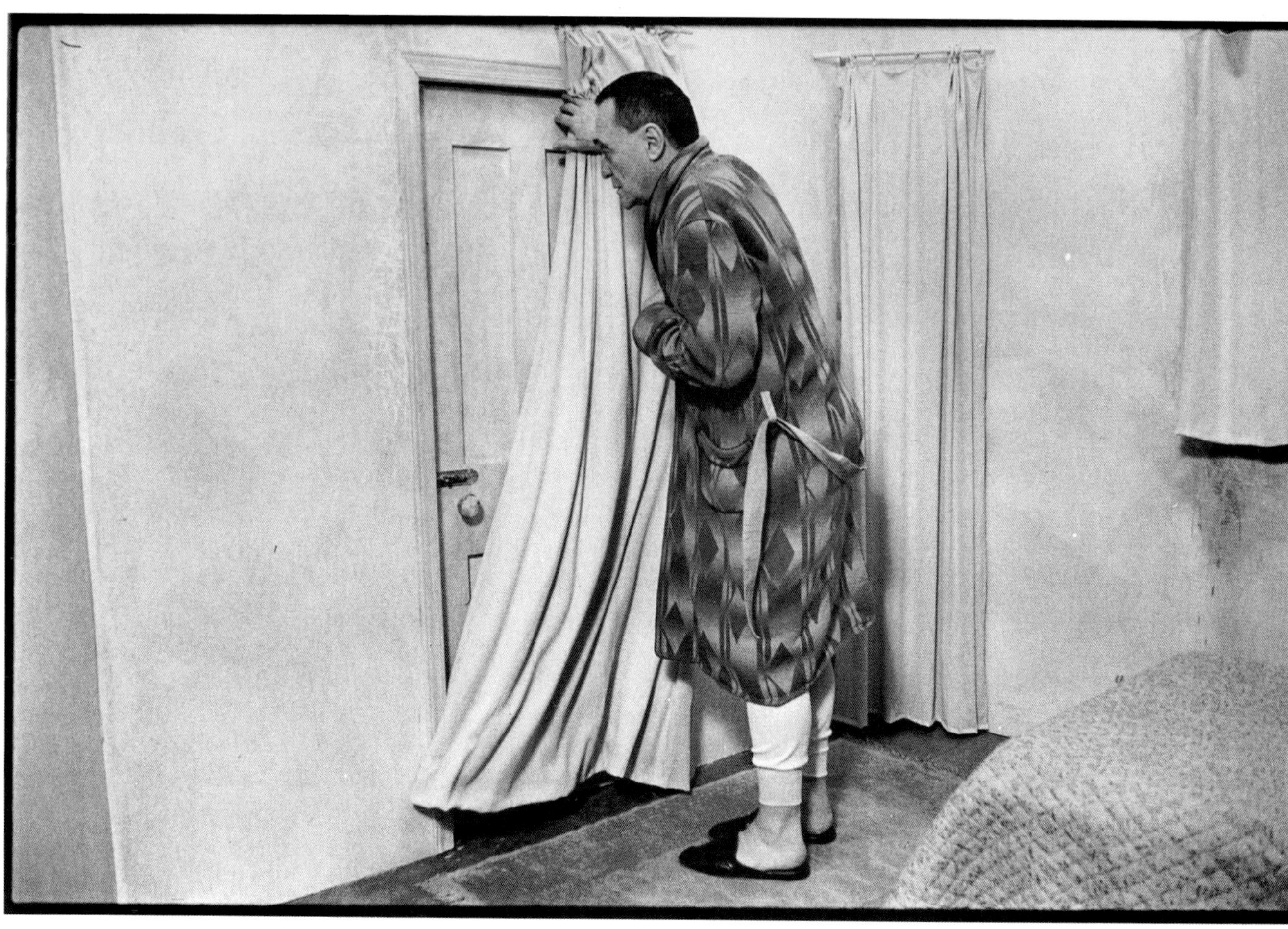

Pages 64-66: John Giorno in Eh Joe *by Samuel Beckett, directed by Erica Bilder, performed in an installation designed by Peter Ungerleider, La MaMa ETC, Annex Theater, 19-29 January 1995, photo Paula Court*

ON PLAYING SAMUEL BECKETT'S *EH JOE*

John Giorno

In November 1994, Peter Ungerleider asked me to be Joe in Samuel Beckett's play *Eh Joe*. He said Erica Bilder had been casting for weeks, and had not found the right person. I did a screen test in Peter's studio, and they loved it. *Eh Joe* opened in the big theatre at La Mama Experimental Theatre, New York, on 19 January 1995, for a two-week run.

Eh Joe was a television play written by Samuel Beckett in 1965-66. There were famous productions of it in 1966, by the BBC in London, as well as American, French, and German television; and it has scarcely been performed since. It was published with *Cascando*, and other short dramatic pieces for radio, television, and film from the 60s. *Eh Joe* and *Cascando* were presented together at La Mama.

Eh Joe was directed by Erica Bilder, and performed in an installation designed by Peter Ungerleider. There was a huge video screen 25 feet square, mounted in a huge wood box, that was seen by the audience sitting in bleacher seats. The audio, heard on infra-red transmitted earphone sets, was Erica Bilder's voice, performing the text in the slow dry monotone, exactly as proscribed by Beckett, which was the inner dialogue going through my head.

Joe is an old man in his late 50s, at the end of his life, alone in a room. I am 58, and live joyously. He moves about briefly, then sits on a narrow bed, listening to his inner monologue, contemplating his meaningless miserable life, devoid of love, kindness and compassion, for about 20 minutes. The thoughts are remembrances of his suffering and the suffering he has caused: anger, desire, loss and the banalities of his discursive mind. I am a Tibetan Buddhist, and I believe the play is a pure view of the first Noble Truth. As I performed the role of Joe, I followed each word with absolute concentration, allowing myself to feel each moment of his mind.

I performed in a small room, off the entrance to the theatre, whilst being broadcast live onto the huge screen. The audience could not see me as they entered the theatre, but at the end, as they left, they could see me through the open doorway. I was sitting on the bed with tears running down my cheeks. I cried every night on cue, within 30 seconds of when I was supposed to, and kept them running until everyone left and the house was closed.

Peter Ungerleider designed the set exactly as Beckett stipulated in the script: a window, a door and a cupboard, each with a curtain that pulled closed. The colours were a lighter shade than pale, and very carefully lit. I wore an old dressing gown from Theodora's closet and carpet slippers. I put on my own make-up every night. I am a man in a straight world and I never wear make-up. I really smeared on the powder, obviously too much because I matched the walls. In the tight camera shots, with just my eyes and mouth on the 25-foot screen, the liver spots on my cheeks were the size of cannon balls.

Peter Ungerleider and Erica Bilder are obsessive perfectionists, and they directed me very carefully, which I really appreciated. I was being released from being John Giorno, and could do anything I wanted. Tell me what you want me to do. I do anything.

It was filmed in black and white, there were ten camera moves, and Beckett was specific about each. We did it exactly as he directed, as we also knew that the estate of Samuel Beckett was very fussy that nothing was changed. Why not? What a great idea, do it exactly as he had wanted. The text was in ten segments, each with a four inch camera dolly move just before it. The move stopped when the text started in each segment. We made it seamless, shot with a Betacam by Eben Mears: walking around, sitting on the bed, then the camera moved in tighter eight times, scored by the narrative, ending up just with my eyes (and the tears).

I had never acted in anything. I had starred in Andy Warhol's movie *Sleep* in 1963, and I have spent my life playing John Giorno in the endlessly ongoing series called John Giorno; but I had never acted in someone else's work. What a break, I thought, I can play somebody else. I have for decades performed the work of John Giorno: gay, pornographic, violent – loving fabulous sex, anger, politics, money, and the stupidities of the world and now I get a chance to play something other than my narrow world. I get a chance to play the vast empty expanse of Samuel Beckett.

When I accepted the part, I did so by intuition and as usual, my intuition said yes. I had read the play quickly, skimmed it and it looked good; and Erica had read some of the woman's part during the screen test. Only when we went into rehearsal two weeks before we opened, came the shock of what it was and what I had to do.

I began each performance with the William Burroughs shuffle. The stage directions by Beckett are that of the old shuffle about the room, going to the window, closing the curtain, to the door and cupboard, doing a routine. I have lived with William Burroughs for decades and I have seen him shuffle about in his pyjamas, dressing gown and slippers, every morning and night, doing the same routine. I began my performance each night as if I was William Burroughs, stooping with my shoulders hunched, frail and pathetic, walking with a halting little stagger, exactly as William does, with the same facial expressions and jerky head movements. This is how I got into character.

It also hit me that I had personally known the girl who had committed suicide, of whom Beckett wrote. In the late 1950s and early 1960s, I had a girlfriend named Marcia Stillman. She committed suicide age 23 in November 1962. She was a brilliant actress (her role was Antigone), had a brilliant mind, lived on Park Avenue with her family, and was very beautiful.

Andy Warhol painted Marcia's suicide in the 'Disaster' painting series in 1963 at my request and gave me the painting. It was called *Bellevue II*, and shows Marcia laying dead on the cobblestones, surrounded by two orderlies and three policemen. The painting is

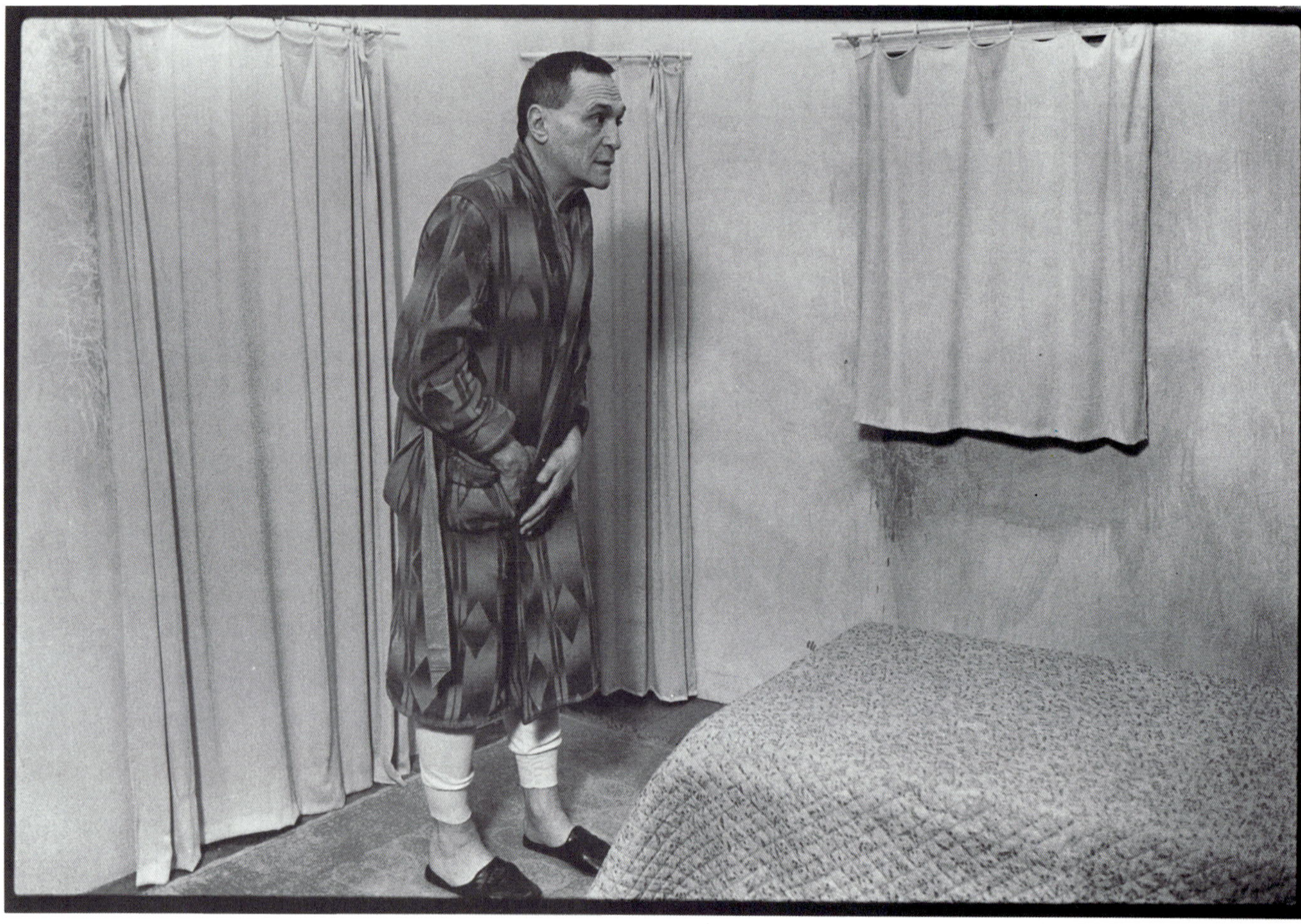

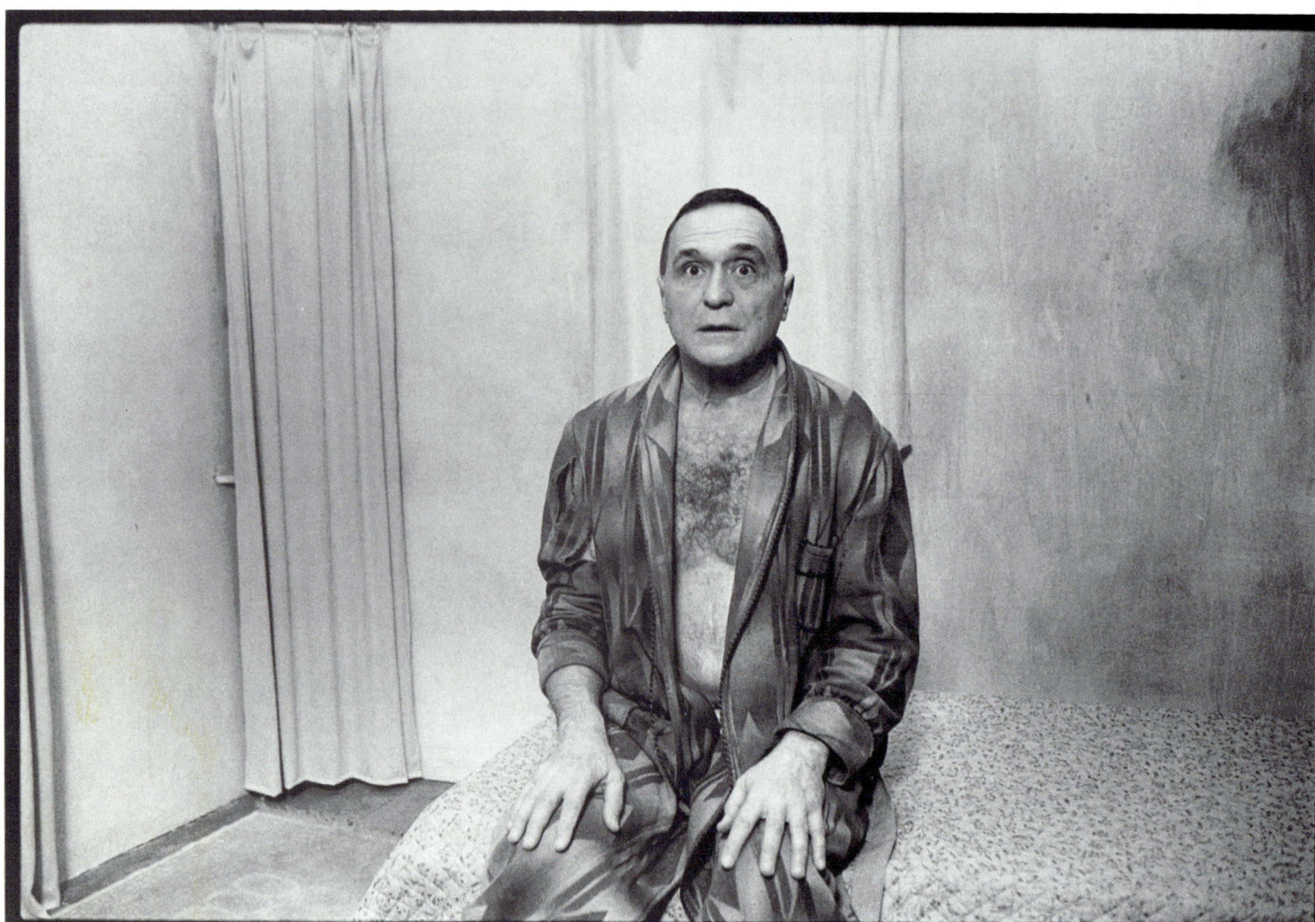

now in the Stedelijk Museum in Amsterdam.

Marcia was also the girlfriend – and later married – another friend of mine, Harry Joe Brown Jr, also known as Coco, who produced *Krapp's Last Tape* by Samuel Beckett. He co-produced it with Richard Barr in 1959, for the Provincetown Playhouse on MacDougal Street. It was a great coup for him as it was the first time it was shown in America. *Krapp* had premiered in the London's Royal Court Theatre in 1958. I actually saw *Waiting for Godot* in 1957 at the Provincetown on MacDougal Street.

Harry Joe would go to Paris and visit Samuel Beckett, always taking Marcia with him. I remember thinking at the time that Marcia was the reason Beckett saw Harry Joe. She was the hook. Harry Joe was a dilettante playboy, son of a Hollywood director and a 1930s movie star. He was a flake who exploited everybody. Beckett was straight, and probably not at all interested in him, except for Marcia. I was sure that Beckett was deeply charmed by Marcia, as everyone was, and was in love with her.

Beckett wrote *Eh Joe* after Marcia's suicide, and the character of the suicide is a composite of every young girl who kills herself. Marcia died in 1962, and as I rehearsed the play in 1995, I could not help but think that Beckett had written about her death and that she had inspired Beckett. Now 33 years later, I was re-acting to her suicide, allowing those feelings to arise every night as I performed the role, and letting it arise strongly to effect a large audience. I had been very much in love with Marcia, and after her death I had been possessed by her spirit or ghost. In 1965, Brion Gysin presided over an elaborate exorcism of her from me.

Each night, as I performed at La Mama, the tears poured down by cheeks but they were not tears of sadness and grief. They came from relaxing the eye muscles. I had looked with intense clarity directly into the camera and into the panoramic space around it for 30 minutes, scarcely blinking my eyelids. When I lowered my eyes at the end of the narrative and relaxed the muscles, the tear ducts just opened, and within 30 seconds, tears poured down my cheeks. There was no pain – there was just joy. The audience read it as tragedy. For me, it was bliss and empty space, and with no thought of anything.

Halfway through the run – and I cannot say I was tired of thinking about Marcia's suicide, because I still had compassion for her suffering, Ray Johnson committed suicide by jumping off a bridge in Sag Harbor on Long Island, in the dead cold of winter, and drowned in the frigid water. This was a shock.

Ray Johnson was a Pop collagist, an originator of mail as an art form and the New York Correspondence school. He was famous for this, but not as famous as he wanted to be. I met Ray Johnson in 1963, when I was with Andy Warhol. I was always a little more famous than he was, and sometimes he was a little mean. In 1969, he bought a house in Locust Valley, and moved there. My family lives in Roslyn Heights. My mother's house is down a couple of roads from him. I was dumbfounded, and said, 'Ray, are you crazy? Do you want to commit suicide?' This was the north shore upper-middle class hell-world from which I had escaped. Barely escaped, since I had attempted suicide myself. Ignorance is a quality of the god worlds. Although very beautiful, it was a deadening, obscured, heaven world from which I had been liberated. It was incomprehensible that Ray Johnson should want to move there. A big mistake. It is strange that 30 years later Ray Johnson should commit suicide there. I knew the Sag Harbor Bridge well.

Each night, I did my meditation practice connecting to Ray Johnson's consciousness, trying to ease his pain and help him go on. I had to reinvent myself each night (two shows on weekends) for the benefit of the audience, as Beckett's boring words describing the girl's suicide droned on.

Suicide is one of the worst kinds of death. If a person is so depressed and frozen in this life, seemingly unable to change anything, then in the moments after death, the consciousness of the person becomes completely frozen, unable to change anything, which continues for a very long time. This is true in all spiritual beliefs: Christian, Jew, Muslim, and Buddhist. Suicide is the cause of great suffering.

Each night, I also did my Tibetan Nyingmapa Buddhist meditation practice. While I did the Beckett play, simultaneously on another level, I did mantra and visualisation practice. Even if nothing was good about the play and the worst was true, if my meditation practice was good enough, maybe Vajra Sarasvati, the Buddhist deity of poetry and art would shine through for an instant and help someone in the audience. I tried to radiate enough compassion to fill the world.

Often during the run of *Eh Joe*, I heard that people stayed back in their seats crying, with tears running down their cheeks, as I did. People did not know that the play was live, most thought it was taped until they saw me sitting there as they left the theatre. One of the them was artist Bruce Witsiepe, who I had never met. I also run the AIDS treatment project, that helps people with AIDS by giving cash grants for emergency situations or when they are in trouble. We gave two grants to Bruce, and he came to see *Eh Joe*. It made a very strong impression on him. He died of AIDS three months later. His friend Racquel Shapira said, 'He thought about you all the time during his last three months. It was the last time he went out'. *Eh Joe* was his last strongest imprint. 'He thought about you when he died.' He thought of Joe when he died. I hope the Buddha Sarasvati came through with the bright light of pristine awareness.

When I was at Columbia College in New York in the mid 1950s, I studied modern drama with Eric Bentley. Samuel Beckett was the most radical, revolutionary theatre – cutting through dumb concepts and liberating the mind with wisdom. This was before William Burroughs wrote *Naked Lunch*, and before Allen Ginsberg wrote *Howl*. Now, 40 years later, I find myself performing Beckett, in this obscure classic from the distant past.

I got rave reviews in the *New York Times*, *Village Voice*, *New York Post*, etc and we packed the house. Just the way it should be.

I will perform Eh Joe *in Rome, Italy, at Teatro Dell 'Angelo, in November 1995, for a two-week run, in a festival of plays that originated at New York's La Mama Experimental Theatre Club.*

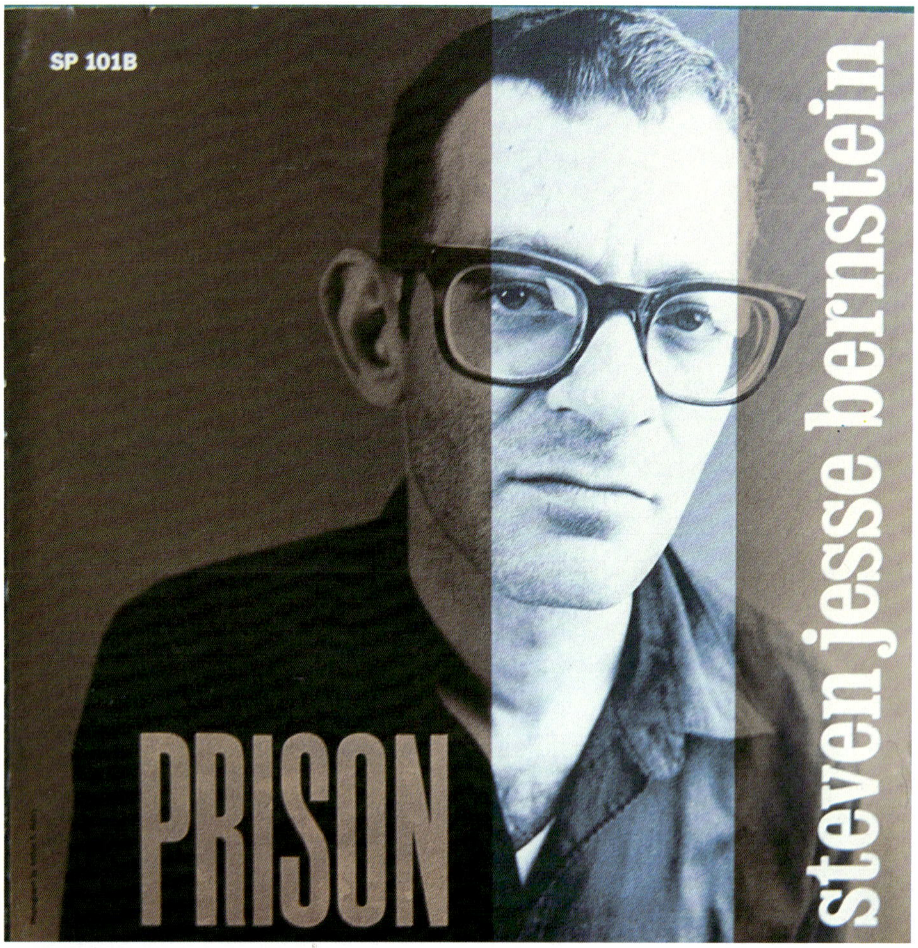

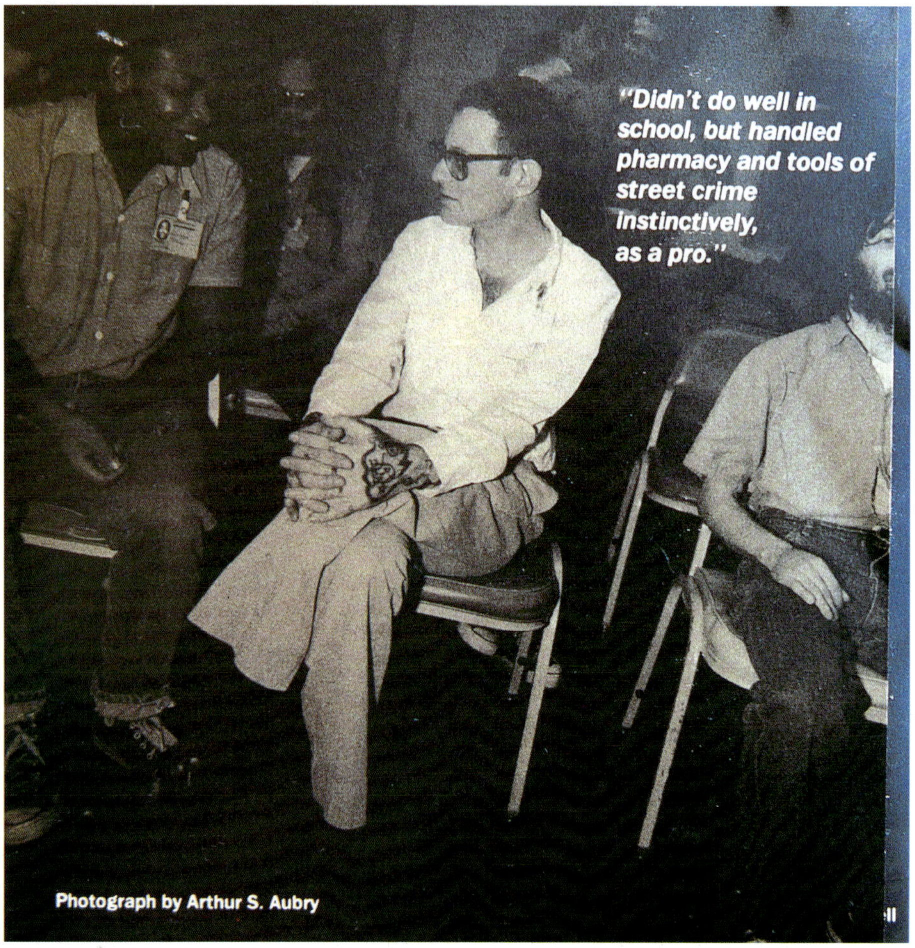

Steven Jesse Bernstein, Prison, *CD cover (Sub-Pop Records, Seattle)*

PUNKS ONE, POETS NIL

STEVEN JESSE BERNSTEIN, LYDIA LUNCH AND HENRY ROLLINS

Jim Krank

> *This then? This is not a book. This is libel, slander, defamation of character. This is not a book, in the ordinary sense of the word. No, this is a prolonged insult, a gob of spit in the face of Art, a kick in the pants to God, Man, Destiny, Time, Love, Beauty . . . what you will. I am going to sing for you, a little off-key perhaps, but I will sing. I will sing while you croak, I will dance over your dirty corpse.*[1]

And now Steven Jesse Bernstein is dead; dead at his own hand, assassinated by society and a witness to forces his own life could no longer reconcile. The remaining CDs will be shredded, recycled in asphalt leading to new suburbs in hell. It was a turf he knew well; he had spent his life charting this terrain, an underground man at the edge of existence. A great man of history, like Adolf Hitler or Joseph Stalin, is honoured by *Time* magazine as 'Man of the Year'.[2] Artists like Bernstein, exposed nerves twitching at the limits of the body politic, are consigned instead to blast furnaces of the historical process.

Bernstein is dead, but there are others, like Lydia Lunch and Henry Rollins, in his wake. Paragons of punk, flowers of evil birthed from the corpse of Western culture. 20 years ago they torched the house that rock built, blazed it to the ground in an orgy of noise and naked aggression. Now they tread gnarly boards as 'spoken word' performers. 'I was publishing books . . . I was 20 at the time and it felt very futile. I wanted to shake up the world. I wanted to make noise, but nobody reads.'[3]

New York City in the early 70s made few concessions to youth. Feeling alone and outside, consumed with the horror of a world they had not made, teenage Rimbauds like Richard Hell, Patti Smith and Tom Verlaine reviled existing forums for the poetry they wrote.[4] Encased in spiritual lucite for the delectation of the privileged few, poetry appeared a noble gesture that was ultimately futile and hopelessly complicit. In any case, their audience lay elsewhere – for Hell's 'nobody', read 'none of my peers'.

And so their voices found a vehicle in punk rock, a form they created out of the most absolute necessity, the usurpation of a popular art form by the only people with anything to say. Maybe no one understood the metaphors – as Joe Carducci has pointed out, the rock audience is 'aesthetically illiterate' – but their intent was as clear as the bloodied nose on your face.[5]

New performers struck both stage and audience in the years that followed. Fleeing a childhood of abuse and abasement, Lydia Lunch played a baby-faced banshee at the fore of a succession of bands, defining a half-dozen aesthetics in as many years. Similar suburban dysfunctions informed Henry Rollins, for years the singer and songwriter for LA's *Black Flag*. If, as Artaud wrote, 'incest is the enemy of poetry'[6] Rollins and Lunch were drumming out their personal demons, reckoning with the cost and the causes of their stolen innocence. Now their attention is turned to other arenas – writing, and performing and recording 'spoken word'.[7]

American dreams are overshadowed by double golden arches, each marking the point of the nearest Moloch franchise. This was not the syndrome Gore Vidal identified as 'M-3' – but it might have been. Vidal elaborated, M for Miller, M for Mailer, M for Manson. To which we might add: M for Morrison. Lunch admits admiration for Henry Miller, and Rollins's chilling declamation of 'Family Man' recalls nothing so much as a lucid but barely restrained Charles Manson.[8]

But the real point of connection between the *poètes maudites* and raucous rock lies in the dirt of the Père La Chaise cemetery, at the site of Jim Morrison's Parisian grave. Morrison was the first (or perhaps the most popular) rock musician to admit what were essentially literary aspirations. A self-styled successor to the transgressive tradition of French symbolism, it was he who alerted Hell, Smith and Verlaine to its existence. It was after sobbing at his grave that Smith renounced rock criticism for rock performance.[9] More recently, Rollins has spoken of Morrison's influence: 'The one thing I have learned from Jim Morrison . . . (was when) . . . he said, "Guns are not dangerous, minds are dangerous. You want a weapon? It is right here" (points to head). You hear that song *Five to One*? That is so incendiary'.[10]

Jim Morrison almost single-handedly valourised the stance of the rock musician as a seer, caustic visionary, intemperate Zarathrustra.[11] As such, he fits perfectly within the parameters of Vidal's 'M-3' category. Morrison pioneered the stance of the rock musician as poetry-of-pain, baring his soul to a bovine herd – he something more than human, his audience something less. And these twin conceits – that the lyrics to rock music might be equivalent to verse poetry, and that rock musicians might be a few rungs higher on the ladder of perception than their audience – have informed much of subsequent rock musings, in the United States as elsewhere.

Vidal never intended 'M-3' to be as flattering epithet; for him, 'M-3' man was exemplary of all that is most loathsome in modern American culture, conditioned to 'think of women as, at best, breeders of sons; at worst, objects to be poked, humiliated, killed'.[12] Like Rollins, Lunch admires Morrison, but has consistently defended herself against accusations of misogyny, claiming instead to be a 'misanthropist'.[13] This equal opportunity hatred provides ample opportunity for angst – especially when the objects of that scorn are paying to be exposed to it. But this bilious misandry was the spine of the punk posture, the fuel that fired the aesthetic engine. 20 years on, it is still fuelling the likes of Lunch and Rollins.

The rock critic, Lester Bangs, once defined punk rock as 'rock honed down to its rawest elements, simple playing with a lot of power, and vocalists who may not have much range but have so much conviction and passion it makes up for it ten times over'.[14] Thus, it becomes tempting to consider Lunch's and Rollins's more recent work as a continuation of the punk project, especially in the light of these words by Rollins: 'I think there is a need for people to hear things without a bunch of racket behind it. To hear a voice, not 80,000 watts'.[15]

Lunch seems to concur that the 'spoken word' is a refinement of punk's minimalist aesthetic: 'It is just nonstop nagging in the face of the public. How can a mere record with guitar, bass, drums, saxophone give me the satisfaction of being in someone's face annoying them'.[16]

It may well be true that poetry, or indeed the whole of modern literature, is ripe for the challenge that punk once provided to popular music. But are writers and performers like Lunch and Rollins likely to be the agents of that renewal? Can passion and conviction alone suffice in the arena of writing and declamation?

As a component of music which was of itself revolutionary, the writing and declamation of Lunch and Rollins could make a virtue of its own weaknesses. Intellectual reductivism and a primal physicality are the essence of rock music – or advertising – but antithetical to literature, whether written for the page or performed before an audience. As literature, the work of Lunch and Rollins looks pretty slight. This is especially so when you compare it with other writing of a similar intent, such as Lautréamont's, or Céline's. Lautréamont's cooking is *cordon bleu*, with equal measure of myrrh and mustard gas at its core. Maintain the metaphor, and Lunch's and Rollins's endeavours might be a Big Moloch burger – all beef (or all ham . . .), raw, and all on its lonesome.

It must also be understood that the internal mechanisms by which we respond to music and speech are fundamentally different.[17] Human response to music is intuitive, emotional and governed by the right hemisphere of the brain. Our understanding of verbal signals is mediated by the left hemisphere, and involves rational, analytical processes. That is why rock concerts can become riots, but poetry festivals almost never do.

Lévi-Strauss found the same opposition between speech and music, but for him the function of speech could be reconciled with that of music when it evoked tribal mythology.[18] But in place of

Notes

1 Henry Miller, *Tropic of Cancer*, Panther, London, 1965, p10.

2 See John P Diggins, *Mussolini and Fascism: The View from America*, Princeton University Press, Princeton, 1972, p26.

3 Richard Hell, speaking at the 'Punk and History Forum', Fashion Institute of Technology, New York, 24 September 1988.

4 Hell, 'Punk and History' Forum. For Smith's response to Rimbaud, see her LP *Radio Ethiopia,* Arista, 1976.

5 Joe Carducci, 'The King of It and the King of Thing', in *The Penguin Book of Rock and Roll Writing*, ed Clinton Heylin, Viking, London, 1992, p150.

6 Antonin Artaud, 'Revolt Against Poetry', *Artaud Anthology*, City Lights, San Francisco, 1965, p101.

7 See for example Lunch's video anthology, *The Gun Is Loaded*, Lytham St Annes, UK, Visionary JE 246; and Rollins' video anthology *Talking From The Box,* Imago 72787210093, New York, 1992.

8 Gore Vidal, 'Womens' Liberation Meets Miller-Mailer-Manson Man', *Collected Essays, 1952-1972*, Heinemann, London, 1974, p390.

9 Lunch, interviewed by Charles Neal, in *Tape Delay*, SAF, Harrow, 1987, p44. Rollins reads 'Family Man' on an *Untitled* promotional video compilation, SST, Los Angeles, 1988.

10 Patti Smith, 'Jukebox Crui-fix', in *The Penguin Book of Rock and Roll Writing*, pp397-400.

11 Henry Rollins, 'No Pain, No Gain', interview by David Fricke, *Rolling Stone*, Sydney, No 491, December 1993, p55.

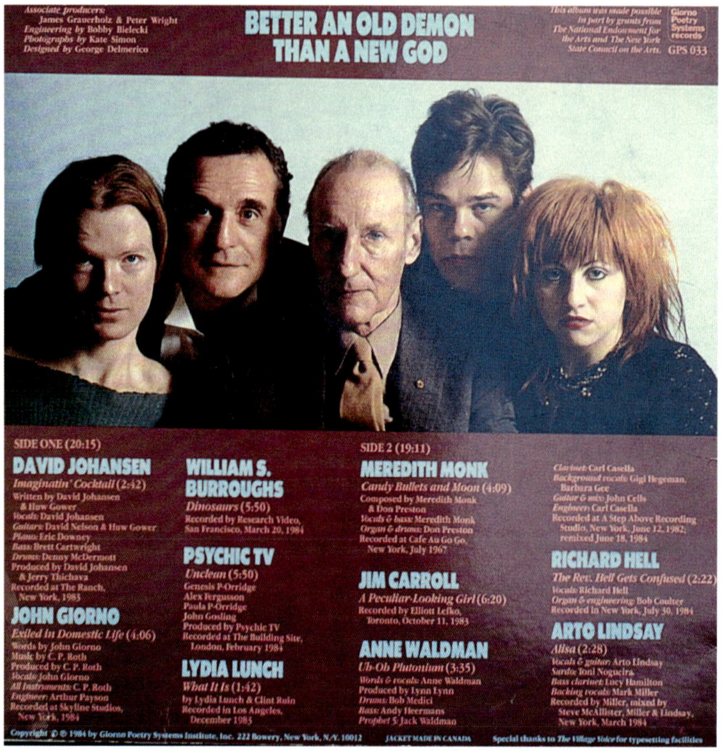

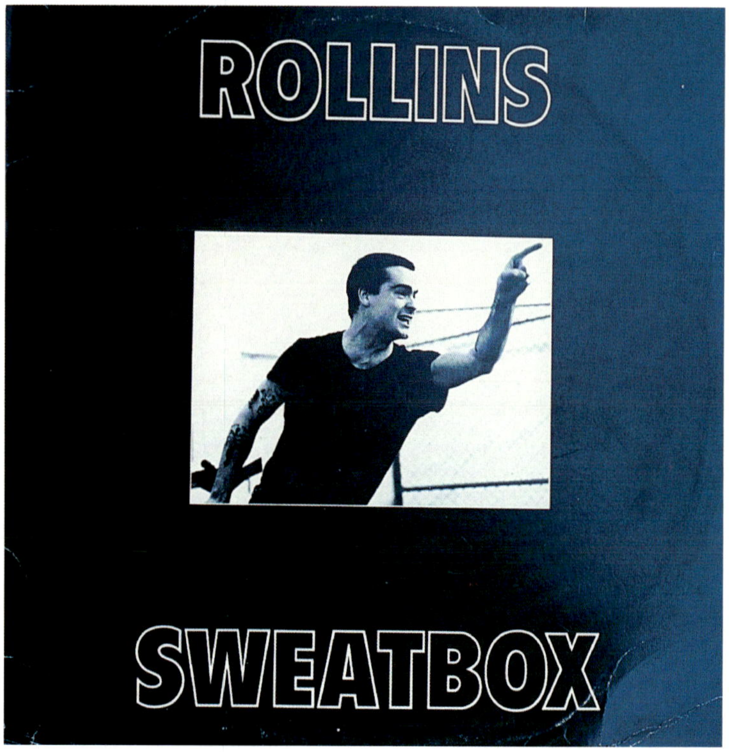

L to R: Jim Carroll, John Giorno, William S Burroughs, Richard Hell, Lydia Lunch, Better An Old Demon Than A New God, *LP cover, Giorno Poetry Systems Records, New York; Henry Rollins,* Sweatbox, *LP cover, Texas Hotel Records, Santa Monica.*

mythology – with all the resonance that myth demands – Lunch and Rollins offer us a steaming pile of macho bullstuff . . . personal anecdote, ironic asides, sneering diatribes, journal extracts. Charles Bukowski (another 'M-3' exemplar) tilled these same fields and became the virtual poet-laureate of America's urban proletariat. Lunch and Rollins are both apt to employ the same loosely-metered vernacular that Bukowski – in the company of Céline and Miller – used to such effect. Whereas this triumvirate turns such base matter into the philosopher's stone of modern myth, Lunch and Rollins give us the misandrist meanderings of superannuated punk rockers; all grown up, and nowhere to retire to.

So, what of Steven Jesse Bernstein? Listen to Bernstein's only recorded work, the CD *Prison*,[19] and hear the cries of a man lost at sea, the sound of someone drowning in the boiling confluence of their own bile and excrement. If the function of literature is redemption and/or transcendence, Bernstein succeeded where Lunch and Rollins never will. Bernstein plumbed his drunken depths. His 'spoken word' performances do not describe his ascent from the maelstrom, but they affirm that his essential humanity was still intact. This is one of the pedagogical functions of great art; that a human being can suffer, and go on suffering a whole lifetime, and yet still retain some empathy and love for his or her fellows. Anything less is quite understandable, but merely banal.

Humanity is the rarest commodity there is, all the rarer for being the only commodity that is not on the market. Bernstein's *Prison* CD is rich with this rare substance. Apart from this solitary recording, I know little of Bernstein's work, and almost nothing of his life. Too unphotogenic for fanzine covers, he never gained the fans his work alone should have merited. He had no personality cult to succour him, no fanzine editors clamouring for interviews or work to publish.[20] 40 years of age at his death, he should have been maturing as a poet, a long and promising career ahead of him. Instead, he fulfilled the promise that Lunch, Rollins and their ilk have been making for years; for what is suicide if not the ultimate act of self-hatred and alienation from your environment? I, at least, would wish that it might have been otherwise.

12 See Jerry Hopkins and Daniel Sugerman's biography of Morrison, *No One Here Gets Out Alive,* Plexus, London, 1980. Morrison's 'spoken word' work appears on the CD *An American Prayer,* WEA, 1995.

13 *op cit*, Vidal, p390.

14 See Lunch, 'As Deep as Pink', interview by Byron Coley and Jimmy Johnson, *Forced Exposure,* No 10, Boston, 1986, p38. See also C Carr, 'Lydia Lunch Faces the Void', in *On Edge: Performance at the End of the Twentieth Century*, University Press of New England, Hanover, 1993, p142.

15 Lester Bangs, 'In Which Yet Another Pompous Blowhard Purports to Possess the True Meaning of Punk Rock', in *The Penguin Book of Rock and Roll Writing*, p56.

16 *op cit*, Rollins, 'No Pain, No Gain', p56.

17 *op cit*, Lunch, 'As Deep as Pink', p40.

18 Douglas Bernstein, Edward Roy, Thomas Srull, and Christopher Wickens, *Psychology*, Houghton Mifflin, Boston, 1991, pp103-105.

19 Claude Lévi-Strauss, *The Raw and the Cooked*, Cape, London, 1970, pp18-29.

20 Steven Jesse Bernstein, *Prison*, Sub-Pop, Seattle, 1992.

21 Comic book versions of a biography of Bernstein by Dennis Eichorn and of an unpublished Bernstein story (both illustrated by cartoonist and editor Pat Moriarty), appear in the magazine *(Your and Your) Big Mouth*, Vol 1, No 4, 1994, from: *Fantagraphics*, 7563 Lake City Way NE, Seattle, WA 98115.

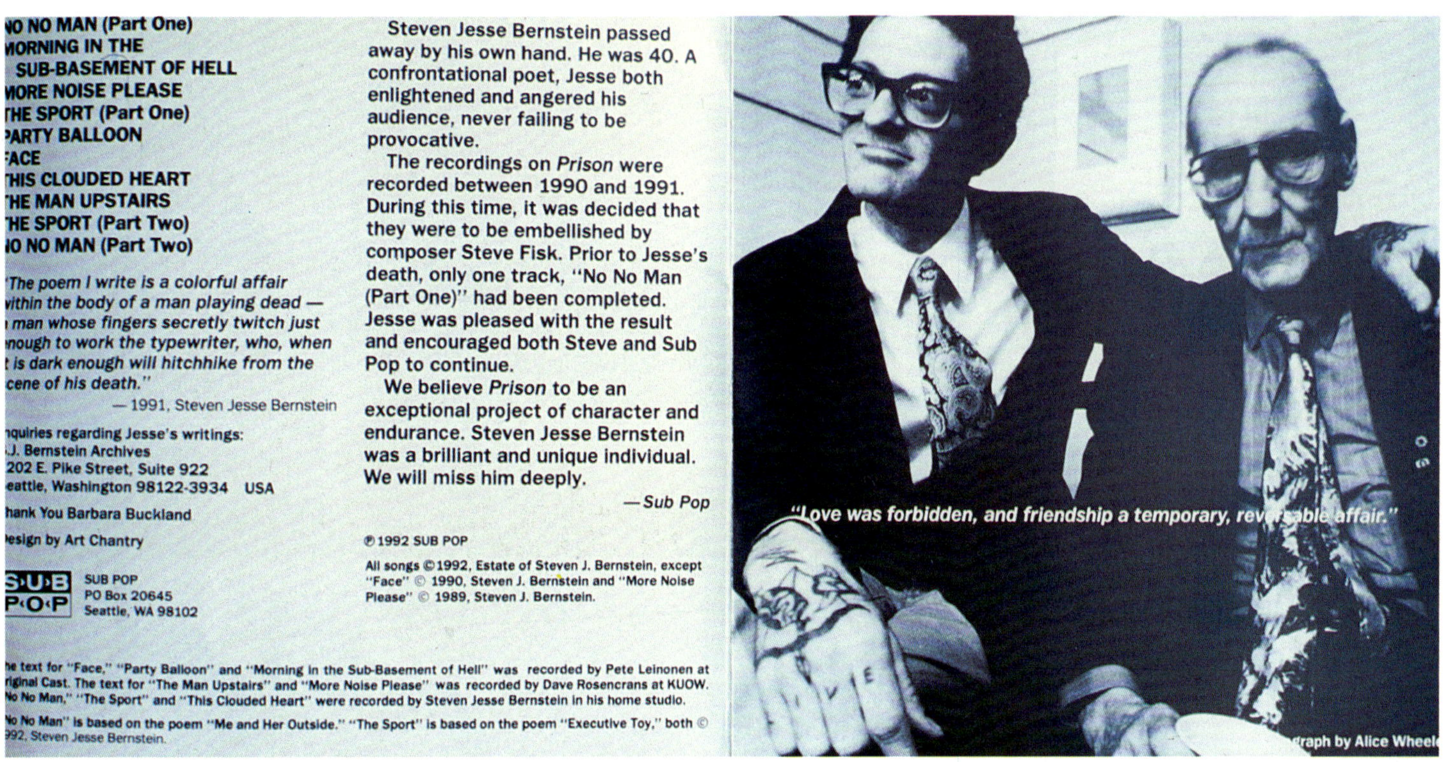

Steven Jesse Bernstein, Prison, *CD cover (Sub-Pop Records, Seattle)*

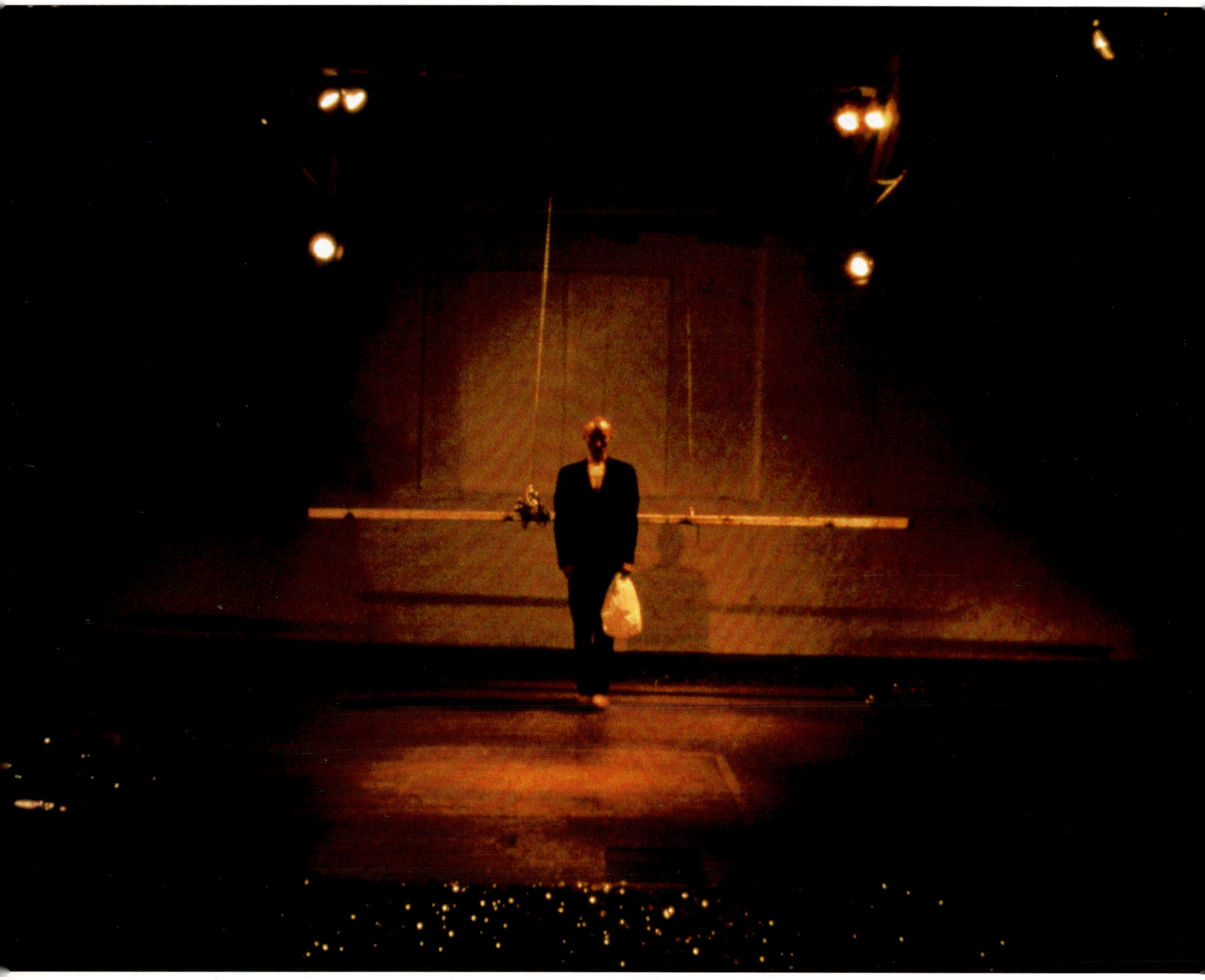

Stuart Lynch in Paradance Fable, *Institute of Modern Art, Brisbane, April 1995*

PARADANCE FABLE

STUART LYNCH

Interviewed by Nicholas Zurbrugg

In the following interview Stuart Lynch discusses *Paradance Fable*, a performance piece in three sections inspired by, and responding to, the French theorist Jean Baudrillard's essay 'Metamorphoses, Metaphors, Metastases', from *The Ecstasy of Communication*. First performed at the Institute of Modern Art in Brisbane, Australia, on 4-6 April 1995, *Paradance Fable* addresses the problem of integrating both Western traditions of multimedia performance, theatre and dance, with Eastern traditions of Butoh dance, particularly the work of Japanese Butoh dancer Min Tanaka and his Mai-Juku Performance Company. As Lynch observes, Tanaka's emphasis upon 'Body Weather' training exercises, and upon 'an objective attitude towards the body and its relation to the mind', seems to coincide very closely with Baudrillard's meditations upon what he calls 'the body of the Fable', or:

> The body of metamorphosis, the one of a pure chain of appearances, of a timeless and sexless fluidity of forms, the ceremonial body brought to life by mythology, or the Peking Opera and Oriental theatre, as well as by dance: a non-individual body, a dual and fluid body – body without desire, yet capable of all metamorphoses – a body freed from the mirror of itself, yet given over to all seduction.
>
> ('Metamorphoses, Metaphors, Metastases', p45)

Paradance Fable attempts to suggest 'an open loose-ended relation to find how . . . theory and practice might join in 'dialogue' with Baudrillard's essay, both alluding to what Lynch calls 'the beautiful clarity of the opening lines' of Baudrillard's essay, and at times playing with, upon and against the subsequent convoluted contradictions of Baudrillard's essay, intermingling improvised video-taped monologue, pre-recorded work by Lynch, by the late Australian composer Jamie Fielding and by the American jazz pianist Cecil Taylor, randomly broadcast radio static, and explorations of what Baudrillard terms: 'Not a psychological body, not a sexual body, a body freed from all subjectivity, a body recovering the animal felinity of the pure object, of pure movement, of a pure gestural transpiration'. ('Metamorphoses, Metaphors, Metastases', p46)

Somewhat as Baudrillard's own photographs propel textual reference to 'the pure object' into the iconic domain of photographic 'pure objectivity' (*The Transparency of Evil*, p154), Lynch's performative dialogue with Baudrillard's essay translates textual reference to 'pure movement' into choreographic projections of the 'non individual', 'dual' and 'fluid body', and like Baudrillard's prose itself, reverberates with the kind of partially sublime, partially grotesque, self-deconstructive energy that East German playwright Heiner Müller associates with 'the androgynous element, this mixture between snake and wildcat movements' in Shakespeare's plays (*Germania*, p210).

Nicholas Zurbrugg – *What led you to conceive of* Paradance Fable*?*

Stuart Lynch One of those classic inspirational moments at the Institute of Modern Art, almost one year ago, at the Baudrillard seminar 'The Art of Theory'. A number of ideas which had been floating in my head suddenly became more concrete, and this impetus led to *Paradance Fable*. I detected a great challenge in the mystery of Baudrillard's work, and also hearing him speak – a sense of it being right, a sense of truth in it. I felt that he had arrived at a point of self-awareness, that he achieved something, that he had gone through things. I was extraordinarily impressed by his general demeanour, by his sense of grandness and generosity, and felt an enormous challenge to try to understand his writing in physical terms and perhaps to reproduce it, or to respond to it, in performance. All this redirected my attention to his essay 'Metamorphoses, Metaphors, Metastases', in which he asks what has happened to the body of the fable, the objective body, as opposed to the self-expressive or subjective body. Baudrillard's text seemed to suggest ways of finding movements within the body which were not so much self-expressive as giving way to something on a grander scale representing something else – the sorting out and finding out of an objective body and the kind of movements that body would make.

Did you feel that Baudrillard's own personal delivery had something of this objective quality?

– Very much so. What I found shocking about his way of speaking was the way it is all-inclusive, an almost religious sense of truth ran parallel with devilishly constructed games and paradoxical webs undermining any sense of orthodox spirituality or dogma. He seemed to have an immense capacity to understand or feel the division or juncture between the objective and the subjective, cutting through all the political correctness that seems to be so prevalent.

I liked this very much insofar as it suggested a kind of performance emphasising what is actually happening in a space, rather than what we want to happen in the space. In a sense, *Paradance Dance* tries to ask the same question; 'What is happening in this space now?' Not, 'What am I showing you?', but 'What is happening? Has something happened? Has something changed?' I also felt that Baudrillard had a very intuitive sense or instinctive sense of – not of what was politically correct – but of objectivity, and I felt that if this feeling could be caught in a dance or in a performance it would be extremely interesting.

How did you begin to work with Baudrillard's essay? Did you try to translate its successive paragraphs directly into dance?

– No. I could have taken this first paragraph: 'Where has the body of the Fable gone?' and made a performance out of it. You know, 'this is a non-individual body', 'this is a body brought to life by mythology', and so on. I just did not want to translate the essay directly. At that

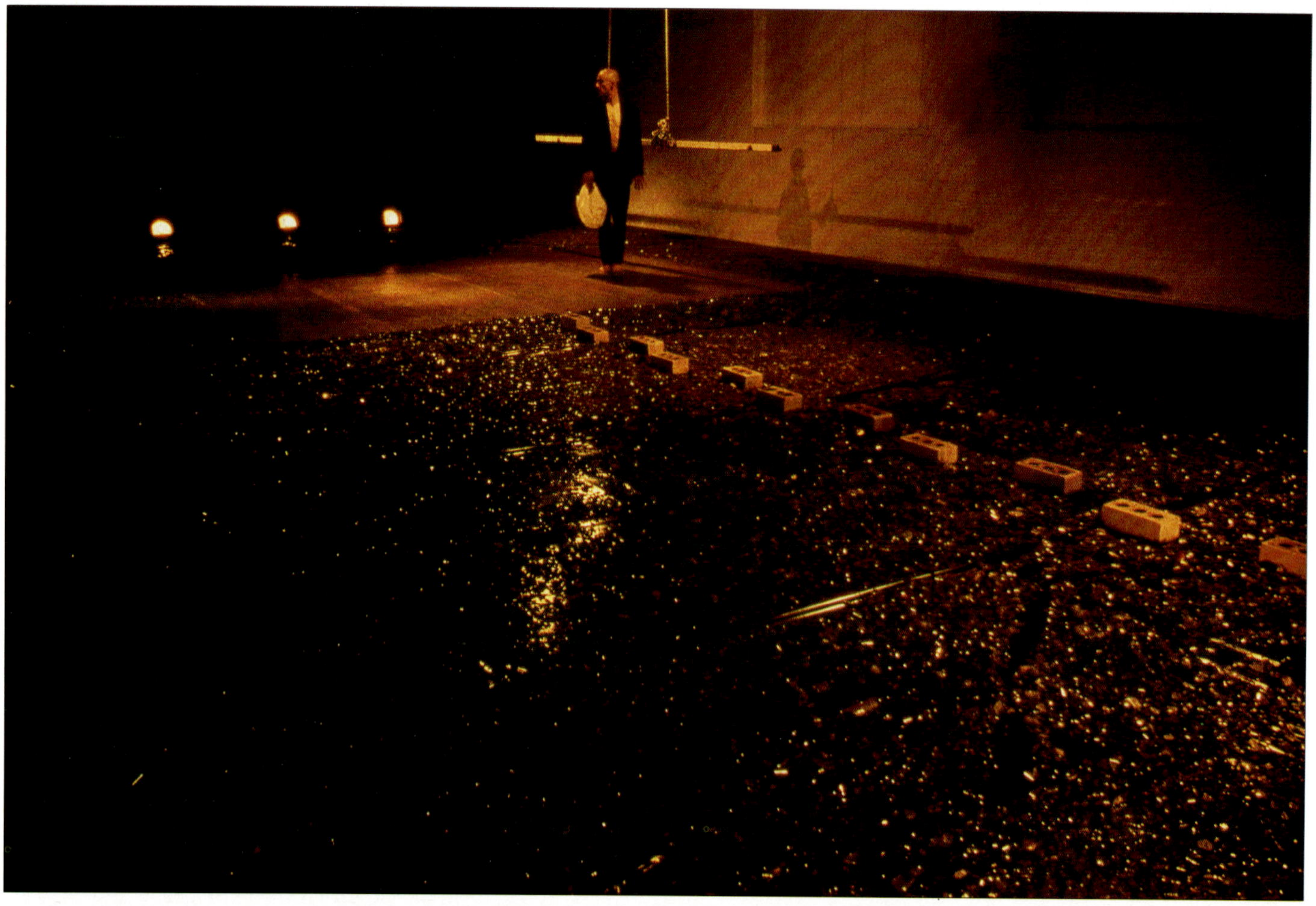

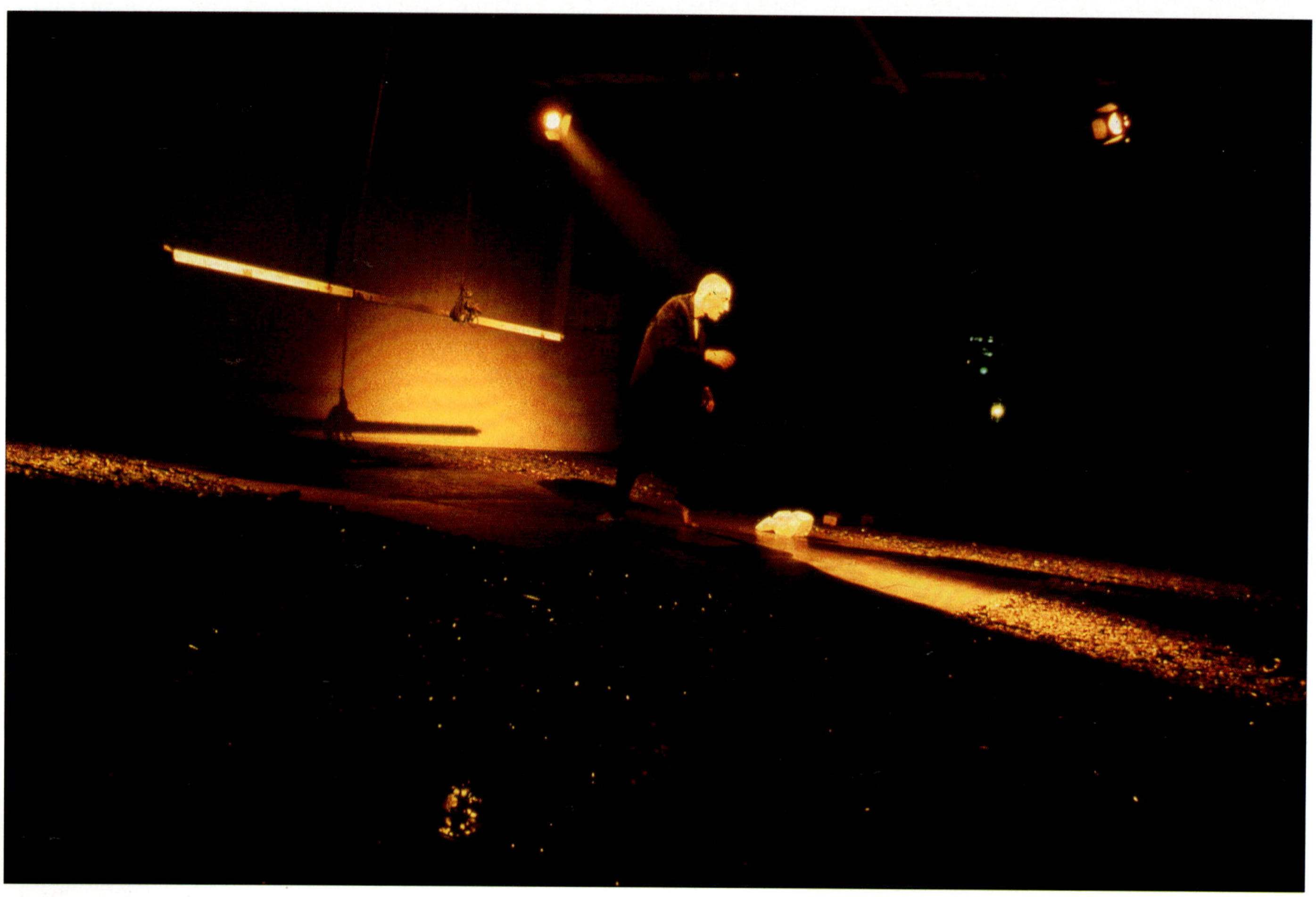

Stuart Lynch in Paradance Fable, *Institute of Modern Art, Brisbane, April 1995*

point I completely gave up rehearsing conventionally, and simply kept up with my Mai-Juku body training.

If you were not rehearsing conventionally or literally, how did you begin to plan the different ways in which Paradance Fable *would respond to Baudrillard's essay?*

– Perhaps my whole problem was that of defining the kind of webbing I sensed in Baudrillard's writing. I am a sculptor by training, so I wanted to build a space that would be integral to the whole piece. This immediately brought me back to the conflict I felt between literal and more interpretative responses to the essay. Should I have created a space for a ceremonial body to perform in, or for a mythological body to perform in? Or should I have created a more general Baudrillardian space? I also practice within theatre, and I wanted to make this a performance. My initial structure for the choreographic aspect of the work came quite quickly. I knew that a large amount of the work was going to be concerned with body speed – with how many different speeds the body has, or how many the mind can 'gear' into the body. Then there were particular aspects of ceremonial bodies – direct ceremonial bodies that exist within the genre of Butoh, and also the language of the Mai-Juku Company, and then a third section which directly related to purely improvised movement. What I would then do within these sections, and how I would approach them, was the problem.

I began by trying to create a very pure ceremonial space, with broken glass as far as the audience could see, leaving a space within it in which to dance. During the prologue I walk to the space from a chair where I am sitting at the beginning of the performance, crossing the stage on bricks which were just slightly above the area of the glass.

On another level, I also used a video projection of myself talking, as if to the audience, about Baudrillard's text in a very derogatory, stand-up comedy manner, often falling into highly caricatured English and French voices. This was prepared the night before, at the last possible moment, to capture my most spontaneous intellectual and emotional response to the essay, as opposed to the more objective and more detached quality of the body on the stage. In the performance itself I wanted to concentrate on what Baudrillard calls the 'body of metamorphoses' and the 'pure chain of appearances' – on the pure nature of what he is suggesting in his first paragraph – whereas the video rather more playfully evokes his essay's contradictory aspects, improvising on certain passages and sounds.

The video goes on for an hour-and-a-half. My performance itself is not that long, but within it there are choreographic elements of variable length, so that the first section, for example, might vary from five to ten minutes. While the video image of my face is present throughout the prologue and the first two sections, my voice is cued to come on and off when I reach certain parts of the performance, so on different evenings the audience hears different sections of this monologue. I wanted part three to offer my most purely improvised work as a body within a space creating a dialogue with an audience, and for this I wanted nothing that was in an any way derogatory, self referential, clever or intellectual. I wanted a pure sense of the body, and so at that point I indicated that the video should be stopped.

Does the relationship between your performance and Baudrillard's text become less obvious at this point? Or do you think that when you are doing this highly detached, depersonalised sequence of improvisations this is in fact a rendition of the sort of the 'non individual body' that Baudrillard has in mind?

– My personal feeling is that it is the purest I can come to his work, because I believe he is working to his utmost to produce the work that he produces. As I said, when talking about his demeanour, he clearly seems to have arrived at something, and at this particular point in *Paradance Fable* I am trying to capture something comparable for myself, as a dancer. I feel it is at that point that I get as close to this quality in his work as I possibly can.

Considered very generally, Paradance Fable *seems to respond to a complex series of self-imposed challenges exploring the fusion, or the tension, between variable sequences of elements from the worlds of Eastern and Western dance, installation, music, comic monologue, Post-Modern theory and multimedia performance in general. And you also have plans to integrate a recording of Baudrillard reading his text in French when the piece is re-presented in Copenhagen in November this year. All in all, it seems a very volatile and very valiant 'translation' of your responses to Baudrillard's own equally volatile ideas.*

– Yes, as Baudrillard suggests in the last paragraph of his essay, it is exciting to look beyond 'dialectical ideas' towards what he calls the 'escalating power expressed by a potentialisation of the stakes' which 'sometimes chances upon us, as it does for things when they are left to their own devices'.

Brisbane, April 1995

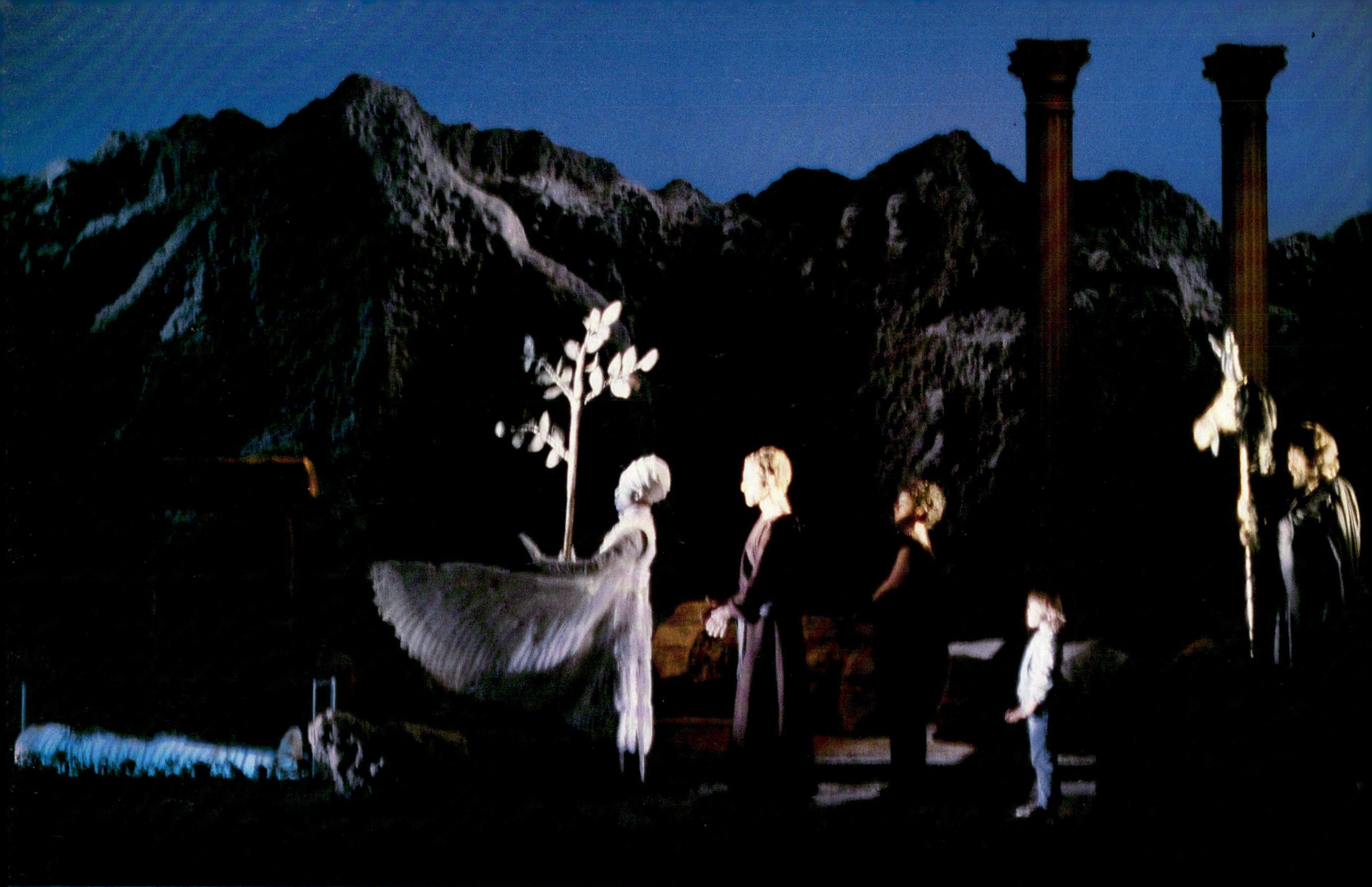

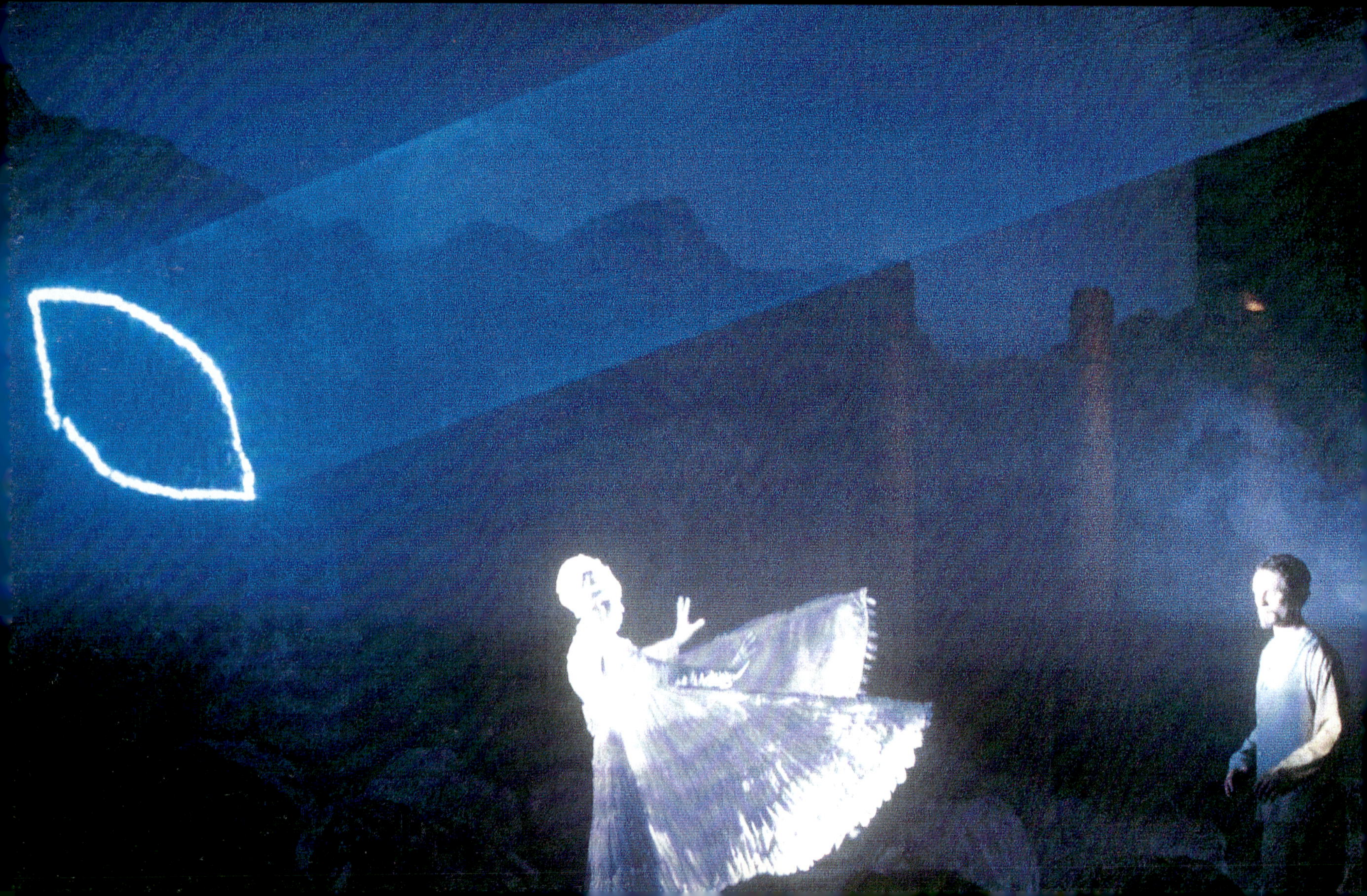

POST-MODERN TIME AND PLACE
WILSON/MÜLLER INTERSECTIONS
Robert Scanlan

Robert Wilson and Heiner Müller – a study in contrasts. Waco, Texas and Saxon Germany; a childhood spent in stark open prairie country and one spent in distressed cities riddled with Nazi brutalities and war; tall and short; American and German; silent and brilliantly loquacious, studiously unlearned and massively erudite; seemingly apolitical and drastically engaged – how could two such men have become the profound friends they are and what is the basis of their repeated and fruitful collaborations? There are no greater or more influential artists than Wilson and Müller working in the theatres of Europe and America. Between them, they command the Post-Modernist aesthetic in the theatre and even the works they create without each other (they work more frequently apart than together) are marked through and through by the deep aesthetic bonds they have formed together since the early 80s.

Wilson's expressiveness is achieved through vision. His art is plastic and dynamic, framed almost exclusively by a collage of the so-called 'visual arts' of painting, sculpture, architecture, lighting, and the rhythm and tempo of live performance. Müller's contrasting and complementary mission as a late 20th-century poet and intellectual has driven him systematically away from the logos which comes so fluently and brilliantly to him; he has come to prize powerful inexplicable images over the shaky ever-questionable assertions of words. The 'death of the author', so cavalierly propounded by French theorists, is for him (as it was for Samuel Beckett) a consummation devoutly to be wished, with all the attendant horrors, night-sweats and interior miseries such a state of affairs really entails when it is lived in the flesh, in the time of one's life; when it describes the tormented real life of the psyche and not some metaphorical theory of art.

Heiner Müller was honoured in December 1994 by the Taormina Arte Festival in Taormina, Sicily, where he was awarded the '*Premio Europa per il Teatro*'. After enduring several days of praise of his life's work, Müller thanked us wryly for giving him 'a dead man's view of a funeral; each tribute a shovelful of dirt in the face'. He added that his writing continues to put the maximum possible distance between him and death. Robert Wilson was also given a prize at these obsequies, and the two friends spoke publicly about each other, something they rarely find occasion to do. What they said was significant, for they both spoke of time and space, and how each finds in the other's art a 'gift' of time and space which seems to inspire and soothe them both. What were they talking about? Some solace, however fragmentary and ephemeral, to be sure, but is this private communion between them, this fusion of metaphor and literal reality an important clue in unravelling the complex psychology of the Post-Modern aesthetic?

It is fascinating to ponder the fact that Heiner Müller's artistic life changed in his 47th year when he visited Texas for the first time in 1976 – an event charged with the bizarre, unlikely and fortuitous juxtapositions which shape contemporary consciousness. For the East German Marxist, the discovery in mid-career of 'the politics of space', as he put it, was decisive and overwhelming. Texas came out of the blue for Müller, and his travels in the Lone Star State as well as in the neighbouring vast states of New Mexico and Arizona transformed his view of the world. Robert Wilson, who grew up under the open sky of east Texas, has spent, by election, the bulk of his artistic maturity working among artists and intellectuals in Germany. It was fascinating to see these two friends collide again at Taormina Arte's award ceremony. Both were surrounded by a swirling international press corps as well as by admiring theatre artists from every corner of the globe, all momentarily united under the midwinter sun of Taormina. Jet-lagged myself on that occasion (I had just left bitter winter weather in New England) the jump-cut consciousness of Post-Modern aesthetics seemed simply to transcribe experiences such as the one we were all sharing. In the midst of all the hubbub surrounding Heiner Müller's *Premio Europa*, Woody Allen arrived with his movie stars and film crews – all of them utterly unaware of the ceremonies in progress – to shoot the final scenes of Allen's latest film (to be released sometime in 1995) in the *teatro antico*. An embarrassed bellhop at the San Domenico Hotel asked me, after seeing me part from Heiner Müller, whether that gentleman I had just embraced was not 'il Signore Woody Allen, perhaps?' Time and space seemed indeed warped and refracted in each other.

There are few more beautiful spots on earth than Taormina, clinging as it does to volcanic cliffs overlooking the Straits of Messina and the Ionian Sea. The town itself is a treasure trove of ancient architecture festooned in riots of flowering vines, shrubs and citrus trees. Ancient villas (most of them converted into hotels) look out over terraced gardens which in turn overlook the sea. Down below along a sweeping beachhead lie the remains of Naxos, the first Greek colony in this part of the world (734 BC); in the distance, Mount Etna smoulders away majestically, a stark reminder of the geological birth of the planet; higher up the jagged cliffs, a Norman 'krak' built during the Crusades culminates the view; it is a breathtaking place. The crown jewel of this paradise (and the chief reason the Taormina Arte Festival is located here) is the *teatro antico* carved into the side of the cliffs. Originally an ancient Greek theatre, the site was reworked by the Romans, and it is the architecture of the high Empire (from Augustus to the second or third centuries AD) which is visible in the picturesque and very usable ruins which remain today.

Robert Wilson had strangely anticipated this multi-layered historical setting for Müller's award: in 1986 in Cambridge, Massachusetts, he staged a visionary version of Euripides' *Alcestis* in which the dream-like scene, inspired by Apollo's shrine at Delphi, unknowingly echoed Taormina's contrast of mountain steeps and classical ruins.

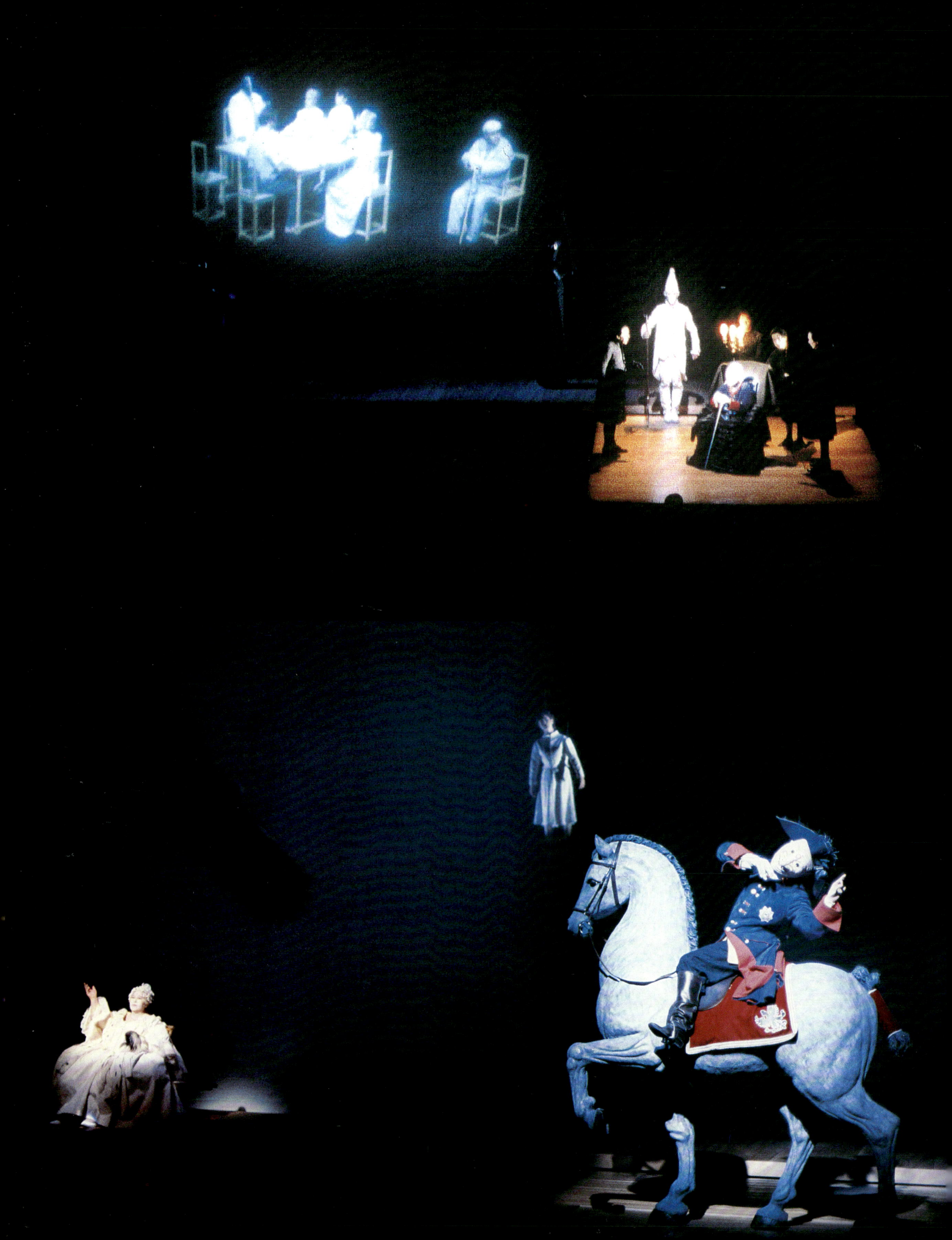

Heiner Müller wrote a disturbing prologue for that production of *Alcestis*: a harrowing text of deep and morbid personal significance, the *Description of a Picture*, which he later referred to as *Explosion of a Memory*. Wilson staged this text as a frame for the *Alcestis*, placing it in the mouth of an actor wrapped like a mummy high over the stage, to the audience's left, held in the frozen embrace of an ancient Cycladic marble idol, copied and enlarged from an artefact of the third millennium BC.

Such historical palimpsests and echoes of dead voices have flowed back and forth between Heiner Müller's work and Robert Wilson's since the Cologne segment of Wilson's *the CIVIL warS* in 1983. For this first collaboration with Wilson, Müller drew on his own recently completed *Leben Gundlings* (1976), a strenuous theatrical meditation on the German Enlightenment and its violent modern legacy. Much of the material in *The Life of Gundling* was destined to shape this Cologne section of *the CIVIL warS*, and the figure of Frederick the Great of Prussia, in particular, was to dominate the scenes of domestic strife and civil carnage in Wilson's play. In Cambridge in 1986, Robert Wilson restaged at the American Repertory Theatre those Cologne portions of *the CIVIL warS* on which Müller had collaborated. This was my first contact with both their work, and the source of the photographs accompanying this article.

One image from *the CIVIL warS*, in particular (among so many), epitomises the relationship between Müller the writer and Wilson the director and designer. In Act IV, Scene A, a figure known as the White Scribe appears on the stage costumed in festoons of writing paper, and sporting an enormous pencil attached at the head. For this fantasy figure of Wilson's – almost a spoof of 'the condition of the writer' – Müller wrote a pensum-text which was delivered in performance (in Carl Weber's translation) accompanied by the sound of labouring machinery:

> Always the same rock always up the same hill. The weight of the rock increasing, the manpower decreasing with the incline. Stalemate before the top. Running competition with the rock which is rolling downhill many times faster than the man can push it up. The weight of the rock relatively increasing, the manpower relatively decreasing with the incline. The weight of the rock in absolute terms increasing with each repetition (pushing the rock up, before beside behind the rock: running down). Hope and disappointment. The rolling stone. Reciprocal attrition of man rock hill. To ultimate exhilaration: release of the rock from the achieved summit down into the crevasse on the other side. Or to ultimate exhaustion: in view of the unreachable summit. Or to possible zero: no one moves anything across a flat surface.

To anyone versed in 'Lit-Crit' jargon, such a text will conjure up Roland Barthe's *degré zero* formulation for an *écriture* beyond the modernist tradition: the exhaustion of means, the exhaustion of the author, the evisceration of authority and authentic message. We are left with pure Sisyphean labour, futility, the life of the author reduced to its quintessential despair. But the strange apparition Wilson created for the delivery of this text: part joke, part nightmare – a figuration of the French expression '*graphimane*', or the demented compulsion to transform self into the act of writing – is both irreverent and amusing. It sets the text and evades it. Wilson's staging smiles gently at the pseudo-despair of the writer, while it 'floats' the text – whole and unadulterated – in the performance medium. Meanwhile, the 'Family at Table' tableau continues its simultaneous and silent evolution. A year letter, in a letter he sent to Wilson, Müller wrote, 'The dead are writing with us on the paper of the Future at which flames are already licking from all sides.' The White Scribe passage was unforgettable in performances of *the CIVIL warS*, and Müller's text now conjures for me Wilson's staging, complete with the wonderful actress who played the White Scribe in Cambridge, the late Shirley Wilber. Any allusion to the image will also conjure the text: Wilson's image and Müller's words (via Wilber) have become perfectly fused as experience.

This fusion of word and image has been repeated with each Wilson/Müller collaboration I have witnessed, and I worked with Wilson as his dramaturge in 1991 when we fashioned similar fused motifs out of the text of Ibsen's *When We Dead Awaken*. In that play (Heiner Müller was not involved) I charted the exact sequence of images in Ibsen's text, deliberately paying no regard to logic, story continuity, or narrative progression. We discovered in the resulting lists a haunting image of night trains pausing in deserted stations which had been cut from Robert Brustein's adaptation of the play. Having decided to restore the image to the production, Wilson asked me to fashion a terse, Rilke-like poem out of a page or two of desultory 'ping-pong' dialogue. Once isolated and made concrete by the formal structure of verse, the image was fully detachable, and Wilson 'floated' it like a geode in the ongoing mass of the performance: the poem became a recurrent motif which visited the play like a returning comet.

Wilson's staging of *Alcestis* in 1986, was the next occasion after *the CIVIL warS* on which Wilson and Müller fused text and image in a production at the ART. This time the Müller text was the disturbing *Description of a Picture* and the setting was the talking mummy, steadily and unemotionally 'voicing over' the 'view from beyond the grave' (as Heiner Müller himself described the text) while we who experienced it in performance heard it as purely cadenced sound in a magical dreamscape of mountain crags and ruined classical temples. The progressive horrors described by the words – something clearly related to Müller's own experience of discovering his first wife's suicide – had no correlative 'build' or emotional interpretation in the theatre. The words were treated as eternally recurring patterns of speech, and the dead figure speaking these words was fixed and immobile, embalmed and mounted on the theatre wall above the fray, like the vestige of a past action. These two artists, Wilson and Müller, were indeed giving each other space – space to be two simultaneous and autonomous entities in the same world. It is not a bad definition of the deepest kind of friendship.

The most extensive and most brilliantly achieved of the three collaborations Wilson and Müller brought to the ART was the staging of *Quartet* in 1988, a difficult work based on Choderlos de Laclos's *Les Liaisons Dangereuses*. In his reworking of the novel, Müller has reduced the two principal agents of the novel, the paired seducers Valmont and the Marquise de Merteuil, to figures of pure machination and analysis. They pick their way through a meticulous autopsy of their deadened feelings and decayed motives. The lusts that once animated them to perform acts of depravity has become pure verbal excess, a sort of horrid dry masturbation with words. There is a baroque over-elaboration to the verbal surface – a huge challenge

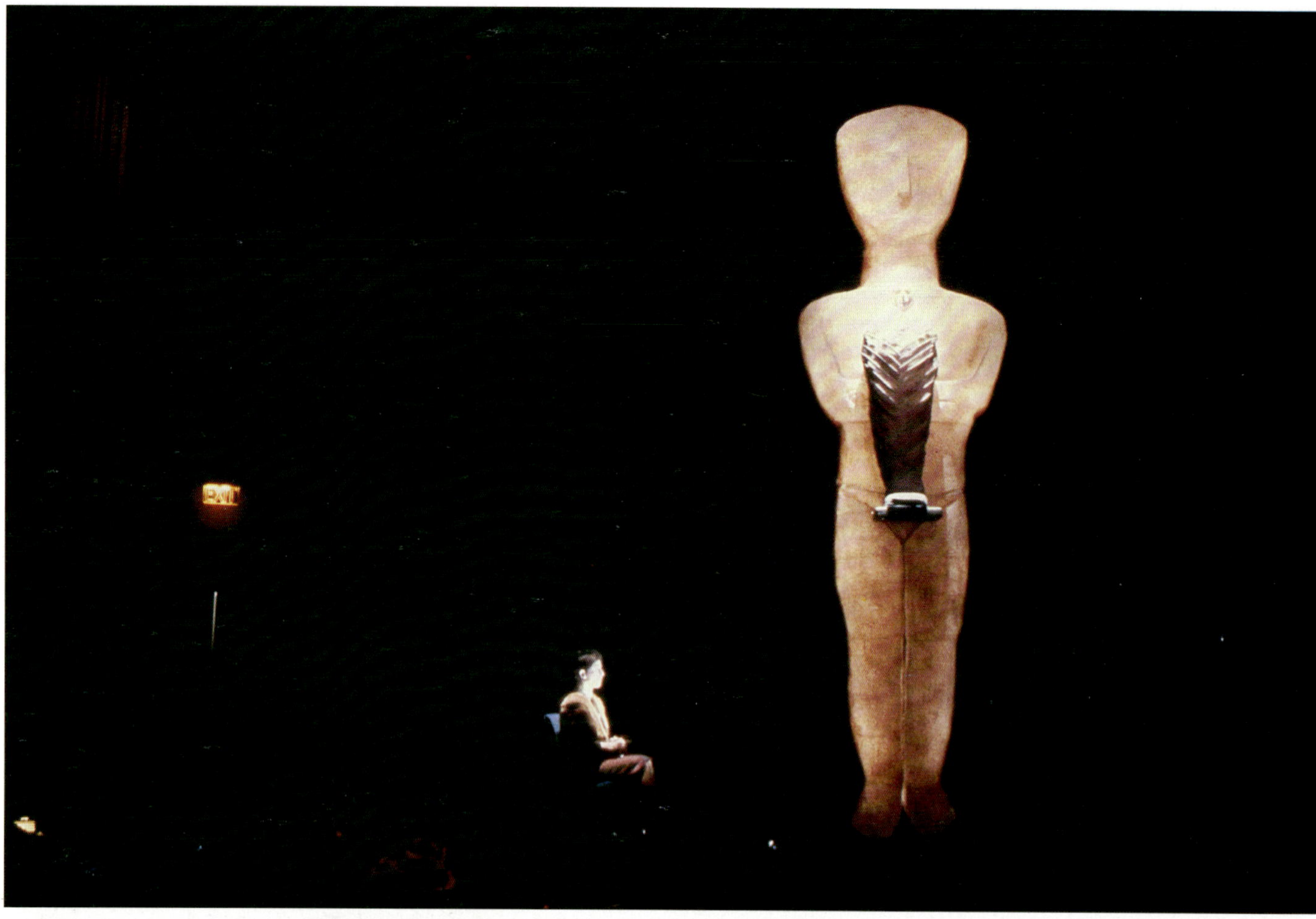

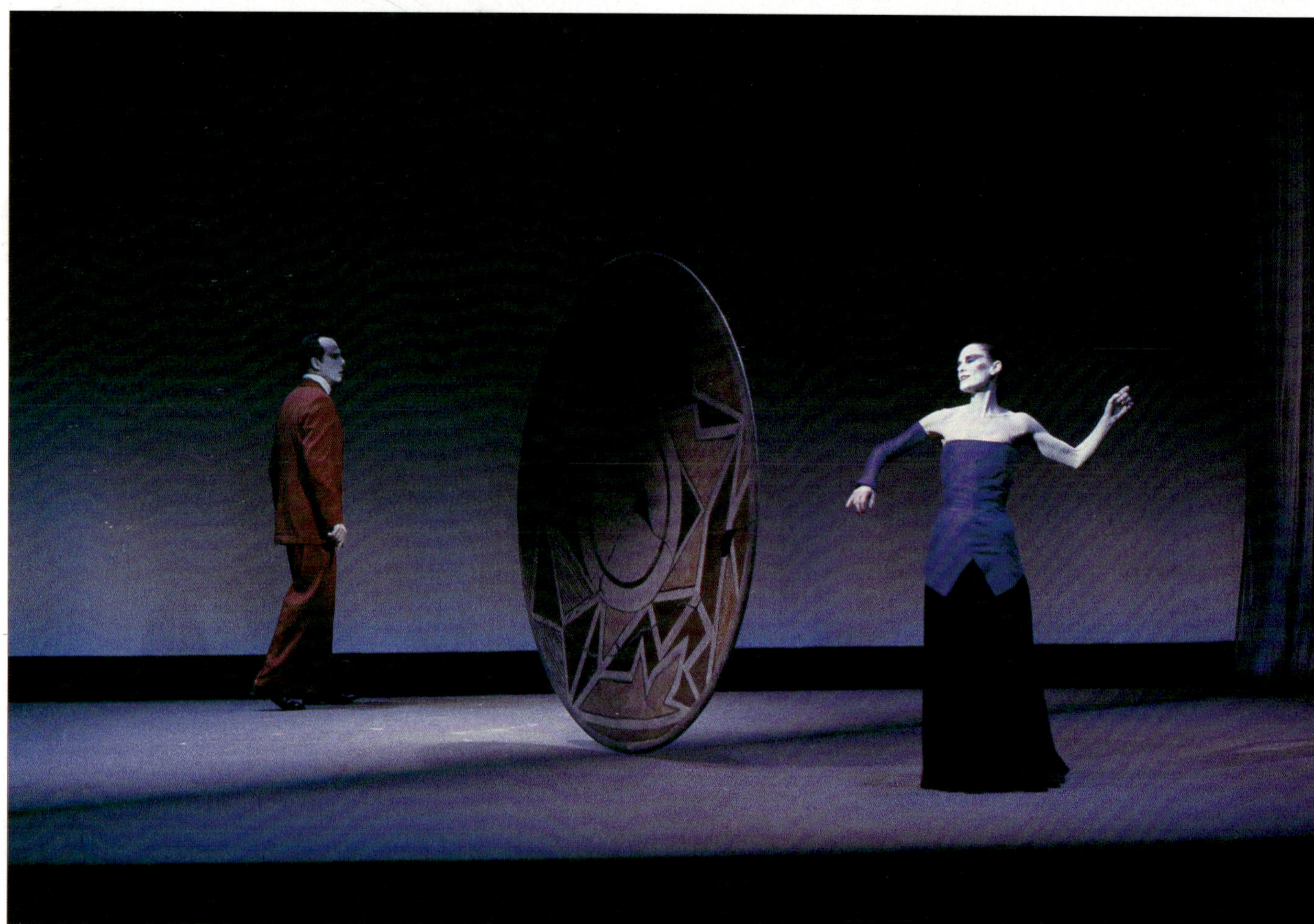

to the translator, Carl Weber yet again, who has been achieving masterpieces of his own in rendering Müller into English.

For this imposing text, scored for only two speakers, Wilson devised a meticulously formal quartet (the mute victim characters were essentially danced in slow mime movements) incised in the theatre with balletic precision. The result was an exquisite chamber concert of movement, light, symmetrical variations and neoclassical balance. No other work of Wilson's that I have seen was so perfect in form, so economical of means and so deeply rooted in the aesthetic of its source 'period.' It revealed the enormous range of a huge plasti-poetic talent, an inner instinct for visual development which is completely equivalent to musical genius. The *mise-en-scène* was as sophisticated, inventive and accomplished in stage terms as the composition of a baroque fugue. *Quartet*, though it was not as popular as Wilson's more sumptuous and operatic spectacles, was one of the finest examples of stage artistry I have ever witnessed. The arduous text of *Quartet* was delivered in clear, dry, cold tones by actors engaged in a stylish, deliberate, enervatingly slow, deliberately cruel and aggressively perverse set of fetishistic rituals. It was like watching insects devour each other in a glass case; it was a view into a still chamber in hell.

It is in contrast to such visions as these that the paradisal Taormina, surrounded as it is with Ionian blue and gold, was surely one of the most ironic of places for Heiner Müller's dark Germanic oeuvre to be celebrated. The usual dreamscape in Müller's work is the nightmare. His imagination is sombre and even macabre, and his work has expressed the frequently unbearable stress and anguish of the German psyche, both in the socialist East and in the capitalist West, since Hitler's downfall. But Wilson's constructions have always lightened this material in the theatre, brought unexpected beauty to the nightmares, and afforded unimaginable relief to visions frequently stifling in their febrile anxieties. From Wilson's point of view, his intent has always been deadly serious – one has only to look at some of the apocalyptic visions he created on video at The Kitchen in New York in the suite of shorts called *Stations* – and yet his artistic disposition in the theatre is cool and detached. In Taormina, Wilson said that his work was 'the opposite of television', and by that he meant that he never makes it his business to illustrate or explicate what is being shown. Wilson is never trying to persuade you that anything in particular is true, but he is doggedly persistent in laying something substantial onto your perception of time; 'My work is full of time . . . Heiner's work is full of time . . . there is no one way through our work'. Here there was one of Wilson's masterful pauses (one of his most powerful resources in the rehearsal hall). As the prospect of reaching his thought with words dissolved in evident futility, Bob Wilson simply added, 'I'm glad you're here, Heiner'.

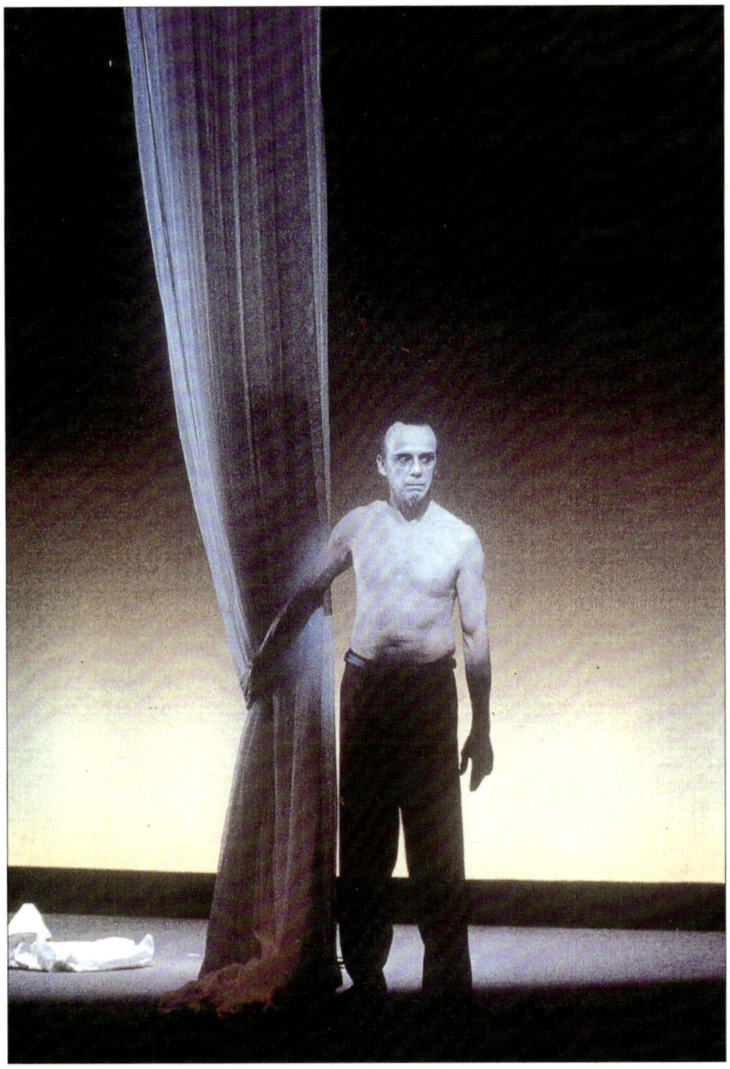

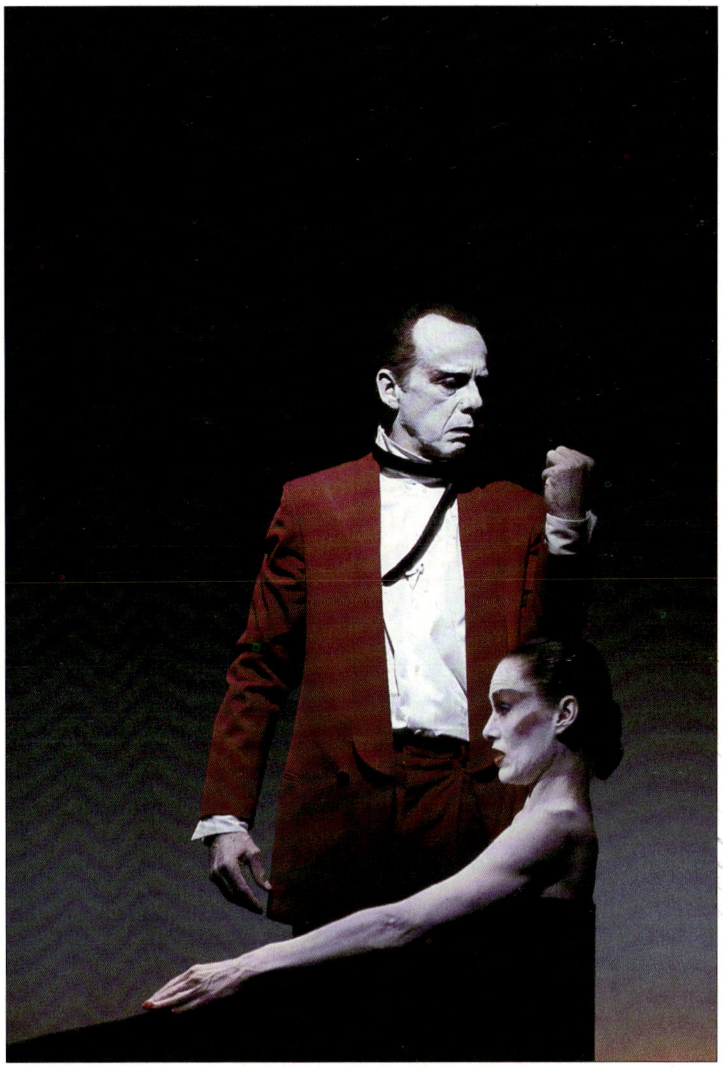

Robert Wilson, PAGE 76: Alcestis; *PAGE 78:* the CIVIL warS; *OPPOSITE, FROM ABOVE:* Alcestis; Quartet; *THIS PAGE:* Quartet

NARRATIVE AND THE WORLD WIDE WEB

Larry Wendt

I feel that the future of writing is in Space, not Time.
William S Burroughs

Artistic endeavours within the electronic media known as *hypertext*[1] have been with us for a few years now; the examples of this way of working describe a specific genre of literature with its own history and particular properties. With the advent of a consumer base for CD-ROM publishing, along with recent developments with its informational big brother, the Internet,[2] activity in hypertext production and theory has recently risen to a fevered pitch. This is particularly the case with the construction and use of the Internet service known as the World Wide Web.[3]

The Web, as it is known casually, makes use of documents that have been prepared with the aid of the hypertext markup language (HTML),[4] and are composed of 'hyperlinks' identified by what is called the Universal Resource Locator (URL). Internet access is now estimated at being around 24 million users,[5] and though only a portion of these have full access to all the Net's services,[6] the numbers who are familiar with this 'new' way of electronic reading and writing has become quite large.

Anticipated by Vannevar Bush's July 1945 essay *As We May Think*,[7] hypertext is a database-like form in which a text, or part of a text, can point towards another part, or any other text or representation. In the digital domain, any feature within a standard file can be made to retrieve another part of the same file, or another text file, a graphic file, a digital audio file, a digital video clip, etc. Access is neither limited by the mere media type that the file represents, nor restricted sequentially to the inherent linear dimensions of older recording forms. In the context of the World Wide Web, access to these various kinds of information files is not limited to a particular location either, but distributed throughout every site which is connected to the Internet. A single Web page[8] has the ability to be a gateway to all the other sites on the Web. In theory and practice, any point in the Web can interpenetrate another; a word can link to another anywhere in the world.[9]

Hypertext author and theorist, Michael Joyce distinguishes two varieties of hypertext.[10] He calls the former 'exploratory hypertext', which is a 'read-only' form that is ultimately fixed in some sort of array. Most of what is available as hypertext presently is of the exploratory variety. The reader is given a finite set of choices from which they must choose from in order to continue the process of reading.[11] A text is presented as a landscape to navigate within; the exploration of such an environment elicits an aesthetic response of sensual discovery and exploration is equated to a form of eroticised learning.[12] Its seductive appeal to the public makes it a form of entertainment.[13]

Hypertext's manifestation as a way of working in art, often betrays this utilitarian history, and it is difficult to see it ever breaking away from these less than aspiring associations, along with even more diminished characterisations of hyper-literature being just a form of 'multiple-choice poetry', 'stories with footnotes', or 'narrative as video game'. In this portrayal, hypertext seduces the reader into believing that their choices are somehow significant to a personal understanding of the material which the author lays forth; that their cognitive association powers have magically been improved rather than being just another Pavlovian knee jerk to drilled lessons of common-practice, sequential logic.[14]

That the initial topography of material does not have to be followed or that some connections between the material which the author did not foresee can be made by the reader, does not particularly mean that a radical displacement between the reader, the author, and the artificiality of age-old hierarchies of power and control has occurred. Rather than being a starting point to allow for new insights into reason through the technique of playful exploration, such a way of working can instead continue to denigrate an objectively critical approach to the personal acquisition of knowledge: the actual processes of non-critical acceptance, low esteem for the individual, and reduced expectations are programmed into the reader (or viewer) with an ever more efficient and chilling technology.

Joyce calls the second form of hypertext 'constructive hypertext', which is a 'read-write' form, where the reader is empowered to give 'birth to the true electronic text'. Constructive hypertext is an alternative, though somewhat utopian vision, of our on-going era of better personal control of individual possibilities through technology. On a practical level, the realisation of constructive hypertext, has much in common with a previous kind of computer programme known as an outline processor. These 'knowledge amplification systems' allowed the user to organise quickly jotted down notes in a conveniently accessible database and from which one could build upon.

By allowing a completely reciprocal exchange between author and reader and breaking down all of the barriers between them, the text is no longer a rigid collection of rules.[15] One is allowed to alter a developing body of knowledge which can continue to be extended by subsequent readers.[16] As technologically extended literature, constructive hypertext can never exist as a self-contained, user-friendly, commodity, but rather it is something which will always be in the state of becoming a revolutionary art that burns itself up as quickly as it is replenished on the forefront of creativity. It can not be extinguished, co-opted, or 'televised' by those ideological forces which have become used up, worn out, or bartered off.

Back in the good old days when the technologies of writing and reading were only available to the select few, oral tradition reigned supreme as a means to impart cultural insight and experience.

Narrative was a living organic thing which articulated and elaborated every complexity of human interaction with each retelling. A single anonymous storyteller would pass their tale to a listener, who would make some subjective response which would change the tale as they themselves retold it. A narrative was transformed slowly by time, parts were condensed, expanded, mixed up, lost, reinvented, etc, until it fit the society like an old shoe, it resembled its original like a river bed resembled the mountain it was carved from. The old-time storyteller weaved a sequence of events in their narratives that would exist outside of time.

Meanwhile, the printed word branded the text onto time. Before the invention of movable type, the text often existed as a floor plan for an illuminated manuscript: ornamental gesture was often given more significance than the textural accuracy of the reproduction, and a lexicography was largely just a pantomime. A committee of monks preserved the sacred integrity of the text despite their lapses in precision by encrusting the printed word with an articulated visual dimension. The emphasis upon the ocular was a celebratory link to that which was deemed holy. The text was transformed by an act of worship into an object of God.[17] Copies that were made of less ceremonial texts were treated with a much more objective brand of processing, and though 'mistakes' were still made, the printed word was less likely to undergo the temporal forces that effected oral documentation. The word as print was an idea that eventually became frozen in time like an insect stuck in amber. The construction of the illuminated book, however, continues to exist in space as an artifact of architecture rather than a catalogue of history.

The Gutenberg Revolution blew this dichotomy all to hell. Movable type, flattened the peculiarities of text to the boundaries of the page. Typos were reduced to just so much noise created by sloppy proofreaders rather than the grit that some scribe could cover up in a pearl of zoomorphic design. The tale was confined within the homogenised rows of fonts within the object of a book – sanitised by such technical processing, narrative became a discrete sequence of events. Like fate in a Greek tragedy, narrative's plodding movement was as immutable as death. The cloning of narratives as an easily handled, mass-produced multiple meant that it could be appreciated remotely as the actual narrator became nonexistent and virtual, just as the ideal listener was to become.

The secular words of humanity, like the words of gods before them, were preserved outside time (though a little less fancy and at bargain basement prices) and narration continued to exist but only as the husk of its former self. The heart and soul had been amputated by the new technology. The social activity of sitting around listening to a teller of tales was collapsed into the solitary activity of an individual reading a book. The true narrator's abandoned real estate was parcelled off and sold to the highest bidder. Hack scribblers became deified as really interesting characters, the cult of the personality, and the talk show host was born. The writings of the select were worn bare by the tweedy banality of committees, to become the foundations for factories for institutionalised learning. That knowledge which could not be codified in print, was liquidated as being insignificant. That which remained of the rest of us, ended up sitting around reading trashy romance novels and wondering what is good on TV tonight.

Near the end of the last century, the electric light was invented.

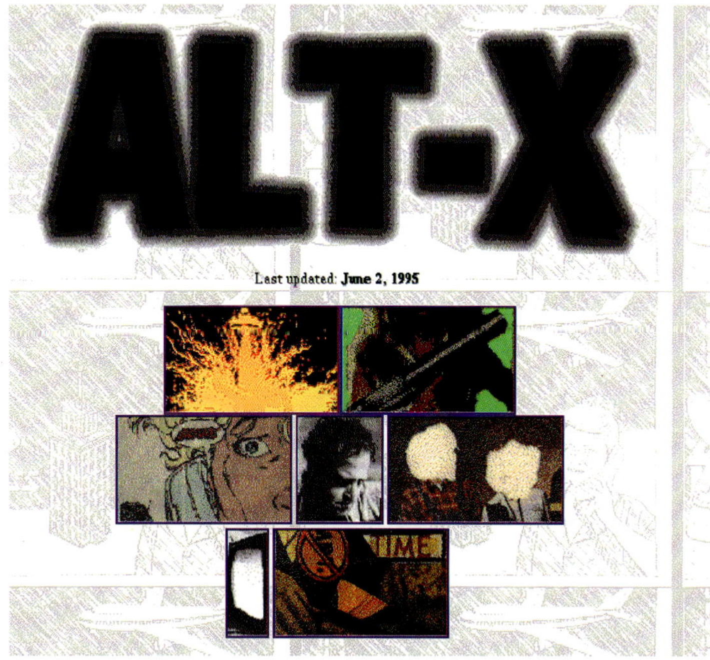

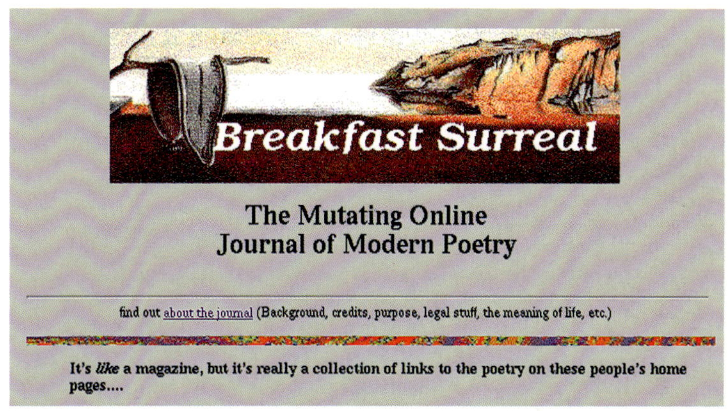

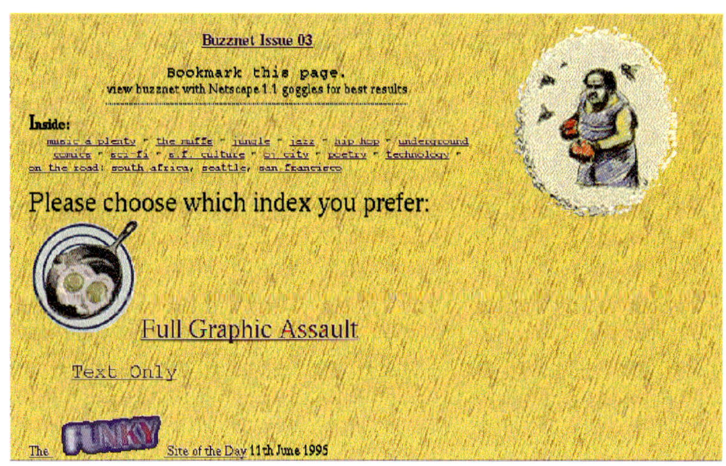

FROM ABOVE: URL:http://marketplace.com/alt.x/althome.html; URL:http://www.indirect.com/www/warren/surreal.html; URL:http://www.hooked.net/buzznet/index.html

The ensuing worldwide electrification which occurred in the 50 some odd years that followed, was fundamentally and pervasively responsible for a change in the way people lived, interacted and thought on a day to day basis.[18] We find a stratifying break in culture before and after electrification, as if some great comet hit and wiped out everything archaic in conception. The lost history of the preceding personal life can be sifted out from the deposits of art and thought that remain.

It is difficult to say at this moment[19] if indeed the invention of digital computers, and the resultant networking of information that they contain, will have a similarly pervasive effect upon culture into the next century. Or, if like the heresy of movable type, we will again be jettisoned to yet another level of indirection between experience and thought, and continue to be lost in that hall of mirrors of mass senselessness. The information revolution may only be a transitional technology to something around the corner. It is a moving target and we have had only a short glimpse of its potentials and its failures. That there is no Hugo Ball, Velimir Khelbnikov, or Marcel Duchamp for the networked age of hypertext is perhaps significant, though there again it is perhaps too soon to tell.[20]

If hypertext had not been used as an organisational feature of the World Wide Web, it is hardly doubtful that some other Internet service would have arisen which would made use of its paradigm. Because of the non-hierarchical, distributed nature of the Net, finding a way of linking up bits and pieces of widely scattered information became a necessity with the increased growth of digitally accessible information. Even though the amount of recorded information which exists in a digital format is a small percent of the total, it became clear from the onset that digital access of materials did not need to be limited by hierarchically-based index systems.

That hypertext is a convergence between computer science and contemporary literary theory is a point which has often been made by George P Landow.[21] He sees hypertext as a kind of a Post-Modern laboratory where the ideas of critics like Roland Barthes, Jean Baudrillard, and Jacques Derrida have a sentient reality. The empowerment of the active reader over the passive reader as the result of being projected simultaneously through every point of a multiplicity in hypertext, signifies the death rattle of the late age of print.[22] Much of what is being written as hypertext theory evokes the ghost of Marshal McLuhan, and the word is conceived as assuming a new sensuality through its electronic conversion in the Global Village. The light passively reflected to the eye from tactile printer's ink on a page is exchanged for digital electronic ink being projected directly onto the back of the brain as if it were a movie screen. The word is televised as something approaching pure information and in the case of hypertext at least, the medium is definitely the message.

In some dim way perhaps, the use of hypertext has moved text back towards the medieval. That aspects of a document can be purposely designed to signify other objects is a form of monkish encrustation. The delimitating features within the quanta of the word, line, page, book, etc are starting to become fuzzy. The concept of publisher is starting to collapse[23] as writers and readers are not as sure about the boundaries and what their responsibilities to the text are. That part of a text can exist virtually as a link that can not be succinctly reduced to a sequential sequence of printed words on a page, is significant of a different way in which we have to perceive and to manipulate language.

If narrative has come to be known as the causal sequence of events since Gutenberg's invention froze the word into multiples of print, then a singular, non-causal, non-sequential flow of ideas can be seen as a form of 'anti-narrative' representing everything which common narratives have come to be known as not to be. It is that aspect of human communication which has been excised, domesticated and sanitised as the print media gained its position of acceptance and predominance as the 'truth'. Anti-narrative has its roots in orality, those things which cannot be written down and that hide in structures of myths and mute gestures. It is expansive, delusional, and self articulating in ways that traditional narrative is linear, compact and succinct. Anti-narrative is both fragmentary and redundant – there are pieces left out. The main part of its action occurs outside the boundaries of the page (or whatever other forms of delimitating structures it might employ). The reader has to 'connect the dots' to make the picture and map out a resonant after image of the narrative from within, rather than being forced at face value to absorb into memory an artifice from without. In the language of the 20th century, anti-narrative is the mechanism of collage and the textual 'cut-up'. It is what 'surfing the Net' aspires to become.

At this moment, the World Wide Web is a particularly conducive environment for a drift upon surface appeals. Following the ebb and flow of fancy on a fragmentary, non-contiguous surface,[24] one is directed towards a multitude of strange attractors, and outside the city limits of recognisable, traditional, knowledge neighbourhoods. Despite the choices of material largely reflecting the social class of those who originally built the Net, as it opens up to more people one finds themselves out into those low-rent neighbourhoods where the buses are not running any more: chased there by the dogs of their desires, to the place where nothing is rehearsed and everything is always new.

That this idealised view of an immersion into cyberspace [25] has to depend upon the continued anarchy[26] of the network is perhaps the downside to all of this. That parts of the Net could collapse in uselessness from the excessive chaos and 'spamming'[27] is a possibility, though substitutes would most certainly take its place. The Net has been in operation too long now: it was designed for defence and it knows how to protect itself. Not only is the Internet resistant to nuclear attack but it has also resisted up to this point any major changes in its distributed power structure. That it is likely to be unplugged, reduced to mush by an overzealous legislator, or sold to a single company in the near future appears to be more than just a little remote.

Commercial concerns are however, rushing in and attempting to cash into the Internet. Their activities are reminiscent of the 'gold rush' of the 80s, when new markets opened up in the Eastern bloc countries after the walls went down. Every inch of the Internet is under construction as the shopping malls of the future are being moved in. The Net is similar to what used to be called East Berlin; what exists this week will be completely different the next. Wads of money are being spent developing imitative exhibits and demonstrations, and the 'provincial', old west shoot-em-up, 'flaming' adolescent atmosphere common to older Net activity and discussion groups, is being replaced by a gentrified and refined self-censored slickness. The hopeful smile of civility from which a quick, smarmy gleam of gold can be seen, has made its presence felt on the Web – entrepreneurs and their bit players madly rush ahead in search of the new hoola-hoop.

Despite all the still tacky paint, eye candy, and 'under construction' signs, there is more to all of this than just a handful of quickly cut-out, cardboard examples. It is rather clear even at this point, that the precepts for this technology have been fully absorbed by our culture, and there is no turning back. Despite its shortcomings, the Net is quickly becoming a practical necessity.[28] Its future lies at the point where it is difficult to imagine how we ever did things without it. Though it is perhaps doubtful to many that life on the Infobahn will ever equal or accede the claims of innovation and totality that has been placed upon it, it nonetheless has had and will continue to have a very profound influence upon our culture.

Notes

1 This was a term coined in 1965 by Ted Nelson in *The Hypertext*, a paper delivered to a national conference of the Association for Computing Machinery, describing a branching, non-sequential form of writing that could exist in a computer environment. A victim of Attention Deficit Disorder (or 'Hummingbird mind'), Nelson invented hypertext both as a specific strategy to keep track of his own thoughts, and as a more general response to his sense that the preservation of knowledge might save humanity from repeating the same destructive errors. Gary Wolf's *The Curse of Xanadu*, in *Wired* (June 1995), p137, documents the ill-fated attempt by Nelson and his associates to realises the 'docuverse' in their 'Xanadu' project. As Stuart Moulthrop's 'Getting Over the Edge' observes, 'Hypertexts cannot be translated into print. They retain a dynamic or "interactive" component which no non-electronic reduction can adequately represent.' (URL:http://www.ubalt.edu/www/ygcla/sam/essays/surface.html).

2 In its present incarnation as the Internet, the digital information network first came about in 1969 as an experiment by a group funded by the Defense Advanced Research Project Agency (DARPA). ARPANET, as the network was known, investigated computerised telephonic information transference strategies which could survive direct nuclear attack by segmenting messages into 'packets' concurrently sent along several routes. Even if part of the network was blasted away, enough of the packets would arrive at the destination site to provide a clear message once it was reassembled. Research scientists in particular found ARPANET useful to transfer information and queries about their latest work in an electronic form imitating short mail messages, known as E-mail. Faster digital telephone equipment allowed larger amounts of data (or any other information converted into a digital format, such as images or sound) to be transferred relatively quickly. ARPANET became the Internet by combining and merging with other regional networks such as JANET (UK) and BITNET (USA). The availability of powerful low-cost personal computers and high speed telephone connections increasingly eroded the high costs of access to the Internet. But true 'backbone' access fast enough to allow real-time video and sound through a T1 or better kind of connection is still fairly expensive (starting at about $1000 a month for lease charges), with resultant effects on the overall Net culture.

3 The World Wide Web has its origins in March of 1989 at CERN, the European Particle Physics Institute in Geneva, when Tim Berners-Lee proposed a hypertext tool to aid the high-energy physics community around the world in the sharing of information. Reformulated with Robert Cailliau in a design document published in November 1990, the first

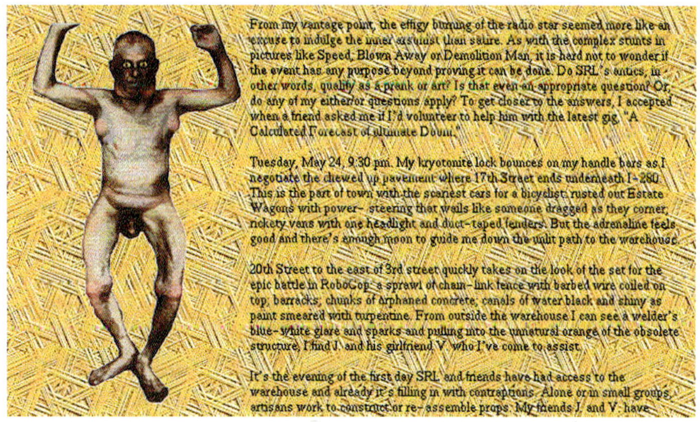

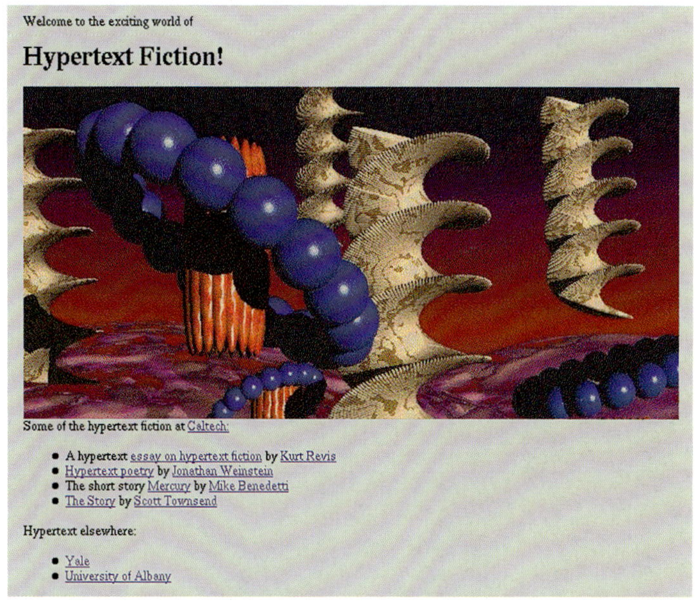

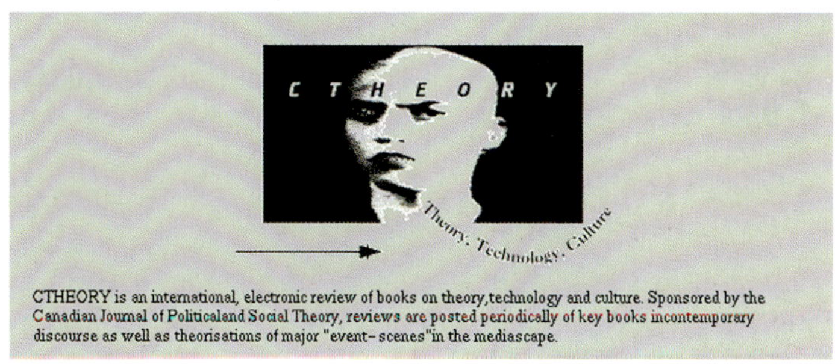

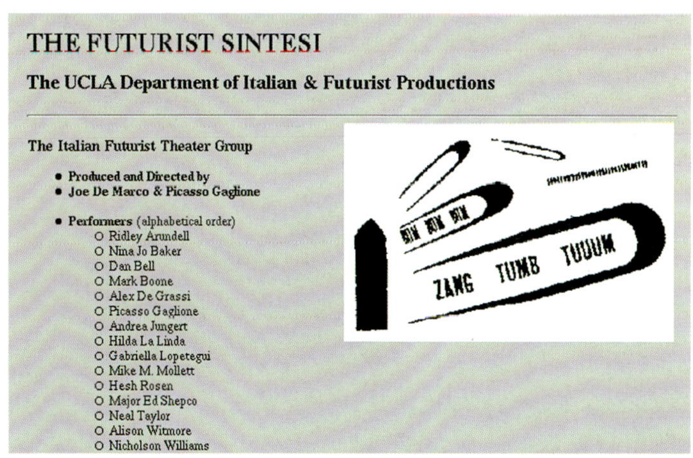

FROM ABOVE: Buzznet number 3; URL:http://www.ugcs.caltech.edu/~benedett/hyper.html; URL:http://english.hss.cmu.edu/ctheory/ctheory.html; URL:http://pharmdec.wustl.edu/juju/surr/Futurism/FUT-MENU.html

working version of the World Wide Web was released by CERN in May of 1991. Widespread interest in the service did not blossom until about February 1993, when Marc Andreessen, then a student in the National Center of Supercomputing Applications (NCSA) at the University of Illinois in Urbana-Champaign, developed an easy to use and maintain, graphical Web browser for X-windows called Mosaic. Among available browsers Andreessen's commercial venture, Netscape, appears the most popular at the moment. (URL: http://www.w3.org/hypertext/WWW/History.html)

4 By 'markup' we mean all the information contained in a computer file other than the text itself, which computer programs are able to manipulate texts in useful ways. The term is borrowed from the history of printing, where markup referred to the notations made in the margins of a text to guide the compositor in the layout of the text. Markup intended to specify the proper layout or presentation of a text is still the most common type of markup in computer files. From *Living with the Guidelines: An Introduction to TEI Tagging* [an excerpt] by Lou Burnard and CM Sperberg-McQueen (URL: http://www.sil.org/sgml/sgml.html). HTML is born into a long standing community of standards for electronic documentation called the Standard Generalized Markup Language (SGML). Any deviations from this standard are met with complex discussions and controversies which bog down any rapid changes. The hypertext paradigm has only been superficially realised in this limiting markup environment. An extension of the capabilities of HTML is being developed as HTML+, and there are other attempts to get around the Cartesian graphical restraints of HTML with such three-dimensional systems like VRML (Virtual Reality Markup Language) (URL: http://www.eit.com/vrml/).

5 *Managing Internet Information Services*, Cricket Liu, Jerry Peek, Russ Jones, Bryan Buus and Andrian Nye, Sebastopo, O'Reilly & Associates, Inc, December 1994, p6.

6 Having a large number of computers with varying features, strengths, and weaknesses, all communicating along a single established channel allowed for a simple and direct control of any digital information available on the network. Following the development of E-mail, List servers allowed individuals to send a message simultaneously to several individuals or subscribers, while readers could E-mail an instruction to a 'robotic' list server to automatically receive a document on demand or perform a complex search function of the site's archives. With the telnet feature one can connect a 'stupid' computer up to a 'smart' one and perform complex operations and searches that the weaker (and less expensive) unit was unable to perform. With the File Transfer Protocol (ftp) feature, one can universally transfer data, graphical files, or whatever, irrespective of concern of how electronically different two computers are. Anonymous ftp archives allow the storage and retrieval of freely available information to anyone with an account on Internet. The Usenet service (developed from the general system 'News' features of the network) became a convenient method for users who shared a common interest to transfer recent ideas to one another. The Internet Relay Chat (IRC) lets one 'talk' (or 'listen' in the case of voyeuristic 'lurkers') in real-time typed messages with other users of the service anywhere in the world. In turn, still more elaborate schemes to locate and retrieve information came about. Archie was developed as a 'search engine' to go through all the anonymous ftp archives to trace the location of a particular topic one was seeking, while Gopher provides an easy to use navigational tool to 'burrow' from one computer to the next and to connect to specified information archives. Specific search engines known as *Veronica* and *Jughead* (of course!), are useful aids to navigate among the Gopher holes. The World Wide Web incorporates all the previous services that have been available on the Internet, as well as providing a functional metaphor to access non-text based information.

7 Published in *The Atlantic Monthly*. A HTML version of the text prepared in April 1994 by Denys Duchier appears at URL: http://www.csi.uottawa.ca/~dduchier/misc/vbush/as-we-may-think.html.

8 That these things are still called a 'page' reinforces the recognisable form of a previous technology and is indicative of the early, imitative phase of this technological art. Generally, the only divisions within a flat document file are subjectively defined by what the viewer can comfortably read on their cathode ray tube at any one time; this often has more to do with optiomology than the resolution limits of the CRT monitor.

9 In practice this is largely inhibited by the type of Internet access a user may have. On the lower-cost kinds of systems popular at this time, access to static pictures and texts on the Web is reasonable with only a short delay in response between the client and the host computer. Sound and video files on the other hand are usually quite large and have to be first downloaded in their entirety to the user's computer before being 'played' at a conventional scanning rate (which is usually much higher than the data transfer rates on the low-cost connections). This is often far too time-consuming for the impatient general user.

10 Notes Toward an Unwritten Non-Linear Text: 'The Ends of Print Culture' (a work in progress) by Michael Joyce, *Postmodern Culture* v.2 n.1, September, 1991 (URL: http://jefferson.village.virginia.edu/pmc/joyce.991). Essay republished in Joyce's *Of Two Minds: Hypertext Pedagogy and Poetics*, Ann Arbor, The University of Michigan Press, 1995.

11 One finds it ironic that after almost 50 years of mind-numbing television, one is expected to read as well as to make choices again. That such activity has become supposedly so extremely popular is also completely mystifying. I have long suspected that our 'decision-making' genes have actually been burned out many years ago by TV emitted X-rays, and most people cannot decide what they want for lunch, much less figure out what they want to read. More books end up being bought than read because we like to buy stuff. Books are a 'cool thing to have laying around' since they remind us of potentials which we are now too lazy to explore. Building a learning environment that is more like play than work, grates against those minds which have been trained to form logical separations between such things.

12 Such exploratory hypertext has a lot in common with the 'programmed learning' texts used in education during the early 60s, where students were led onto the next stage of instruction within a 'work book', depending on how correctly questions were answered within the present lesson. As a form of mechanised learning it was easy to convert into a crude hypertext-like format once inexpensive personal computers became available to educators. The educational acceptance of Computer Assisted Instruction (CAI) soon became widespread in grade school and high school environments where it was believed to be a realistic alternative to decreasing public education budgets. The superficial promise of this type of educational approach far exceeded its meagre results.

13 'Net Surfing' is a variant of 'Channel Surfing' that is popular among those television viewers who can afford a TV with an infrared remote control. In channel surfing, one is only given one dimension to move in – channels are selected sequentially (non-sequential selections are usually too much of a bother for the experienced channel surfer/couch potato). The operator uses the remote control as a tool to go up and down the

television dial seeking the thrill of the ride. The trick is to find something which attracts the attention longer than it takes to select the next channel. In the case of Net surfing there is an array of multiple dimensions which can be selected non-sequentially. One explores the surface appeals of a more or less infinite field (since the variety of documents, finite as it is, is generally beyond most human attention spans now). However, since critical decision making powers are at an all time low, this nomadic activity is largely a passive response to boredom: it is being directed in absentia by the Net which like TV, guides the choices of viewing (usually through elaborate, eye appealing, graphic images). The viewer accepts what they see uncritically as the truth. For those decisionally-impaired individuals who are still overwhelmed by the number of TV channels available, there is on the Web a 'roulette' page which selects Web sites at random, allowing total non-decision by the viewer (URL: http://kuhttp.cc.ukans.edu/cwis/organizations/kucia/uroulette/uroulette.html).

14 Even the more positive aspects of the exploratory approach are suspect. Michael Joyce (see note 10) describes a form of 'transitional exploratory hypertext' in which 'the text does not transform or rearrange itself to embody (any) current state', but remains 'a marriage without issue'. 'Each of the reader's additions lies outside the flow of the text . . . The text may be seen as leading to what she adds to it, yet her addition is marginal, ghettoized.'

15 That precursors to this idea of constructive hypertexts have existed in the arts of the past is something which can be firmly speculated upon. The commentaries around the main body of the text in the *Talmud* is a well-known example. Another example which instantly comes to mind is that terminus at the end of the Modernist novel, James Joyce's *Finnegans Wake.* See Donald F Theall in his essay, 'Beyond the Orality/Literacy Dichotomy: James Joyce and the Pre-history of Cyberspace', *Postmodern Culture* v.2 n.3, May 1992 (URL: http://jefferson.village.virginia.edu/pmc/theall.592). A proper reading of this 'cross-word puzzlers' bible' requires a group of an indefinite number of speakers talking simultaneously. The *Wake* has inspired others to create pieces as a form of reading. For example, John Cage used it as a meta-text to create mesostics for *Writing Through Finnegans Wake* as well as a meta-score for *Roaratorio.* The *Wake* prompts individuals to fill its narrow margins with notes about all kinds of arcane references as well as to notate repeated resonances to other sections of the work. The 'Joyce Industry' which has employed many, pumps out volumes and volumes of dictionaries, lexicons, censuses, and gazetteers. As students we carried arm loads of books to our *Wake* seminars, and our copies of the text were split open like an over-ripe watermelon from all the inserted notes – held precariously together by a peculiar arrangement of rubber bands, paper clips and gaffer's tape. The text educated us in the intricate and arcane philosophies of Giambattista Vico and Giordano Bruno, in linguistics and world myth, in operas and bawdy drinking songs, in Irish politics and Dublin street maps, and a myriad of other things. We dreamt the dream of hypertext long before we ever knew that it was there.

16 Historically this ability has not been necessarily restricted by inadequate technologies or low public interest but rather by certain antiquated economic notions which date back to at least the mercantile trading companies of the 17th century. As worn out as they may be, these concepts are probably immutable within our society. There is a similar problem in music which can be exemplified with John Oswald's development of 'plunderphonics': a compositional technique which manipulates pre-existing recorded materials in order to produce a completely new

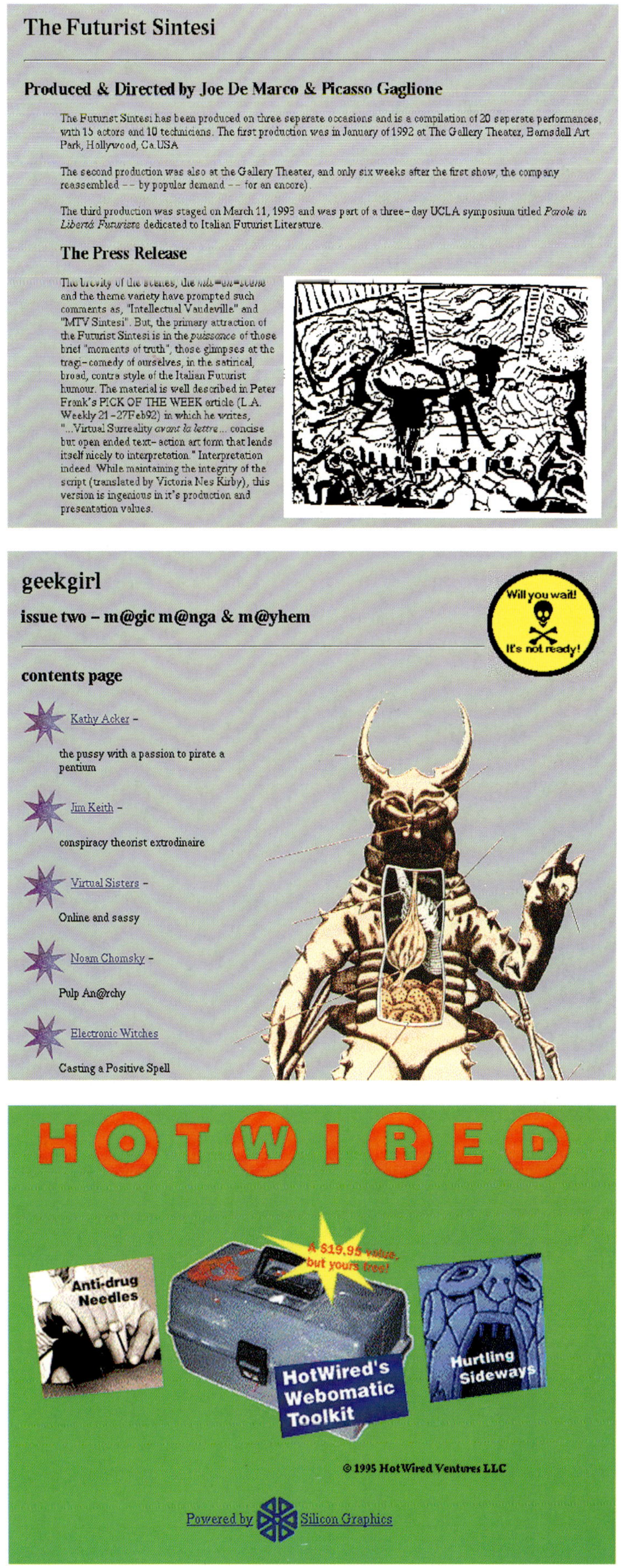

FROM ABOVE: Futurism; URL:http://www.next.com.au/spyhood/geekgirl/index.html; URL:http://hard.wired.com/

composition. A few of his pieces got him in trouble with a particular record company and his work was destroyed. Pretty good methods of securing copyright information by encryption have existed on the Net for some time now. Despite what some journalists may think, the Net is neither more nor less secure in the old-fashion sense than any other form of commercial exchange.

17 In her comments about one of the more famous Western illuminated manuscripts, the 11th-century Irish Gospel, *The Book of Kells*, Françoise Henry comments upon 'the extraordinary carelessness with which the text has been handled'. 'It looks as if the Kells scribe did not care very much, knowing that nobody was going to use the volume for reference, and that it had, first of all, to be a beautiful object . . . the fantastic lavishness of the decoration and the unusually large size of the book show clearly that it was an altar-book, made to be used for liturgical reading, and probably intended to be displayed open as a sumptuous ornament during ceremonies when pomp was especially required'. *The Book of Kells: Reproductions From the Manuscript in Trinity College Dublin*, Alfred A Knopf, New York, 1974, p153.

18 A technology is not merely a system of machines with certain functions; it is part of a social world. Electrification is not an implacable force moving through history, but a social process that varies from one time period to another and from one culture to another . . . Put another way, each technology is an extension of human lives . . . its social history has almost no limits, traversing histories of the city, transportation, labour, the professions, industry, business, engineering, physics, women, agriculture, medicine, advertising, art, architecture, and more'. From the preface of David E Nye, *Electrifying America: Social Meanings of a New Technology*, Massachusetts Institute of Technology, Cambridge, 1991.

19 In the more 'established' and 'accepted' forms of mass media, not a day passes without some wild promise or fearful forewarning about how access to the Net will effect the human race. Self-appointed media 'experts' project two models of our soon to be networked future. In one, people enter an elevated state of electronic grace as they jack into the totality of recorded human experience, simultaneously flitting around all points along the matrix of human endeavour. The other model depicts a Hieronymus Bosch-like hell of utter banality in which the latest trendy info gimcracks and gewgaws wreak havoc along the informational thoroughfares and human byways of interaction, as civilisation collapses into just so much random static. As I wait for something 'better than TV' to appear, I suspect that the reality is somewhere in between these two visions.

20 Back in the late 50s, Henri Chopin, in an attempt to extend the power of his own personal poetry, created a type of sonic work which he called *poésie sonore* with the aid of a tape recorder. The commercial availability of audio recorders which used plastic tape were barely ten years old at the time and even though the technology was new, the piece of equipment Chopin used was second-hand and well-worn. He would use this piece of equipment 'improperly' by doing such things as defeating the erase head with match sticks to overlay one recording over another or switching the worn-out, no longer discrete, tape speed changer to achieve a glissando. But with this ill-used, worn-out technology, he was able to produce a completely gestural, unique and non-semantic poetry by recording his own vocal utterances many times. Fellow Parisians François Dufrêne and Bernard Heidsieck made similar literary experiments around the same time, initially largely without knowledge of one another. Dufrêne discovered a new sonority in amplified vocal recordings which he was able to develop acoustically in a vocal technique which he called *crirythme*: much like indigenous people vocally mimicking the sounds of their musical instruments, Dufrêne was a modern primitive mimicking the processes of a new technology, and in the process created another form of gestural poetry that was completely different from Chopin's. For Heidsieck on the other hand, the tape recorder became a means to amplify semantic gestures rather than vocal gestures, allowing the projection of words off the *poème partition*'s printed page, into a highly individual sonic space, replete with multiple readings. Offering unique responses to a new technology, Chopin, Dufrêne and Heidsieck were just three of the many sound poets extending conventional literary forms beyond recognition. Though highly marginalised, most of these practitioners became known to one another by the late 60s, and a 'network' was created among them by the old fashioned ways of physical travel and mail. Publications, manifestos, translations, histories, anthologies, recordings and international festivals consolidated their research, and second and third generations of sound poets continue to provide new ideas and material for a still, somewhat obscure area of literary experimentalism. The number of individuals active in this area are relatively small and are often obscured and hidden by slightly more accepted and somewhat similar experiments in performance poetry, visual poetry, avant-garde jazz and computer music, though often these areas are equally unknown and misunderstood by many. We have seen that hypertext has much to offer in technological latitude to provide a similar breeding ground for extended literary experimentalism. That much of it is still stuck representing older, more recognisable forms is disheartening. Like the early phases of most technologically influenced art of this century, much of hypertext art is largely imitative and demonstrative of the 'weird stuff' that it can do, rather than forming a cohesive way of working. Its theoretical documentation and manifestos promise far more results than are evident so far. One thinks back to Italian Futurism at the heart of all this century's technological art, and of Franz Marc's observation to Wassily Kandinsky: 'I cannot free myself from the strange contradiction that I find their ideas, at least for the main part, brilliant, but am in no doubt whatsoever as to the mediocrity of their work.' In attempting to dispute such statements, one dreams that there is another Chopin out there: secreted away in cyberspace with a beatup old laptop computer and a cheesy modem, living in a place that is as far away as can be like DeView, Arkansas or Lübbenau, Lusatia. Producing jaw-dropping work and waiting to link up to another Dufrêne and Heidsieck.

21 George P Landow, *The Convergence of Contemporary Critical Theory and Technology*, The Johns Hopkins University Press, Baltimore, 1992. See also George P Landow, ed, *Hyper/Text/Theory*, The Johns Hopkins University Press, Baltimore, 1994, and Paul Delany and George P Landow, eds, *Hypermedia and Literary Studies*, The MIT Press, Cambridge, 1991.

22 I have been to the places where books go when they die. No book over $5. Sold by the pound or by size. Handy for speaker stands, shim stocks, land fills and flower pressing.

23 For a couple of thousand bucks for gear and some spare change for monthly access fees, any self-proclaimed thinker who believes that they really have something important to say, can 'broadcast' to an audience of millions, 24 hours a day on the World Wide Web. A homepage can easily be registered on significant Web search sites, and the individual is empowered to reach everyone on the Net. An individual's homepage is often a personalised and unique attempt at constructive hypertexts, and is historically derivative of the personalised 'signature' boiler plate at the

end of E-mail messages. But there is still only a small percentage of public 'space' in this society in which an audience for new or 'difficult' works can exist. In regards to electronic distribution of contemporary poetry, Charles Bernstein writes, 'I don't believe that technology creates improvement, but rather that we need to use the new technologies in order to preserve the limited cultural spaces we have created through the alternative, nonprofit literary presses and magazines.' From 'WARNING – POETRY AREA: Publics Under Constructions' (URL: http://gopher:// wings.buffalo.edu:70/hh/internet/library/e-journals/ub/rift/authors/bernstein/publics).

24 That such a partial reflection of the body of human information is being passed off as a totality under the Emperor's new clothes of technology is another quagmire that the Net can fall into. One would hope for more contiguity as the Net matures, rather than just displaying a view of information that is distorted by the limitations of the particular social group which accesses it. That the succinct anecdotal 'sound bite' and 'buzz word' acronym is replacing the encyclopedia fits well with the now popular world theme of the 'dumbing' of the public mind. Keeping up with the increased fragmentation of a continuous surface of knowledge is indeed the same problem which first led Bush, Nelson, and others to formulate their concepts. At some point, the associated links stretch beyond their breaking points and intellectual connections spill out like quicksilver and into a thousand directions of dissipation, exhaustion and entropic heat death.

25 Phillip K Dick's amphetamine-fuelled, 'Can-D' visions of parallel universes and conspiracies of the 60s were translated by William Gibson into the cyberpunk milieu of the 80s, via the images of the future portrayed in Ridley Scott's cinematic adaptation of one of Dick's stories that was given a title borrowed from William S Burroughs: *Blade Runner*.

26 The hypertext metaphor, like many such metaphors, is a particularly Utopian view of information retention in the late age of literacy. Its attempted realisation has led to a chaotic sphere of human interaction that has all the sensibility of a boom town. Whole 'cities' of marginalised and 'outlaw' interests have been thrown up over night on the Net 'badlands'. In this regard such organisation resembles the 18th-century social structures of 'Pirate Utopias' as described in Hakim Bey's essay 'The Temporary Autonomous Zone', *TAZ, Autonomedia*, New York, 1991 (URL: http://www.uio.no/~mwatz/bey/taz/taz_contents.html). A TAZ, according to Bey, is a transitional state on the total information network where islands of functioning anarchies appear fleetingly only to eventually fail in their development as fully-fledged universal autonomies and Utopias. He sees much of what is going on now with Internet reverting into just another class war by the 'lumpen yuppetariat' attempting to blow up and burn down their own 'electro-sweatshops'.

27 Spam is one of the more odious examples of bad Netiquette. It refers to the practice of posting the same message on a multitude of Usenet newsgroups. The term refers more to the classic Monty Python skit 'Eggs with spam, spam spam . . . and spam', than to the unspecified, grey pig Jell-o that had inspired the skit. Often spam is produced by 'nubies' (arrogant beginners) or is of a commercial origin. What is particularly annoying about such messages is that they have nothing to do with the particular newsgroup that they are on, and if one is scanning through several newsgroups of interest, one is liable to run into the same spam many times. To ignore spam eats up time and having thousands of copies of the same message uses up valuable Net resources. With the aid of a simple programme known as a 'spambot', the spammer can send copies

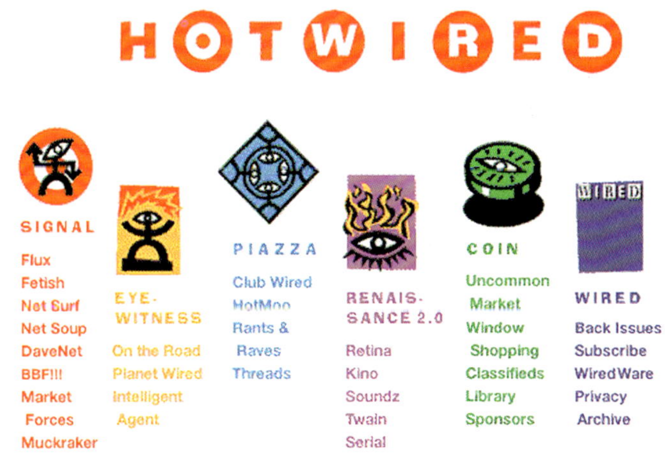

Hotwired

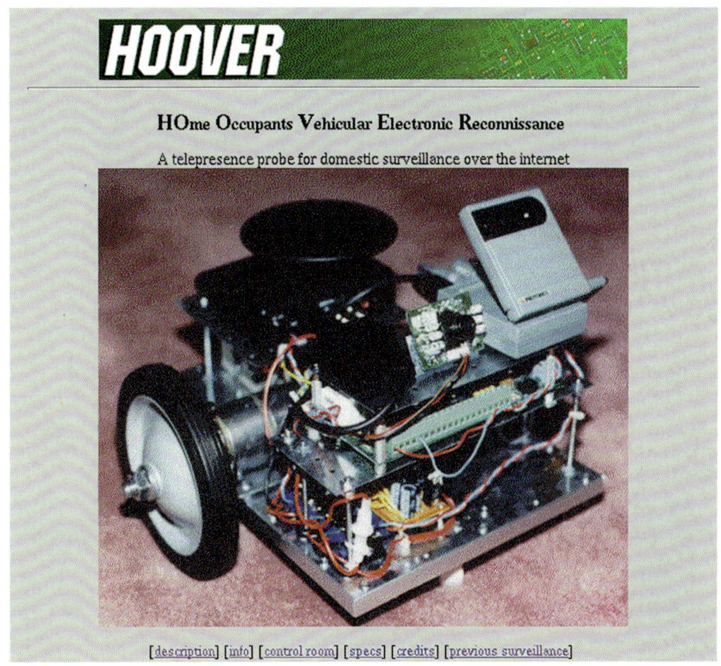

URL:http://cadre-cia.sjsu.edu/info/personell/chan/hoover.html

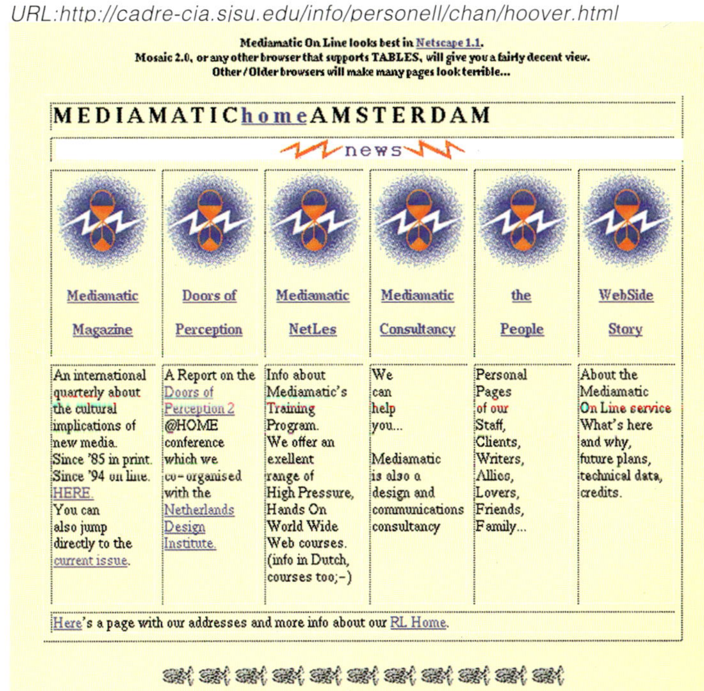

URL:http://www.mediamatic.nl/Default.html

of spam to thousands of locations in a single spamming. In turn, several Netizen have taken it upon themselves to wipe spam off the face of the Net in vigilante fashion, often devising more elaborate programmes called 'cancelbots' to eliminate all traces. This has led to charges of censorship in some cases with resultant counter measures and counter-counter measures. Owing to the easily spoofed nature of the identity of a specific user on the Net, it is not so difficult to post or cancel a message pretending to be someone else. This has also lead to some curious Net holy wars and increased Net noise.

28 The power of the Net to disseminate messages as well as making available the wide variety of documentation has already been alluded to several times here. Electronic journals and 'zines devoted to hyperinformation are starting to spring up all over the Web. Of particular interest are electronic publications which list and review other sites on the Net. These can take the form of a 'Cool Links' list such as the one maintained at Stanford's Yahoo site (URL: http://www.yahoo.com/Entertainment/ COOL_links). However, sometimes what is more insightful about Net culture and the direction which it is going is 'Mirksky's Worst of the Web' (URL: http://turnpike.net/metro/mirsky/Worst.html) that gleefully punctures those Web sites which are truly distasteful in terms of content, graphical layout, and egocentricities. There are also reviews which treat the material on the Web as just a continuation of other forms of media. A fine example of this which is applicable to the topic discussed here is Taproot (URL: gopher://wings.buffalo.edu:70/hh/internet/library/e-journals/ub/rift/journals selected/treehome/treehome.html). Though not particularly exploitative of the hypertext format, and published in a paper format first, Taproot contains mini- 'capsule' reviews and short 'blurbs' about many contemporary poetry 'zines, visual-literature, audio art, and intermedia, that exist in both paper and electronic form. In particular, the reviews cover the more experimental varieties of language art. Each issue is an informational gold mine and the number of reviews which are available at their Web site is extensive. It provides one with a quickly accessible reference list of an ever-changing and widely dispersed literature. Taproot provides information about current ways of working with language that are often difficult to ever learn anything about from conventional sources. Another area where the Web tends to shine is the ease which it allows some degree of audience participation. This is perhaps where the future of experimental art on the Web lies. At present such interactivity is fairly basic and often focused around simple science demonstrations, such as the Virtual Frog Dissection Kit (URL: http://george.lbl.gov/vfrog/). The viewer can strip off the skin and subtract (or add) various frog anatomical systems such as the circulation, digestive tract, skeleton, and nerves, by making selections with hypertext button objects and a 'refresh image' switch. The ability to allow for 'remote sensing' is another natural dimension which is relatively easy to implement in HTML. These can take passive forms such as Fishcam (URL: http://www1.netscape.com/fishcam/). By using the Netscape browser one can be treated to a constantly updated (the rate depending largely on the speed of the Internet connection one uses), 'real-time', digital video image of fish swimming in an aquarium. A somewhat more curious remote sensing site can be found at Vanderbilt University, with their Restroom Utilization Measurement Program (URL: http://entity.vuse.vanderbilt.edu/project/). Both the men's and women's restroom on the fourth floor of their computer science building is outfitted with a variety of motion and pressure sensors. It is part of an ongoing project funded in part by the National Institute of Sanitation to aid in 'improving the work load distribution' in high-use restrooms. A 'reload updated status' button selected by the reader of the hypertext exactly locates all the users of the restrooms at any particular time by displaying a small yellow 'happy face' within a representational map of each restroom site (selecting the 'live video feed' button, one is greeted with a 'get a life' message and a count on the 'sucker counter'). An example of remote sensing that contains a more active form of interaction and is a little closer to performance art than science is Kelvin Chan's Hoover project (URL: http://cadre.sjsu.edu/info/personell/chan/hoover.html). During a week beginning with 14 May 1995, a completely Web-accessible robot, named Hoover (HOme Occupant Vehicular Electronic Reconnaissance) the first 'wireless domestic telepresence probe controllable on a Web Browser' was placed in various homes in the San Jose area during the evening to 'experience occupant lifestyles'. Hoover would send a constantly updated, digital image and sound of what it could 'see' and 'hear' which in turn could be accessed from its homepage. Further, the reader had the ability to move (it was designed to negotiate such things in a domestic situation as carpets, tiles, obstacles, kids and pets) the robot by means of hypertext buttons. However, since many other people could log on to the same Web site, a tug-of-war as to the robot's location would often occur between the Web's readers. A waiting list now exists in which interested parties can have a Hoover placed in their homes for an evening.

Site Examples

Homepage image 4

The Morpo Review *http://morpo.creighton.edu/morpo/*. This journal is published electronically on a bi-monthly basis, and largely concentrates on fairly conventional, though 'unhinged', poetry, prose, and contemplative essays. It makes minor use of the linking capabilities of hypertext, however its graphical layout is a fine example of the possibilities which electronic publishing has to offer to small press. Despite the large number of restrictions in the present HTML format, there are still many things which it can do that would be difficult, or rather expensive, to duplicate in a paper media environment.

Homepage image 6

WAXWEB 2.0 *http://bug.village.virginia.edu*. WAXWEB is the largest narrative document presently on the World Wide Web. This extensive hypertext site is based on David Blair's 1991, completely digitally-edited film *WAX or the discovery of television among the bees*. The film also has the distinction of being the first to be 'broadcasted' digitally to viewers on the Internet (23 May 1993). The Web site version of *Wax* contains 3,000 hypertext pages, approximately 25,000 hyperlinks, 85 minutes of digital video which includes the entire film, 5,000 colour stills, and sound tracks in several languages. There is also a VRML (Virtual Reality Modeling Language) accessible interface to the site which allows the user to interact with thousands of hyperlinked parts in a three-dimensional environment. The user can interact with WAXWEB and add their own narratives and scenes to allow for 'the synthetic creation of a DYNAMIC, 3-D INTERSTORY on the network'. This is an enormous project and to make adequate use of all its features, one has to have one's computer connected via a fairly high-speed interface.

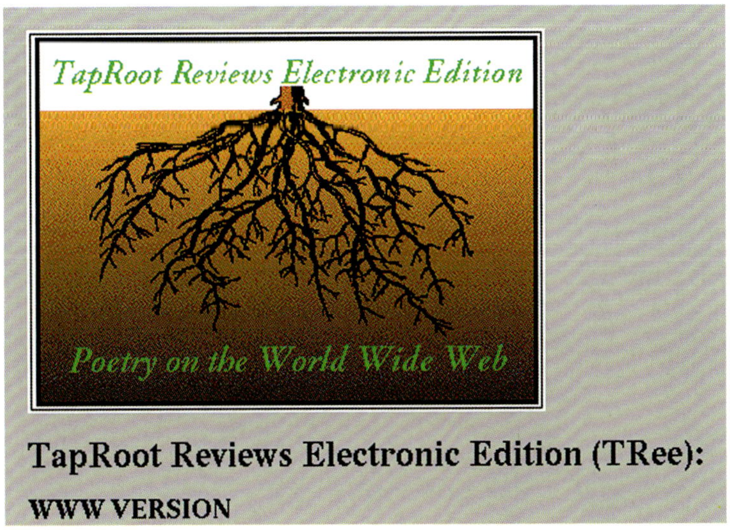

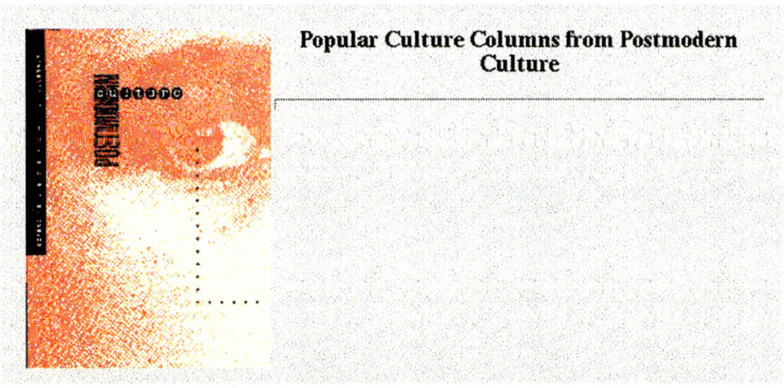

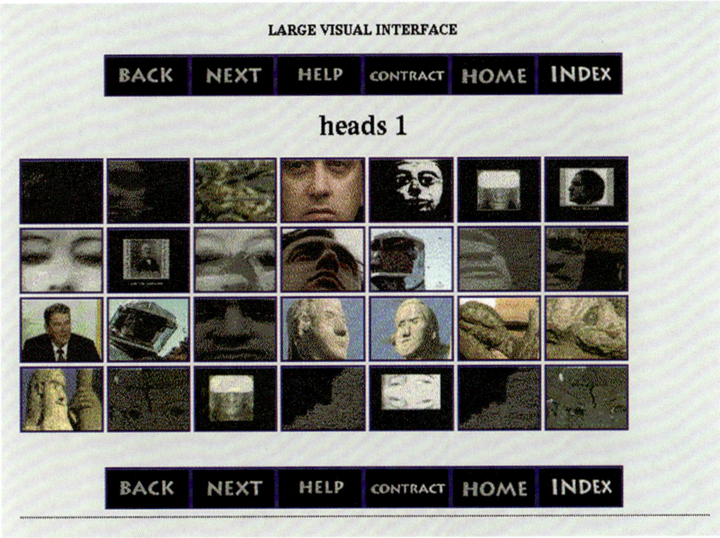

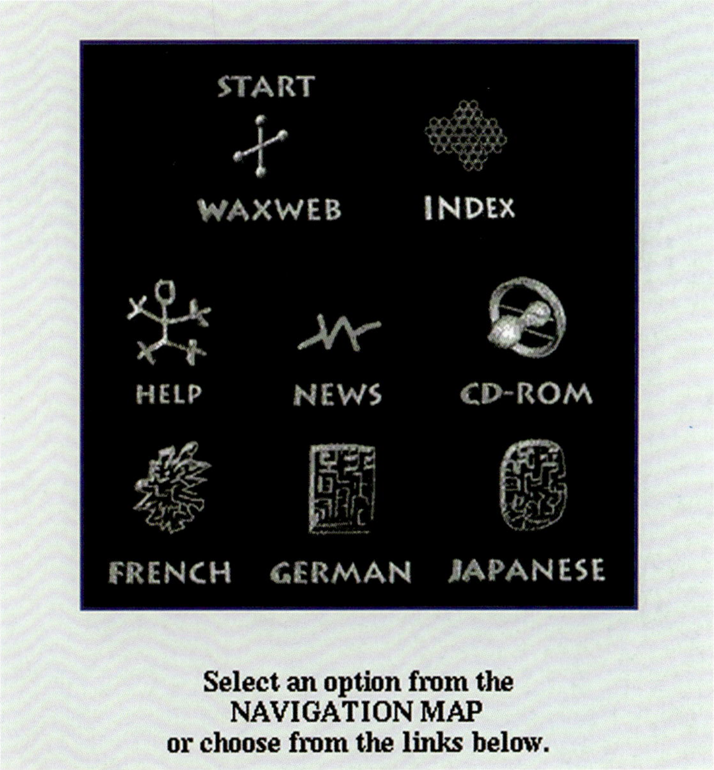

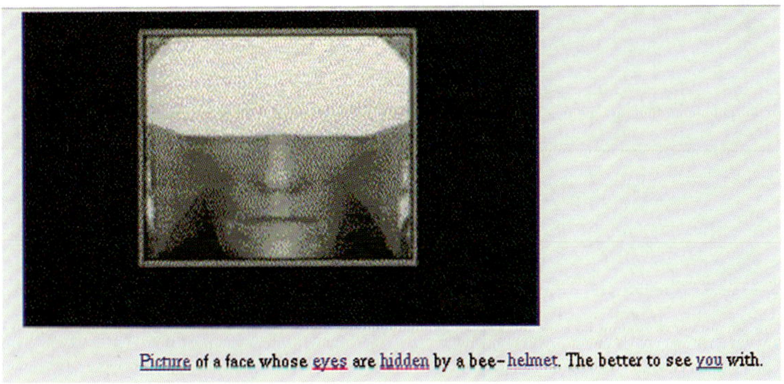

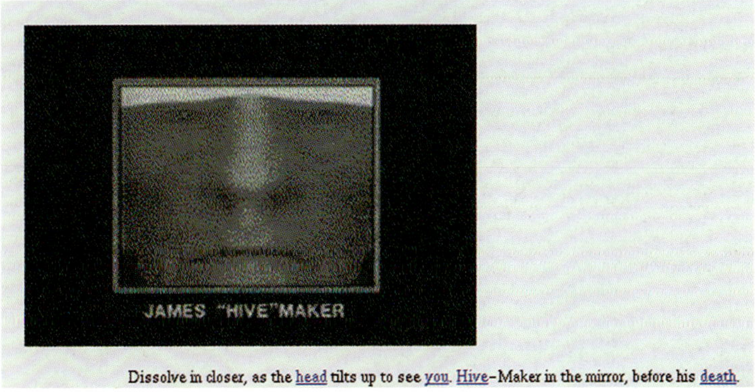

FROM ABOVE, L to R: URL:gopher://wings.buffalo.edu/hh/internet/library/e-journals/ub/rift/journals/selected/treehome/treehome.html; pmc3.gif; Waxweb; URL:http://bug.village,virginia.edu; Waxweb; Waxweb

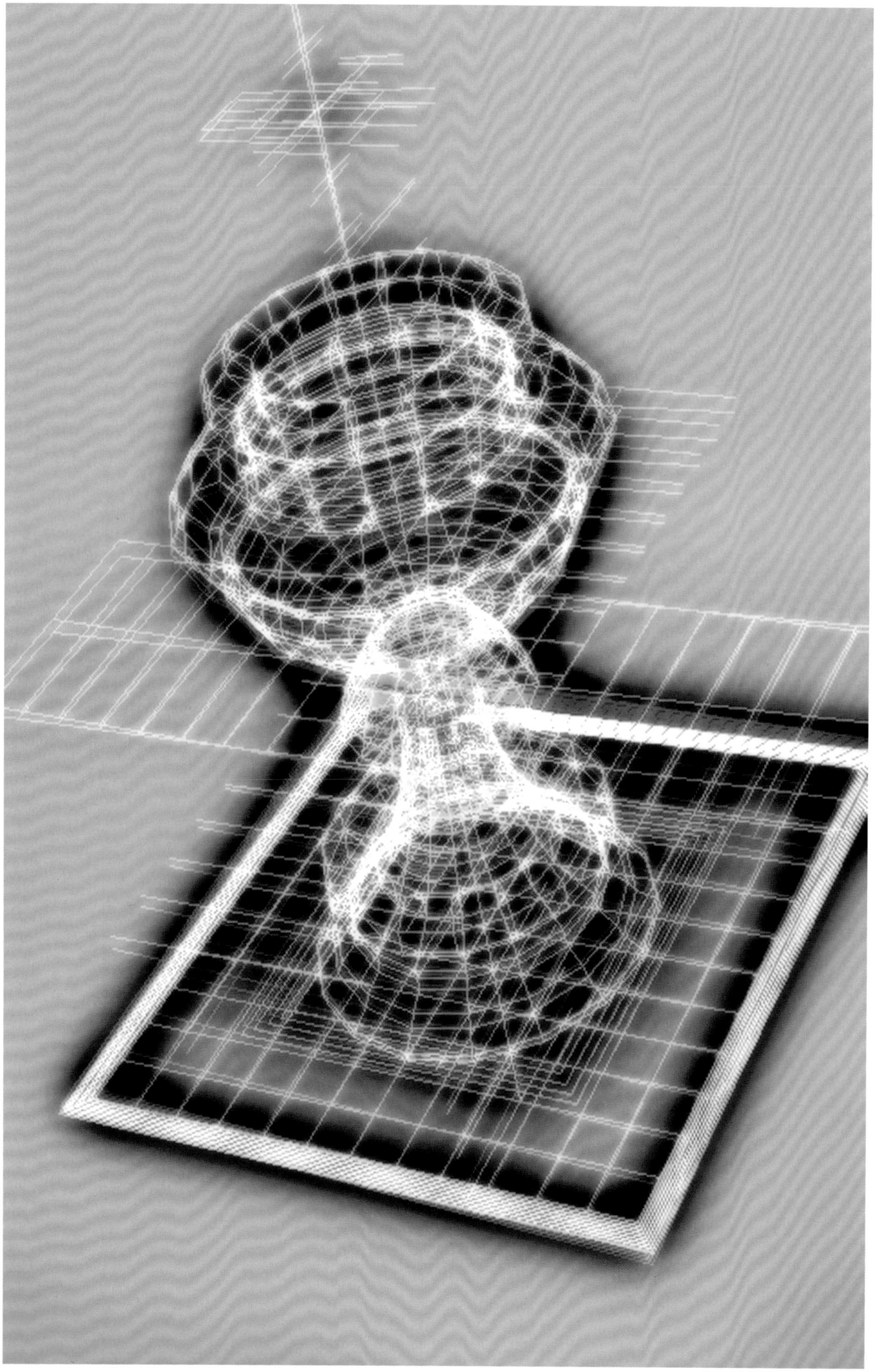

Adam Wolter, Mesh *installation, Institute of Modern Art, Brisbane, October 1994, photo: Prudence Cumes*

ADAM WOLTER

'FAIRLY STRICTLY A COMPUTER ARTIST'

Interviewed by Nicholas Zurbrugg

In the following interview, Brisbane computer artist Adam Wolter discusses the inseparability of computer textuality and computer imaging in his installation *Mesh* (first exhibited at the Institute of Modern Art in Brisbane from 27 October-19 November 1994), speculating that the parity between this machine and 'your machinery' implies that 'to some extent we are all machinery together'.

Nicholas Zurbrugg: *Adam, you have worked predominantly with computers.*

Adam Wolter: I have always worked with computers, I am fairly strictly a computer artist.

How would you fairly strictly define computer art? What, for you, are the challenges or advantages of the computer?

– Well, I suppose generally speaking you would say that computer art is art that could not be made without a computer. But these days that takes in a wide range of practices. There is so much very powerful, very easy to use application software available that with almost no training whatsoever you can sit down and start making pictures with a computer. My practice started a long time before that sort of software was available – so in fact you had to write your own software. And although I have absolutely nothing against using big powerful pre-existing programmes to make pictures – I often do use such programmes – I still pursue a practice of writing software to get exactly what I want. The benefit of that is that you can have very close control over exactly what the machine does. In many of my works, such as *Mesh*, I have always been very keen to include the actual programme text of the artwork. I have managed to do that, I think, quite successfully in this work. It fits in with the underlying themes and the rest of the aesthetics of the work to have the programme text up on the screen.

What do you think it adds, to put the programme's text on the screen? Proust, for example, wrote somewhere that 'an artwork that has its explanation with it, is like a hat to which a price-tag is still attached'.

– The programme text does not really fit into the work like that – it is hardly an explanation and may well seem a little confounding. It is a demonstration of what the work is, without any explanation, so it is revealing the internal clockwork, without telling you how the clockwork works. I think it is certainly got a lot of visual impact and also some poetic impact. It is not ones and zeros although it is still symbolic. This sort of software is written in *Modula 2*, which is quite a high level symbolic object-oriented programme, so it is not completely opaque, although its general audience will not be able to understand the intricacies; in fact, you would have to be a computer to understand all the intricacies of such a programme.

So in a sense, what you are doing is highlighting the textual essence of seemingly three-dimensional computerised images' existence?

– Yes. It is very much orchestrated in a linear, linguistic way, and the imperative here comes from the computing machinery – that is the way the machinery works. You have got to work that way if you want the machinery to understand you. I am particularly interested in this mechanised way of producing visual objects and the *Mesh* installation deals yet again with one of my favourite objects, which is Uccello's chalice. I see this particular figure – which was realised by Uccello in the form of a line-drawing drawn in perspective – as being very consistent with a machine-based way of working, inasmuch as Uccello realised that perspective was essentially a mechanical process. If we were talking about it in current terms, we would say that the process that produces perspective drawings via certain rules is a virtual machine. Uccello realised fairly much that his task was to provide a substantiation of that machine, so his working to those rules was really acting as the engine-room to the conceptual machine of perspective.

How exactly will your installation combine computer text and three-dimensional computer-drawing?

– The work is a triptych, with the rotating three-dimensional figure as a central panel, and the text of the programme used to produce both this figure and the display of the text itself will be used within another panel. There will also be a third panel which will be a fairly highly rendered version of the same thing – but more realistically. It will have effects like optical flares and shadows and so forth, so it will look quite solid. So generally, the three pieces will span the conceptual level of one strictly textual panel, one obviously visual but still not quite real rendering, and a third panel which will be more realistic and yet obviously related to the other figures. Significantly, all these panels will be projected in colour-separated stereography, so you will be wearing goggles and seeing these figures in a three-dimensional setting.

Were you wearing goggles and seeing these images three-dimensionally all the time that you were working on this piece?

– Certainly not! It would have driven me crazy! In fact, while I was doing the textual work – which, surprisingly, took longer than the solidly rendered work – during 95 per cent of the time I was working on it, there was absolutely no evidence of any stereographic effect whatsoever, so I was fairly much trusting my understanding of what was going to happen. It was quite a complicated thing to be doing and I did not actually see the result until I was almost finished.

That makes me think of Cage's comment that when he was working on Europera *it was a type of complex improvisational theatre with*

which he was 'unfamiliar', and which he 'looked forward' to seeing.
– Well, this is not quite like that, I dare say that Cage would have been happy with a very wide range of possible results. I was aiming at a very strictly defined result – it was like trying to get a hole in one.

How strictly defined is the temporal span of the work? Do you envisage a situation in which the viewer will watch the work in terms of the duration of its most extensive component – the projection of the programmed text?
– Well, it would probably take ten minutes or so for the text to go through its cycle, and you do not really need to see it all go past in order to get the gist of the installation. Overall, *Mesh* is the coming together of several different aspirations. I wanted to work with stereopicity, I wanted to have programmed text, and I wanted to have animated three-dimensional objects. Another thing I wanted to have was a deep, rear-projected video space. This work is going to be in a U-shape with video projections from the rear, so the viewer will actually step inside a certain sort of enclosure, looking out into the enclosed space – the viewer will step into a space and look out of that space. The screens might be about two metres wide – maybe three. I would think that two people could stand in it reasonably comfortably.

Could this space be described as a kind of virtual environment?
– You could say that I might be incorporating stereography to get on the virtual bandwagon. But I think my reason for doing this is because the work is really a landscape showing both the way that the computer functions to produce visual objects at three different levels, and the way that we see things – the machinery that we use to perceive things. I have incorporated stereography as part of this demonstration of what is in our perceptual apparatus in a completely unconscious way at all times. I am an artist who is trying to make people aware of what they are. That is a prime function for art. A lot of artists get very emotional about their work and do very emotive work, and when asked about it, say, 'I am just trying to make people aware of their own scope.' That is all I am trying to do with this installation. What I am saying to people is, 'You are machinery that works in a particular way. Cognitive machinery is part of yourselves and works in this way, and over on the side, you have the computer – which is obviously machinery – which in working in a way that is consistent with your machinery, which produces these dimensional effects for you, without actually having the dimensionality involved'. So I am saying to people, 'Here is a machine that is like your machinery, so to some extent we are all machinery together.'

Are you saying that we are just machines?
– No, I am not suggesting this is a reductive function. I am pointing this out, but I would not regard this as reductive.

All the same, what would you see as the difference between a scientific demonstration of parallel mechanical processes, and this kind of artwork? Is it both art and science?
– It is both, definitely. It is a demonstration, but that does not present a problem to me. My approach is always scientific as well as artistic.

All the same, a lot of your work is also very humorous, so in a sense your work is a very subjective kind of fusion of art and science.
– Definitely!

And like Uccello, you are not indifferent to subject matter – you are not just taking the iconography of a brick rather than a chalice.
– I myself see the chalice as an obvious symbol for virtual machinery, because Uccello used it himself and because I think Uccello was fairly much obsessed with the machinery of perspective. He was always more interested in making things look solid than he was in any other form. And he would have been the classic computer-fiend in modern times – he would just be obsessed with the machinery.

Are you at all worried that visitors to your installation will miss the substance of its textual panel? Or are you hoping that this panel will have a more general, immediate impact, insofar as it highlights all the work that went into programming the rotating stereoscopic image?
– It highlights something very profound to me which I have wanted to show for a long time, that a lot of people do not know. You would not normally call the words of a book machinery, but here you have this textual thing that fits together almost literally like cogs and gears and wheels – this machinery made of words and texts and symbols to which most people do not have any access at all. I want to show them something which when they take the stereoscopic glasses off, is flat and blurred, green and red, and when they put the glasses on, seems to be a solid thing. So I want them to think, 'this is something different', 'this is something about me', 'this is something about the relationship between me and the glasses'.

In other words you are addressing a more complex perceptual relationship than Joseph Kosuth's conceptual meditation upon photography, solid materiality and dictionary definitions, in One and Three Chairs?
– Yes, there is some similarity, except that Kosuth is addressing different kinds of familiar definitions or encoding – the photograph, the object, the dictionary entry – whereas the aspects of people that I am showing in this installation are completely unconscious. They are well below any sort of Freudian idea of what might be subconscious – they are really wired into what we are. The dictionary definition is at a very high level – at the top layer of things that we know, whereas what we have here at a stereographic level is very low. This is more like perceptual meditation, it is saying, 'Here is a piece of machinery, it is in you; it is so fundamental to yourself, but you are not aware of it. And here is a visual display of all aspects of it; it happens all the time, it is obviously mechanical, because it is being reproduced by all this machinery, these things are happening to you all the time, and this is what you are'.

Brisbane, 8 October 1994

OPPOSITE, FROM ABOVE: Adam Wolter, Mesh *installation, Institute of Modern Art, Brisbane, October 1994, photos: Prudence Cumes; OVERLEAF, FROM ABOVE: Adam Wolter,* Mesh *installation, Institute of Modern Art, Brisbane, October 1994, photo: Prudence Cumes; Adam Wolter,* After Uccello, *1993, computer image*

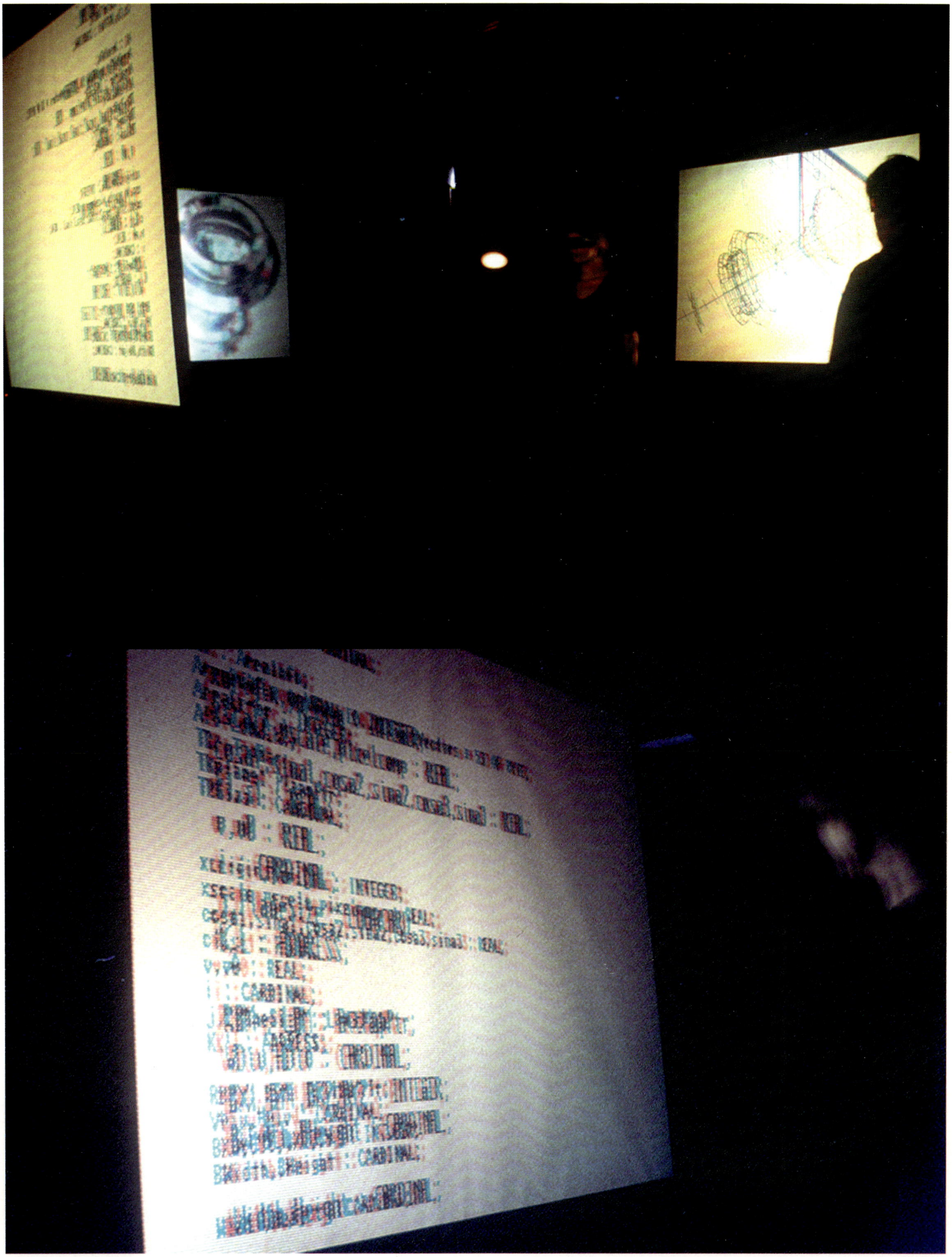

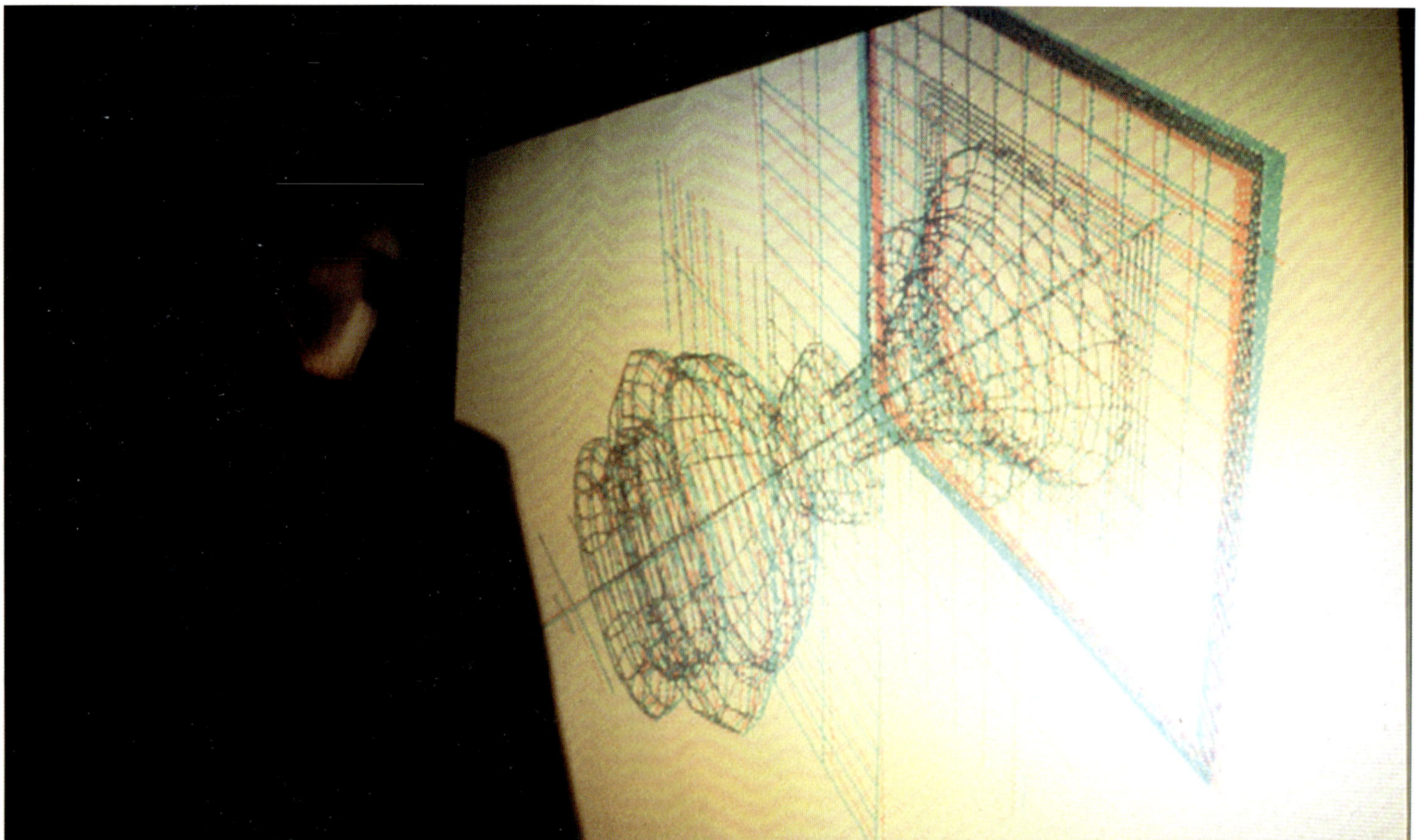

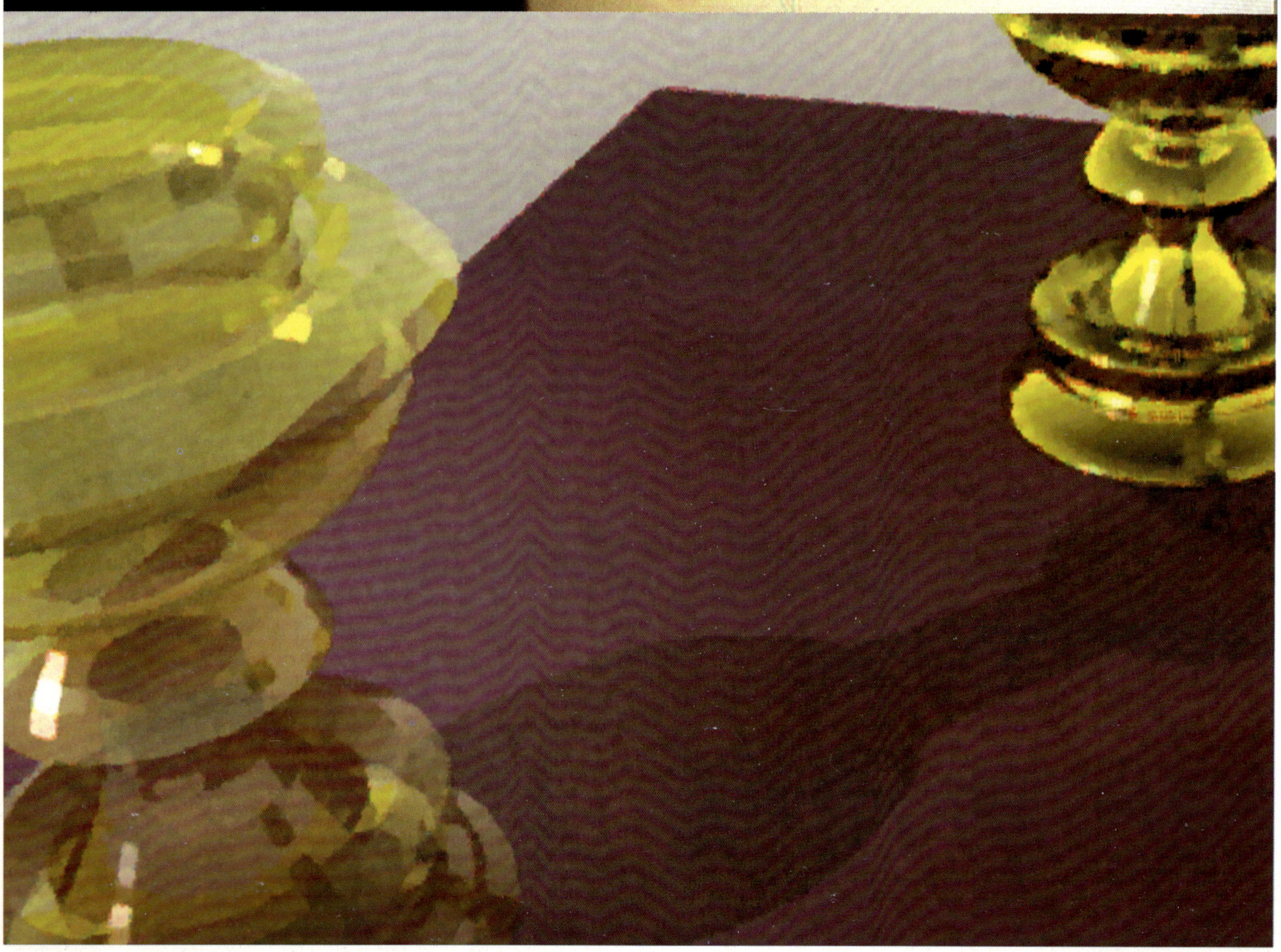